People Solutions for School Leaders

Focusing on the many challenges faced by school leaders in different contexts, including primary, secondary, rural, and urban settings, this book helps you find practical solutions that work for your circumstances, align with your values, and support your relationship with yourself and your people. It shows you how you can keep well, manage workload, accept differences, confront what is unacceptable, break through what's uncomfortable and awkward, collaborate, and rediscover your joy in the profession.

Based on over twenty years of lessons learnt from coaching headteachers and school leaders, *People Solutions for School Leaders* builds on the foundations of respect, adaptability, a coaching approach, and embedding habits. It gives you what you need to know about leading people in this rapidly changing education system. Chapters feature:

- Themed coaching questions for yourself, your staff, and the people 'above' you.
- Activities for team meetings and training days with access to free resources and downloads.
- Headteachers' shared experiences – in their own words.
- Ways to connect effectively with others, so people 'get you' and you 'get them.'
- Principles of emotional intelligence you can put into practice across your school community for stronger working relationships, successful teams, and community cohesion.

Full of practical insights and actionable strategies, this is essential reading for school leaders across all phases, governors and trustees, and all those with a coaching or mentoring role in education.

Maureen Bowes is an Executive Coach and Leadership Mentor specialising in coaching for Headteachers and Senior Leaders in Education. She offers advice on personal development along with practical coaching questions through her website: www.solutions.peopleintelligence.com

People Solutions for School Leaders

What they didn't tell you and you really need to know

Maureen Bowes

LONDON AND NEW YORK

Designed cover image: © Getty Images

First published 2026
by Routledge
4 Park Square, Milton Park, Abingdon, Oxon OX14 4RN

and by Routledge
605 Third Avenue, New York, NY 10158

Routledge is an imprint of the Taylor & Francis Group, an informa business

© 2026 Maureen Bowes

The right of Maureen Bowes to be identified as author of this work has been asserted in accordance with sections 77 and 78 of the Copyright, Designs and Patents Act 1988.

All rights reserved. No part of this book may be reprinted or reproduced or utilised in any form or by any electronic, mechanical, or other means, now known or hereafter invented, including photocopying and recording, or in any information storage or retrieval system, without permission in writing from the publishers.

Trademark notice: Product or corporate names may be trademarks or registered trademarks, and are used only for identification and explanation without intent to infringe.

British Library Cataloguing-in-Publication Data
A catalogue record for this book is available from the British Library

ISBN: 978-1-032-94540-8 (hbk)
ISBN: 978-1-032-94539-2 (pbk)
ISBN: 978-1-003-57132-2 (ebk)

DOI: 10.4324/9781003571322

Typeset in Sabon
by Deanta Global Publishing Services, Chennai, India

Access the Support Material: www.routledge.com/9781032945392

Contents

Acknowledgements ix

Introduction 1

SECTION 1
Foundations 9

1 Respect – valuing yourself and valuing others equally 11
2 Adapting the way you communicate and motivate 19
3 Empowering others through coaching questions 29
4 Embedding habits: Keeping the momentum going for lasting change 35

SECTION 2
Wellness 43

5 The life-changing benefits of self-compassion 45
6 Choices for everyday well-being 55
7 Personal organisation 61
8 Mental and emotional fitness 69
9 Responding to anxiety 81

CONTENTS

SECTION 3
Reducing workloads — 91

10 Workloads for everyone's well-being — 93
11 Living the school values — 101
12 Clarifying expectations — 109

SECTION 4
It's all about relationships — 113

13 Sharing responsibility — 115
14 Resilient relationships — 121
15 When parents get angry — 133
16 Necessary conversations — 145

SECTION 5
A sense of belonging — 155

17 Adding the human element to Inset Days — 157
18 I, me, or we? Criteria for being a team player — 171
19 Buzzing: Emotional intelligence in teams — 179

SECTION 6
Raising morale — 183

20 Getting real about low morale — 185
21 Overstretched: Leadership and the widening parameters of inclusion — 193

SECTION 7
Self-reliance — 209

22 What really stops you prioritising your well-being? — 211
23 Finding fulfilment — 219
24 Creative self-compassion — 227

SECTION 8
Navigating towards a hopeful future   **233**

25 Consolidating your personal development   **235**

Recommended reading   **241**

List of download files   **243**

Index   **245**

Acknowledgements

I want to give the sincerest thanks to those people who have enthused and supported me at different stages on this journey.

Simon – my very own editor-in-chief. Thank you always for being there every single step of the way. 'We share the load.'

Dr Julia Reid – my fabulous mentor from across the time zones – thank you for your invaluable perspective and feedback.

Siobhan Goffee – my Partner in Joy – thank you for your fresh pair of eyes.

Special thanks to Dr Paul Van Walwyk and Anwen Foye for your expertise and advice.

To Jonathan Hannam, Joy Squibb, Alison Story-Scrivens and Nicola Pearce for your time, support and feedback.

To those headteachers who added another dimension to the book through their Shared Experiences. You know who you are.

To my self-compassion peer group – Aimée, Anne, Anwen, Hilary, Imke, Jo, and Sam #quietrevolution.

To my graphic designers helloDODO for many years of playful collaborations.

To all the Solutions members, past and present, and those who responded to the survey for the title.

Thank you.

Introduction

The book's back story

Over the past two decades, I've coached hundreds of headteachers. This means thousands of hours listening and asking questions with the aim of enabling them to find their solutions. From this experience, I realised I am uniquely placed to share what I've learnt with you, especially if it can contribute to keeping you and other school leaders well and motivated to stay in the profession you love – or once loved.

My background is in applied emotional intelligence, so my coaching revolves around how you feel about your work, your relationships at work, how you understand differences (especially when the emotional climate is tough), and learning how to remain true to yourself and your principles. You can imagine the conversations and the stories over the decades about the emotional roller coaster that is school leadership.

When I first started coaching headteachers, I followed up a coaching session with an email and attachments on topics relevant to our discussion. Then one day, I thought how much better it would be if any headteacher could access this information at any time, anywhere. And so *Solutions'* was born.

Pre-dating Substack, *Solutions* is a website with a search function where subscribers can find practical information related to leading people in schools. But it's much more than a growing library of blog posts; it has a reassuring sub-text of 'You're not alone in this.' Its content saves you, the school leader, time and energy. It brings insights, clarity, and more harmony to your work and life choices.

Today, there are over two hundred Solutions that you, and any school leader, can access online. I've created this book by taking the most used and best loved Solutions, informed throughout by the words of the people I've coached, their situations, and their challenges.

The book's backdrop

The 2020s have seen the education system stretched to breaking point. 'Perfect storm' is the term most frequently used to describe the complicated and unsolvable problems facing school leaders and their increasing role responsibilities.

In any one week, you could be attending the funeral of a pupil's parent, working through an attack by a pupil on a teacher, managing racist comments between pupils, teaching in the classroom to cover staff absence, investing hours of your time processing a parental complaint, as well as trying to have a home life and dealing with your own personal and family issues and conditions.

Times are tough, and for many, life is becoming increasingly complicated. School life in particular is becoming increasingly complicated, not least because of difference and inclusivity. As humans, we need to feel safe, to belong, and to connect with others – simple factors that can be tricky to provide. If we are to gain a fair understanding of the complex challenges facing school leaders, and keep you in the profession, it matters that we recognise how difference and inclusivity impact your life, and that we give you the wherewithal to cope well.

This book is about you and the adults you work with across your school community. Whether implicit or explicit, your school's vision and values require your school community to foster awareness and acceptance of people, for the future. All the people – pupils, staff members, parents and carers – with all their different circumstances and challenges. With this awareness, you have choices that can prevent tensions and misunderstandings, minimise performance management issues and conflicts, and reduce loneliness and unconscious bias.

Personal development and adaptability

Accommodating difference requires adaptability, and respecting difference brings lifelong personal development. For you as a school leader, this means, for example, considering to what extent your communication is inclusive of all members across your school community: those who are neurodiverse, those who have difficulty reading and writing, those from a different culture where English is not their first language, and those facing mental and emotional health issues.

It means considering how you respond when you find yourself surprised by a colleague's behaviour or comments; when you feel shocked or confused by a parent's approach to you; or when you find yourself making judgements about individuals or families. It means considering how readily, in those moments, you pause and challenge your assumptions.

It's hard to be the person you want to be, or believe yourself to be, when you're under ongoing emotional pressure from others and feel like there is nothing left to give. At those times, showing compassion to yourself and to others often seems like a distant aspiration.

These complicated times and circumstances are part of the backdrop, and in your role, you only have part of the picture. You cannot be expected to know what is really happening in pupils' family homes, nor what is behind how adults present themselves to you, especially when your focus is more on the child, and when your role is teacher or colleague morerather than social worker.

No staff member can know what trauma or mental health issues a parent is having to live with, nor the stress levels from coping with any family member's dysfunctional or abusive behaviour. This applies in exactly the same way to your staff, in their homes, their family members' dysfunctional or abusive behaviour, their trauma, their conditions, or their mental health issues.

A parent with Oppositional Defiant Disorder (ODD), for example, will struggle to cooperate with a headteacher since the very nature of the role comes with a position of authority. In these circumstances, it's quite difficult not to judge them for arguing and defying reasonable instructions. It's natural to feel frustrated by a parent who doesn't engage with their child's learning when you are unaware that they are experiencing domestic abuse. It's understandable, through lack of awareness and knowledge, to feel disappointed or annoyed with a carer, parent, or step-parent, without realising the real reasons why they are avoiding you – sometimes the shame, fear, or desperation that accompanies addiction or past personal trauma.

Neurodiversity, in particular autism spectrum disorder (ASD) and attention-deficit/hyperactivity disorder (ADHD), has only become more widely known since the 1990s. Given how recent this awareness is, there are likely to be some individuals among your staff and parent groups who were born last millennium, who may be unaware of their own neurodivergence. It's reasonable to assume there are parents, grandparents, and staff within your school community who have learnt to mask their neurodivergence and whose neurodivergence you don't recognise.

Similarly, teaching staff may be unaware of tough family circumstances until parents or pupils start to open up about these. And of course, from your perspective, the people in your school community cannot know your backstory – your personal life, your neurodiverse states, your trauma, or your mental health situation. You need a source of compassion too. When applied in practice, the chapters in this book can go some way to providing this.

Ethos

In three words – *People Solutions for School Leaders* is about difference, courage, and peace.

Difference

We are all different, our circumstances are all different, and so our solutions are different. Your solutions are inside you. The strategies and questions in each chapter serve as catalysts enabling you to find your solutions.

How we are different is so complex. In one staffroom, playground, or school community, there is a kaleidoscope of difference when you consider gender, cultural background, ability, race, socio-economic status, sexual orientation and identity, and how neurodiversity intersects with these.

Courage

It takes courage to break out of patterns that prevent you from taking action. Courage to venture more readily into those awkward zones in relationships and power dynamics, right through to the more terrifying levels of risk involved in righteous indignation. Courage to push back and speak truth to power. To assert what you believe is right for your school's vision. Courage to disrupt compliance.

Peace

Being at ease with who you are, confident in what you stand for, and having the energy and wellness to fulfil your purpose. These are within your reach through personal development practices.

I care about headteachers and school leaders and your potential to influence society. My hope is that you use this book to find your solutions; reacquaint yourself with your truest values; face up to your strongest feelings; and align these so you can step or stride in that uncomfortable direction.

My approach

I'm a pragmatist. I focus on 'how to'. I take theory and experience and translate them into applied practice so that you can answer your own questions – 'What do I need to do?' 'How do I need to be?' *People Solutions for School* Leaders offers you 'how tos'. Step-by-step options. Choices to empower yourself and your people.

I am not an academic. I am not a researcher. I have never been a headteacher. My style is conversational. My work is informed mainly, but not entirely, by white, south of England, mainstream primary headteacher experiences, so inevitably this influences my perspective. I have written *People Solutions for School Leaders* with the firm belief that as a school leader, you will relate to the human emotions and relational dynamics presented here and be able to adapt and apply them within your demographic.

The language of these times is evolving rapidly, particularly within politics and intersectionality. I have aimed to show awareness and respect in these areas.

I use 'headteacher' to mean the person responsible for leading a school. It can be used interchangeably with 'principal.'.

How to use this book

It's unusual to find a straight-line course of action in situations that involve the wonderful complexity of individuals. The patterns and dynamics around people at work are multifaceted, so here's how I've put a structure around this complexity to offer you 'people solutions.'.

Foundations – START HERE
Respect
Communication
Coaching questions
Habits

These four components influence every situation you face with people at work. We're all different: what works for me is unlikely to work for you, and what works for you probably won't work for the next person. Though there are common denominators.

To get the best out of individuals at work, you need to:

1. Develop a demonstrable attitude of respect for yourself and towards others.
2. Be adaptable in the way you communicate with them so you can more readily match their differing communication needs and thereby build rapport.
3. Enable learning and growth so they become empowered to take responsibility.
4. Facilitate change so your people know how to develop, how to change (and sustain) more effective ways of working.

Chapters – Themes and challenges
Building on these foundations, the chapters in each of the eight sections cover the main topics that headteachers and school leaders bring to coaching and want from courses and conferences.

Wellness
Keeping yourself well physically, mentally, and emotionally, and enabling your people to keep well physically, mentally, and emotionally too.

Workload
Ways to make workloads manageable. You don't want to lose staff, so how do you ensure workload and wellness are not precariously balanced?

Relationships
You get things done with and through, people. If you focus too much on the task, people don't engage with you. If you focus too much on the people, less gets done. Managing the balance between performance and relationships within the school system, including staff, services, and families, requires a high level of personal awareness and interpersonal skills.

Belonging
As social beings, it's important we feel accepted and connected. What's needed to ensure those qualities across your school community – from playground to staffroom to classroom?

Morale

Your leadership is needed more than ever when the truth is bleak, and morale dips. You don't have to be Winston Churchill, but you do have to find inspiration, keep your people hopeful, and remain true to yourself.

Self-reliance

'The joy has gone' was a frequent statement among school leaders after the pandemic. Once you have developed your inner resources, it's much easier to find joy from the inside and sustain hope on the outside. This level of personal empowerment means you can make choices that bring a completely different perspective to the challenges you face.

When you are in search of a solution, you are unlikely to have all the information you need to guarantee the right decision, but these chapters will get you out of decision limbo. You'll be able to find the next step from what you know so far, the next right action at any given point, and then keep revisiting and refreshing your approach as things progress.

Zooming in

There will be permutations for each challenge you face and for every solution you want to find. What might work for one team member, parent, or lunchtime supervisor won't necessarily work well for another. To help you take account of these different responses, reactions, needs, and wants within each challenge, I give you developmental prompts and reminders at the end of each chapter.

Coaching yourself

Theme-related questions to reflect on for your personal development in the given situation.

Coaching others

Questions you can adapt and apply for your people and their development in context.

Coaching upwards

Questions to ask, where appropriate, to those in senior positions to you.

Perspectives

Ask individuals to describe the same situation, and the chances are each person will see things differently. This is usually a good thing. How we interpret and express those differences is where it gets complicated.

The *Perspectives* section at the very end of each chapter prompts you to see things from different angles, so you can minimise misunderstandings and get better outcomes.

INTRODUCTION

Shared experiences
There is a range of shared experiences from headteachers and school leaders. Each one is anonymised. Each is intended to add a reality check to those chapters.

Consolidating
The final section hands over your personal development to you.

When it comes to people and change, the permutations and dynamics are endless. In a school community, each academic year brings new year groups and different people. The consolidation process enables you to review the challenges you've faced over the terms and years and see the progress you've made. That year when you took the social media comments far too personally – and now you feel more robust with effective strategies. That term when there were conflicts that went on way too long, not least because you didn't intervene early enough – and now you have more clarity about how to manage similar situations. And so on.

People Solutions for School Leaders involves applying emotional intelligence in practice. Relationships and circumstances at work change year on year. How you apply your awareness, knowledge, and skills changes year on year too. Now you can log your personal development progress through your challenges, and these can inform your performance management reviews for years to come.

In summary
At one end of a continuum, *People Solutions for School Leaders* is a pragmatic guide for school leaders developing themselves and growing others. At the other end, it offers you a transformative personal development process (see Figure 0.1).

The style of the chapters mirrors this. They are not uniformly written. Some chapters are like pages from a training manual, while others take you down a more reflective route. There are chapters that include shared experiences from headteachers in their own words, and some that include learning and insights that are personal to me.

Some chapters are quick to read, linear, and action focused. Some are reflective, harder to absorb, and will take longer to get through. They reflect the book's backstory and will all mean very different things to you at different points in your career.

All of the chapters, at some level, are about difference – how we are different.

How to use People Solutions for School Leaders
It's your choice to dip in and out and use it like a manual or to go further and take your leadership to another level, with emotional intelligence practice as part of your personal development, in your own time.

Figure 0.1 maps out the continuum starting with the foundation chapters, followed by the practical chapters, the developmental and the transformational chapters.

My recommendation is that you start by reading Chapters 1–5 because they underpin every chapter. Then, you decide which chapters meet your current needs, go there and capture those moments, words, and reflections that resonate. Capture them in whatever way works for you. I'd recommend a paper notebook (of course I would) as its contents will really contribute to your personal development and aspirations over the years.

How to use
People Solutions for School Leaders

START HERE — **Foundation chapters**

1. Respect – valuing yourself and valuing others equally
2. Adapting the way you communicate and motivate
3. Empowering others through coaching questions
4. Embedding habits: Keeping the momentum going for lasting change
5. The life-changing benefits of self-compassion

Practical

6. Choices for everyday well-being
7. Personal organisation

Developmental

INDIVIDUAL

8. Mental and emotional fitness
9. Responding to anxiety
14. Resilient relationships
15. When parents get angry
16. Necessary conversations

TEAMS

10. Workloads for everyone's well-being
11. Living the school values
12. Clarifying expectations
13. Sharing responsibility

17. Adding the human element to Inset days
18. I, me, or we? How to be a team player
19. Buzzing: Emotional intelligence in teams
23. Finding fulfilment

Transformational

20. Getting real about low morale
21. Overstretched: Leadership and the widening parameters of inclusion
22. What really stops you prioritising your well-being?
24. Creative self-compassion
25. Consolidating your personal development

Figure 0.1 How to use *People Solutions for School Leaders*

SECTION 1

Foundations

This book is about school leadership – how you get results through people in an educational setting. Results that keep people well, bring fulfilment, and keep them (and you) choosing to stay in this remarkable profession.

The guiding principles for *People Solutions for School Leaders* are:

- Mutual respect.
- Adaptive ways of communicating.
- Empowering through questions.
- Turning intention into everyday actions.

These principles underpin every chapter.

CHAPTER 1

Respect – valuing yourself and valuing others equally

Respect as a fundamental value

Mutual respect is a British value that all schools are required to promote. It's no surprise that if you look on any school website, and walk in most school foyers, you'll quickly find the word 'respect'.

Unfortunately, the reality all too often fails to match the words. Whether that's staff interrupting and talking over one another in meetings, pupils being divisive in the playground, or parents ignoring school rules on timekeeping.

Mutual respect can be incredibly difficult, especially when you're faced with strongly opposing views, behaviour that you find offensive, or the pressure to get quick results. It can be harder again if, for example, you are neurodivergent, trans, or a minority ethnic person in a largely white geographic area – all of which can be used by others to unsettle you.

A lived value is quite different from a stated one. Where there is a commitment to behave with respect, and a willingness to make changes when respect falters, then the whole school community benefits. With respect, we can address difficulties and differences without evasion or aggression.

Simply representing respect

These three characters (Figure 1.1) offer a simple way of communicating and understanding the complexity of behaving with respect. **Big-i**, little-*i*, and **Equal-II-se** bring alive the value of mutual respect through a visual metaphor.

When discussed in context, everyone, from early-years pupils through to governors, understands these visuals. When teaching staff use Equal-II-se to explore what respect means, from the classroom to the playground, it raises everyone's awareness, making it easier to exemplify respect and highlight disrespect.

Applying the Equal-II-se metaphor, situation after situation, offers a highly effective way to embed the value of respect in your school culture, not least because it takes into account different perspectives, the impact of a given behaviour, and the possibilities for behaving differently next time.

An attitude of respect

Values influence behaviour. As you and your school staff live and teach the school values and behave respectfully, your pupils experience respect and learn how to show respect. Over time, this experience develops attitudes where pupils demonstrate a respectful approach. Underpinning the value of respect is an attitude of respect.

The Equal-II-se model (Figure 1.2) takes you further than your agreement with, and understanding of, respect. It probes your attitude, particularly your attitude

Figure 1.1 **Big-i**, little-*i,* and **Equal-II-se**

RESPECT – VALUING YOURSELF & OTHERS EQUALLY

Figure 1.2 The Equal-II-se model

under pressure, which is when **Big-i** or *little-i* are more likely to make an appearance. Underpinning these characters are these attitudes:

Big-i

- I feel I am more important than you.
- I have less respect for you than for me.
- I think I'm better than you.
- Your views count less than mine.

Reflect on your behaviour under pressure. If challenged, do you become aggressive or dismissive? Do you talk over others or insist that you are right and they are not? Do you undermine or belittle people? It takes a certain kind of courage to acknowledge these behaviours which are typical of **Big-i** (Figure 1.3).

Figure 1.3 **Big-i** – I am more important

little-*i*

Then there are those times when your attitude towards your differences can be one, or some, of the following:

- I feel I am less important than you.
- I have more respect for you than for myself.
- I don't feel good enough or as good as you.
- Your views count more than mine.

Once again, reflect on when you feel under pressure. Do you avoid confrontation? Do you stay quiet even when you have something to say? Do you doubt your judgement and tend to defer to others? These behaviours are typical of 'little-*i*' (Figure 1.4).

The aim here is to develop an attitude of Equal-II-se:

- I value myself and I value you.
- I feel equal to you (as one human being to another).
- I respect our differences even when we disagree.
- We both count.

Respect in action

Think of an incident, altercation, or situation where you, or the other person, got upset or angry. Then consider these questions:

- In that situation, which *i* i I were you?
- How did the other person feel as a result?
- What could you have said or done instead to be more Equal-II-se?
- What could you do differently another time?

Attitudinal development is hard for both adults and children throughout life. Schools play such a crucial part in cultivating an attitude of respect across a community.

Living the value of respect, developing an attitude of respect

Attitude takes a long time to shift, but here are some resources to start with. After you have discussed the concept of Equal-II-se with your people, and contextualised it within the school values, you can display and discuss the most suitable version, for the

Figure 1.4 little-*i* – I am less important

RESPECT – VALUING YOURSELF & OTHERS EQUALLY

people and the situations, as a visual reminder for everyone. All the resources can be downloaded from www.routledge.com/9781032945392

Equal-II-se for children
1 – Children's version

An excellent approach for reaching everyone is to start with the pupils. Exploring this simple graphic (Figure 1.5) with its simple questions (Figure 1.6) has the potential to impact everyone's behaviour – teaching staff, pupils, and families.

Equal-II-se for adults
2 – Adults' version

This version (Figure 1.7) works well when displayed in meetings. It offers a verbal shorthand that everyone can use fairly and without fear. Instead of awkwardly taking time to address tensions in the way people are talking, it's much easier to remind people – 'Can we please remember Equal-II-se here?'

Whenever you see signs of, or experience, *little-i* behaviours (avoiding, hesitating, being passive, self-doubting, or withdrawing) and, whenever you see signs of, or experience **Big-i** behaviours (controlling, criticising, being disrespectful, being judgemental, or behaving self-righteously), you can cut through the tension with the request – 'Can we get back to Equal-II-se now?'

Figure 1.5 Equal-II-se – children's version

PEOPLE SOLUTIONS FOR SCHOOL LEADERS

Equal-II-se Questions

In that situation – which i-I were you?

How did ………. feel as a result?

What could you have said or done instead to be more in Equal-II-se?

What could s/he have said or done instead to be more in Equal-II-se?

What could you do differently another time?

resilience habit : mutual respect

© maureen bowes

Figure 1.6 Equal-II-se – children's version with questions

Figure 1.7 Equal-II-se – adults' version

RESPECT – VALUING YOURSELF & OTHERS EQUALLY

Equal-II-se advanced
3 – Advanced version

The advanced version (Figure 1.8) enables you to discuss where Equal-II-se stops and aggressive or passive behaviour starts. This exploration is great for one-to-ones, and useful discussions arise when the advanced version is on display in the staff room and meeting rooms.

You can facilitate attitudinal development in individuals by making the advanced version a frequent reflective habit by asking them to consider, routinely:

- When you tipped into **Big-i** today.
  Note the thoughts, feelings, words, and behaviours that reflected this.

- When you tipped into *little-i* today.
  Note the thoughts, feelings, words, and behaviours that reflected this.

- When you lived the Equal-II-se value today.
  Note the thoughts, feelings, words, and behaviours that reflected this.

This personal reflection process is a compelling way of changing behaviour and embedding the attitude and value of respect.

In your role as a teacher, it's easy to be perceived as **Big-i** at those times when you have to take control of a situation or when you have to be directive with pupils. The advanced version enables everyone to explore the 'courage' column, particularly the confronting and challenging behaviours, and understand how these differ from **Big-i** behaviours.

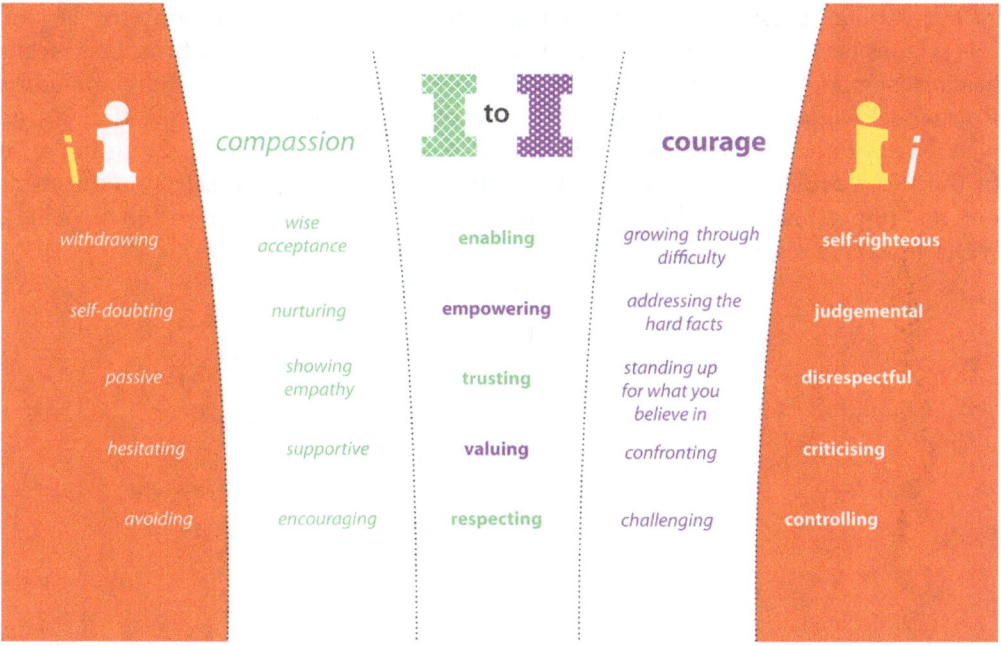

Figure 1.8 Equal-II-se – advanced version

Once the situation has settled and calm is restored, it becomes easier for the pupil(s) and you to reset. When you explore 'We both count' in that situation, it becomes clearer how effectively (or not) you managed the situation respectfully and effectively.

These discussions that hinge on power dynamics help everyone understand how each person counts, that we are equals as human beings, even when things can seem unequal because of our roles and positions of authority.

All these versions can be downloaded from www.routledge.com/9781032945392

Equal-II-se in leadership

Attitude is often distorted by authority and pressure. When you have a **Big-i** attitude, you tend to control and dominate others, and others perceive your behaviour as *controlling*. When you have a *little-i* attitude, you allow others to control and dominate you, and consequently, others perceive your behaviour as *avoiding*. **Big-i** and *little-i* attitudes are often the culprits when relationships at work are buckling.

If, instead, you have an Equal-II-se attitude, you are confident enough to cope with criticism and to stand your ground, so that others perceive your behaviour as *enabling*. Enabling brings engagement and empowerment – so your people find their own solutions and have space to grow.

We each deserve respect

Since the 1980s, respect for professions, particularly in the public sector, has declined, sinking especially low post-pandemic and during the SEND crisis. The lack of respect from some parents towards headteachers and teaching staff shows up in the increase in complaints, the tone and vocabulary of emails, and playground confrontations.

The attitude of respect is fundamental to changing society, so it's clear to see the vital role schools play in growing respectful individuals as citizens of the future. This means headteachers and teaching staff are crucial role models within a school community. Role models who can resolve issues reasonably by communicating and negotiating, and who take both parties into account by enabling people and restoring relationships. To be this kind of role model, it's important to practise respecting yourself from the inside out, and respecting others through courage and compassion because, as human beings, we each deserve respect.

CHAPTER 2

Adapting the way you communicate and motivate

Relationships at work are different
Relationships at work differ from all other relationships because:

- You don't choose the people you work with.
- You're judged on your performance, and your livelihood may depend on this.
- You can be required to do things you don't want to do as part of your job.
- You must deal with people in authority.

These four factors hugely influence how you relate to people at work, particularly when the pressure is on. You don't usually get taught how to navigate your way through the dynamics of relationships at work; you're expected to just know how to get along and perform well together!

'We don't see things the way they are, we see things the way we are.'
You have a vision. You have a strategic plan. You have goals, and you have the passion. How do you actualise all this? Through your people. Through all those multi-faceted individuals whom you have inherited or appointed, through their strengths, their competence, and their potential.

You make it happen through your communication with them:

- How you speak to them to motivate and inspire them to commit their time and energy to action.
- How you communicate your expectations about the work you hope they'll do, their responsibilities, and their accountability.
- What you say to determine the right level of challenge so they engage.
- How you give them feedback so they develop and grow.

How do you accomplish this with a fast-paced, task-focused, rational teacher who wants to be left to get on and do things their way? Or a reflective governor who wants time and more information to be sure everything is right? Or a senior leader who doesn't want anyone to feel uncomfortable? Or an enthusiastic early career teacher who wants to share ideas and get recognition for them?

How do you communicate with each of them to get buy-in, build rapport, prevent misunderstandings, and minimise conflicts?

It's not just the same repeated approach that's needed here; it's an adaptive approach. Words, tone, and styles that match the communication needs of the individual you are communicating with, so you become more aligned.

They don't 'get' me
Think about a time when a dialogue at work didn't go well, possibly with someone not on your wavelength, where the outcome wasn't what you'd expected. In your mind's eye, recall what happened between you and observe the interaction. Aim to be objective in what you notice about how you both came across. Consider the following:

ADAPTING THE WAY YOU COMMUNICATE & MOTIVATE

- Did the other person understand your vocabulary? (To what extent did your words match the words they were using?)
- How much do you think you understood of what the other person was talking about? How do you know?
- How was the pace? Too fast (couldn't keep up and got lost) or too slow (got bored and drifted off).
- How much detail? Too much (went on too long) – or not enough (too concise)?
- How was the tone? Hesitant, apologetic, abrupt, sarcastic?
- What impact did you want to have on the other person?
- What could you have done differently to have the impact you wanted?

Next come some important clues for how to improve that interaction and your workplace communications generally.

Coaching means the way you relate to people at work

Coaching means the way you relate to people at work. This simple model (Figure 2.1) serves you like a compass so you can navigate your way through conversations, meetings, and discussions across your whole school community.

If you observe the people you work with, you'll find that some are more emotionally open and demonstrative, while others are more emotionally guarded. Neither way is 'right'.

You'll also find that some people are more inclined to consider all their options and guard against making mistakes, while others are more decisive and prefer to get things moving, even if they have to correct mistakes. Again, neither way is 'right'.

These two ways of behaving result in four Coaching Styles. In the diagram (Figure 2.1), the top half of the picture has two styles: Innovators and Harmonisers. Both are emotionally open, and in any given situation, they are comfortable with the people involved as well as the task they are doing.

In the bottom half of the picture are two more styles: Achievers and Perfectors. They are more emotionally reserved and, in any given situation, tend to focus on the task and what needs to be done rather than the people doing the task.

Figure 2.1 Coaching Styles quadrants

In the same diagram, on the right half of the picture, are two styles: Innovators and Achievers. Both tend to make up their minds quickly, are more 'black and white' in their approach, and like to get things moving.

In the left half are two more styles: Harmonisers and Perfectors. Both tend to be more measured, take time to make decisions, be more 'shades of grey' in their thinking, and want to make the 'right' decision rather than a quick decision.

The combination of these drivers gives us the four fundamental Coaching Styles (see the title page for Chapter 2) – Innovator, Achiever, Perfector and Harmoniser:

- Innovators are enthusiastic and great at coming up with ideas and fresh approaches. Their optimism is refreshing. They are the least troubled by change and the most likely to see the possibilities. They can help you move forward when stuck.
- Achievers are tough, resilient, and expert at managing their time to get lots done. They are common in senior leadership positions as they are unafraid to act and push through difficulties. They can help you with mission critical deadlines.
- Perfectors are reserved, often quiet, cautious about making mistakes, judgemental, logical, and good with systems. They are fundamental to good administration and getting the detail right. They can help you with records, systems, and policies that work and get results.
- Harmonisers are helpful, compassionate, and supportive. Schools often have a high ratio of Harmonisers because of the caring nature of the roles and the relationships involved. They can help you work through a range of people issues.

Crucial points to remember
- The Coaching Styles model is NOT a psychometric tool. And it doesn't put people into boxes. It's a simple way to make sense of how people relate to you and their colleagues in the workplace. It supports you in communicating with them in ways that work for them.
- Coaching Styles is NOT a personality diagnostic. It's a model that guides you towards being a more effective communicator. It raises your awareness of, and changes your approach to, how you relate to the people you work with. It gives you a shorthand way of making rapid sense of people's differences.
- Few people are purely one Coaching Style. We are all a unique mix, but it's surprising how often our major preference is visible to us and, especially, to others.
- No Style is better or preferable or more important. Simply different.
- All the Styles are able to do what the others do, but not as easily and generally not as well.
- Your Coaching Style is likely to change as you change roles throughout your career and adapt to the pressures and demands made of you.
- The Styles don't just apply to schools as workplaces. They can be found in every workplace. Each Style brings benefits and challenges.

Each Style has its drawbacks
While each Style brings benefits, it also has a 'flip side':

ADAPTING THE WAY YOU COMMUNICATE & MOTIVATE

- Innovators incline to get bored with detail and with being held to account when their work gets dull. They love beginnings but can struggle to finish things they have started. They interrupt easily and can disrupt simply to keep your attention.
- Achievers can become impatient with what they see as the 'niceties' of communication. They can be uncompromising and brusque, especially if they think they are right and don't agree with you.
- Perfectors worry about quick decisions or changes of policy, particularly if they have to get it right. Their worry can lead to long hours at work and poor health as they try to master the detail. They can appear critical of new ideas and can easily deflate others' enthusiasm.
- Harmonisers believe that people are at the heart of the school and that change should be negotiated rather than imposed. They can be surprisingly obstinate if opposed and are willing to undermine you rather than confront you. They avoid awkward situations and uncomfortable conversations.

Think about how you are at work

Are you someone who's emotionally warm and engaging? Or are you someone who's emotionally reserved (perhaps until you get to know someone)? Are you someone who's quick and decisive? Or do you prefer to gather the facts and take more time over your decisions? None of these positions is preferable, they simply reflect your Coacting Style:

- People with an Innovator Style are drawn to the new. They are typically big picture thinkers, talkative, and engaging. They are happiest at the start of a project. They are optimistic and early adopters. They like the next big thing. They don't like to get bogged down in detail. They want you to entertain them or let them entertain you.
- People with an Achiever style focus on results. They are decisive, robust, productive, and unafraid to speak their minds. They are prepared to make mistakes and then put them right rather than wait to decide. They will judge you by your own focus on results.
- People with a Perfector style at work focus on getting things right. They are all about the detail. They prefer a calm and measured environment. If they are uncertain about something, they'll delay a decision until they have all the facts. They will ask you for detail and say 'that won't work because…'
- People with a Harmoniser style at work focus on relationships between people and are the 'glue' in a group. They are alert to conflict and either avoid it or try to resolve it. They don't like upsetting other people. They are likely to tell you what they think you want to hear.

Each of us has our own Coacting Style, our own combination of the four main Coacting Styles. The model doesn't require you, or your people, to fit one of the four styles. Instead, it assumes that we all have our own unique style, which is a composite of the four. Some people do, indeed, make almost exclusive use of one style. Others use two, three, or all four. As an aid to navigating day to day workplace interactions, the four styles do a pretty good job.

An effective way of clarifying your own Coacting Style is to think about your colleagues, especially the people you find most difficult, like those who you find annoying when you're having a bad day. Generally, the styles opposite to your own are the most difficult for you to deal with, and, thereby, give you clues about your own style.

If you are a Harmoniser, you'll want people to be happy. You'll take care of people, remember birthdays, spot when they're feeling low, chat in the corridor, and put others at their ease. Your opposite, the Achiever, is much more concerned that people get the job done. Achievers aren't so interested in putting you at ease, or in chat that slows them down. They see the people stuff as time consuming. They can seem hard and unaware.

If you are a Perfector, you'll want people to explain things to you in detail. You'll be good at spotting potential difficulties in plans and procedures. You take work seriously and worry about things going wrong. You'll value being an expert. Your opposite, the Innovator, is attracted to new ideas, doesn't worry about getting everything right, and has surges of enthusiasm but hates getting slowed down by detail. Innovators like the limelight.

It's easy to see how the opposites misunderstand each other and don't meet each other's needs. It's tempting to see the flaws in the other styles and to overlook the flaws in your own. In fact, each style offers something that the others don't. And, importantly, you need all those variations to keep work alive.

Working with the different styles

You will get better results through your people if you adapt the way you communicate with them, verbally and electronically, so you meet more of their communication needs. Knowing what you know now, how can you adapt the way you communicate to those people who have very different styles to you, so you are less irritating to them? (See Table 2.1 Adapting your Coacting Style.)

Coacting Styles and teams

Teams perform well together when all four Coacting Styles are present; when there is the right balance of ideas, robust action, quality and detail of implementation, and ways of engaging people.

This does not mean each style has to be represented by one individual, it does mean team members need to adapt to what the situation requires.

When team members are familiar with Coacting Styles, they can use the language to direct the team's discussion and action towards a specific style or to change styles. This is especially useful for the team leader. For example:

'I'm conscious of how long we have taken on this topic. Can we go into Achiever mode now to agree our conclusion and decide our next steps?'

'We've been fine-tuning the improvement plan for the last two hours. I suggest we shift into Harmoniser mode now and consider people's ability to take this on, their workload and their wellbeing.'

ADAPTING THE WAY YOU COMMUNICATE & MOTIVATE

Table 2.1 Adapting your Coaching Style

How to adapt your Coaching Style

	Innovator	Achiever	Perfector	Harmoniser
How to prepare	Start with key, high impact points.	List bullet points, priorities, & action. Have evidence.	Full picture briefing with detail at the ready	Show awareness of the impact on the people behind the task.
Open with	Upbeat icebreaker / story.	Time check. Agree how long is necessary.	Context setting. Clarify aim.	Genuine 'How are you?'
When face to face, be	Enthusiastic, optimistic.	Task focused, keep to the point.	Precise, allow time to think.	Pleasant, conversational.
Keep in mind, they like	Appreciation of their ideas, optimism, high energy.	Progress, authority, deadlines.	Facts, evidence, thoroughness.	Interaction, involvement, inclusion.
To get their best, give	Attention, recognition, fresh ideas.	Progress updates, propose solutions to problems.	Thought through plans.	Dependability, loyalty, and trust.
Keep them happy by	Making things interesting.	Solving problems, getting results.	Keeping to schedules and systems, explaining changes.	Keeping in touch.
On the phone, be	Fun, lively, upbeat, share stories.	To the point, respect their time.	Precise, prepared, logical, volunteer information.	Willing to listen, ask open-ended questions.
Close with	Action check – what have you agreed?	Clarity of action & timescale.	Reaffirm priorities. Check they're OK.	Assure co-operation. What's agreed? Thank them.
Email style	Creative, spontaneous dialogue.	Clarity, brevity, no surprises.	Sufficient information, ordered and with support data.	Personable, friendly. Dear… Add tone e.g. with emoticons :)
Email content	Visual, broad brush layout. Big picture first.	Bullet points, headlines. Point out issues for attention	Provide attachments, references, links. Double check for accuracy.	Acknowledge people, give recognition, thanks.

Using the language of Coaching Styles in these ways offers a shorthand that both depersonalises the process and empowers people to take ownership with no sense of chastising or offending colleagues.

Coaching Styles and leadership

We are all a blend of Coaching Styles. We have preferences but these preferences can morph into other combinations for the situations and roles we face:

A Governance meeting will take much longer if the members are predominantly Perfectors/Harmonisers. They are prone to seek ever more information and detail and are too courteous to address how much time it's taking or to suggest the meeting doesn't overrun. Detail has its place, but some items may not require it. This is where Achiever traits, keeping efficiently to time and keeping items to the point, encourage progress at the right pace.

Cutbacks and subsequent lack of resource result in difficult messages. There's no softening the reality of the spreadsheet, yet this reality needs to be communicated to individuals whose work (and possibly life and livelihood) will be impacted. The leader has to access their Achiever to deliver the truth of the hard facts, clearly and concisely, while realising the human element requires Harmoniser traits. The situation demands authenticity, and this means soul searching. That essence needs to be translated into a combination of facts and pragmatism combined with acceptance, reassurance, and compassion.

Your leadership meetings have become stuck in a repeat pattern of people thinking the same and doing the same. These times cry out for some Innovator influence, and you realise there's no Innovator present. This situation needs some facilitation, some group activity to enable people to tap into their inner Innovator and generate ideas. Or a visiting Innovator as a catalyst for stirring up possibilities, stimulating different ways of thinking and stretching levels of acceptance for change.

We can't get away from the differences between Coaching Styles, but we can recognise the differences, value them, and adapt to others' styles rather than become upset or annoyed by them. You, and your style, are living and the Coaching Styles process is deliberately flexible – because it needs to be. So, the key question for coaching yourself, coaching others, and coaching people senior to you is What does the *situation* need?

What does the situation need

When you recognise what the situation needs, you can adapt the way you work, and the way you communicate, to suit those needs in order of priority:

- Sensitivity towards people? Play to the strengths of a Harmoniser.
- Ideas to see things differently? Bring in an Innovator.
- Action and speed? Get into Achiever-mode.
- Caution and consideration? Tap into your 'inner' Perfector.

In what order of priority? How will you adapt and manage your response?

Coaching Styles is a labour-saving device, a time and emotion saving device, that enables you ultimately to move people towards your school's vision. Adapting the way you communicate is important and that's why you'll find pointers and prompts for remembering this at the end of most chapters in the **Perspectives** section.

ADAPTING THE WAY YOU COMMUNICATE & MOTIVATE

Coacting Styles resources

You can download the following resources from www.routledge.com/9781032945392
What are you like at work?
How to adapt your Coacting Style.
They will enable you to introduce the Coacting Styles model to your teams:

- To raise awareness with your people of how the different styles impact on one another.
- To offer simple ways for each individual to adapt the way they communicate.
- To fast-track how people in key working relationships can minimise tension between themselves.

Perspectives

What helps, and hinders, in getting the different styles to adapt how they communicate:
Innovators – enjoy adaptability when it brings in the new.
Achievers – enjoy adaptability when it saves time.
Perfectors – enjoy adaptability when it ensures we get things right.
Harmonisers – enjoy adaptability when it keeps people happy.
Keep in mind – the styles are 'broad brush' and there are people who may not readily fit them. Some who are neurodiverse do not interpret emotions like neurotypical people. Again, if a member of staff is depressed, they may not be as emotionally open as they are when well. The key point is to observe, and ask questions if needs be.

CHAPTER 3

Empowering others through coaching questions

Helping or developing your people?

As a leader, the most beneficial way to truly develop your people is to empower them through a range of coaching and mentoring approaches. You need people to respect your strategic time and not interrupt you with operational, day-to-day issues they can manage themselves. You need them to use their initiative, take responsibility, and stop depending on you so much for permission and approval.

You also know that when the pressure is on, or when time is tight, it's all too easy for you either to slip into doing the task yourself (you can develop them later) or to take charge and help them with the task. Both approaches usually have the same result – you end up doing it. As if you don't have enough to do…

There are five ineffective habits that are very common among busy leaders, particularly leaders under pressure. These habits highlight the gap between helping and developing. You know what you're supposed to do, but what you actually do in practice, especially when stressed, isn't developing anyone. Brace yourself.

Habit 1 – Giving the answers

You immediately give people the answers instead of getting them to take ownership, work it out for themselves, and stretch their thinking. You do it automatically because you think it's helpful, because you have a need for speed, or you feel impatient or uncomfortable with the silence.

The cost is learnt dependency – 'Next time I'm stuck, I'll come straight to you for the answer.' Or 'If I keep quiet long enough, I can be sure you'll take over.'

Habit 2 – Telling people

Telling people what they need to do instead of asking questions. Asking open questions enables people to work things out for themselves and articulate what they need to do. Instead, you do it automatically because it's quicker and easier and saves you time (in the short term).

The cost is frustration when people don't think for themselves. They don't change, and they certainly don't take ownership. This adds to your stress.

Habit 3 – Repeating

You repeat what you said before instead of checking what they understood or remembered the first time around. You do it automatically – to take the weight off them, to show your knowledge.

The cost is a loss of effective leadership. You're dominating. You're not adapting to what the situation needs. You're not empowering anyone, and they are not learning. Everyone is becoming less effective.

People remember more and retain more if they articulate their understanding. (You're a teacher at heart, you know this!) In the security of your presence, your knowledge, and your authority, people will behave like they understand, they'll believe they understand, but they may not have retained very much at all. They need to demonstrate that they understand, for example, by summarising back to you. This might feel a little patronising at first, but if you communicate well and request respectfully ('What are

Habit 4 – You do it for them!

You do it for them to help them out (and to be sure it's done right). Your workload is high, and you automatically add to it – instead of saying 'no', instead of adding to their workload, or risking some mistake.

The cost is that they don't learn. They don't develop. They fear making a mistake. (How does that stack up in a growth mindset culture?)

Habit 5 – You do work that they could do

Instead of delegating, you do something you don't need to do and that others could do because explaining how it needs to be done takes longer than if you just do it.

The cost is a chunk of your time and, in the long term, your well-being. Estimate all the minutes you spend repeating this kind of approach alongside how long it would take to delegate the task effectively. Ask yourself, as a person with a high workload, if you're not the only person who can do this, why are you doing it?

Help or develop? Helping someone can easily come at the cost of developing them so they can do it themselves.

Five effective habits to develop your people

1. Instead of giving the answers, talk much less. Ask questions and listen carefully for their responses. 'What do you think?' 'What might work?' 'What options do you have?'
2. Instead of telling people what they need to do, step back for a moment and give space for others to share what they've learnt so that you can hear where the gaps are.
3. Instead of repeating yourself, empower people to take responsibility and use their initiative – either through asking them questions or facilitating (or creating) opportunities for them to shape up.
4. Instead of doing it for them – determine the right level of risk to grow and stretch people. Without some degree of stretch, all of us stop learning, and then it's only a matter of time until complacency sets in.
5. Instead of doing things others could do, manage your time better. Let go of control. It's not at all efficient if you keep doing something because you don't invest time to show someone else how to.

Action plan

Replacing these ineffective habits with more effective ones is easy to intend but much harder to accomplish. You'll stand a greater chance of success if you:

- Choose one of the five habits – write it down and keep it close by as a reminder.
- Tell your intention to someone you trust. Ask them to check in on it with you.

- Reflect on your new habit each day, and on how you're developing your people.
- Do a friendly progress check on yourself each week.

Once your first ineffective habit has been replaced with a more effective one, move on to the next one. Continue to be vigilant around these ineffective habits though, because when you're under pressure, you can be certain they'll reassert themselves automatically.

You don't know what you don't know…

It's natural to assume that people have the levels of competence to match their roles. Sometimes, though, there are gaps in knowledge, awareness, and skills, where things somehow have slipped through the net. The gap seems strange and awkward, so people often hide the gap because they can't pinpoint what's missing or what they don't know. Others who see the gap feel confused because they expect and assume competence and then start to doubt it. You might see this in others. Others might see this in you.

Find the gap together. Start with coaching and mentoring, but if that doesn't take you very far, go back to basics. Find the blind spot in an accepting, non-judgemental way and practise instructional coaching (*What is instructional coaching?*, no date) together, step by step, on this aspect of leadership.

Coaching approaches

Embedding a coaching approach is so important for leadership effectiveness. Coaching enables you to lead more strategically, with fewer operational distractions, because you are developing your people to take ownership and responsibility – and grow.

This is why, at the end of most chapters, you'll find a section dedicated to themed coaching questions for coaching yourself, coaching others, and for coaching upwards – like those people in senior positions to you. These questions are intended to save you time, facilitate a coaching mindset, and ease your way into a coaching habit.

A coaching approach pays dividends – over time (Bungay Stanier, 2016).

Coaching approaches
Questions for reflecting and coaching yourself
- Write your name in the middle of a circle.
- Write the names of the people you work most closely with around the circle.
- Write a number beside each name to represent the extent to which you help or develop them.
    - 5 = I empower this person. I delegate willingly. I support their decisions. I trust them.
    - 4 = I find opportunities to empower this person. Mistakes are made and we both learn and grow from this.
    - 3 = I want to empower this person. They are capable. I don't prioritise developing them.
    - 2 = I control this person. They depend on me for permission and approval.
    - 1 = I micromanage this person. I don't trust them to do the job well enough.

EMPOWERING OTHERS THROUGH COACHING QUESTIONS

- What's your plan or next step, to move each individual a little bit closer to a five rating?
- How will you remain consistent in your approach?
- Over what timescale?
- How will you hold yourself accountable?

Questions for coaching others

- What does empowering mean in this school for pupils? And for staff?
- How do you empower the people you work with/the people you are responsible for?
- In what ways do you not empower them?
- How could you empower them more?
- What would be the benefits to you and to them?
- What would be the costs of not empowering them?
- What would be some valuable next steps?
- How will you take this forward?
- When will you start?
- How will you keep track of progress?
- What habits do you need to change? What do you need to do differently?
- How will you manage yourself to ensure you keep behaving the way you intend rather than repeat your current patterns of behaviour?
- What are the key points you're taking away from our discussion?

Questions for coaching upwards (those in authority to you)

In the situation you are facing:

- What do you want to achieve with this person?
- What does this person need to discover in themselves to deliver the results you need?
- How might you enable that?
- What approaches could you take to develop the individual(s)? For now and in the long term?
- How could you develop the individual(s) for the best results?

Perspectives

Leaders with different Coacting Styles control or give direction when under pressure according to their style:

Innovators – will talk too much and take up too much space/time, creating more work for themselves.

Achievers – will fix things, be the superheroes, and create more work for themselves.

Perfectors – will hold on tightly to their expertise and create more work for themselves.

Harmonisers – will protect or prevent others from making mistakes and create more work for themselves.

Keep in mind – some of the Coacting Styles are less people-focused. Achievers and Perfectors tend to focus more on the task than the person doing it. This is often a strength, but it can quickly become a problem if one of your people has particular needs, is going through a difficult time, or simply finds your style intimidating.

References

Ambition Institute (no date) *What is instructional coaching?* Ambition Institute. Available at: https://www.ambition.org.uk/blog/what-instructional-coaching/ (Accessed: 12 January 2025).

Bungay Stanier, M. (2016) *The coaching habit: Say less, ask more & change the way you lead forever.* Toronto: Box of Crayons Press.

CHAPTER 4

Embedding habits

Keeping the momentum going for lasting change

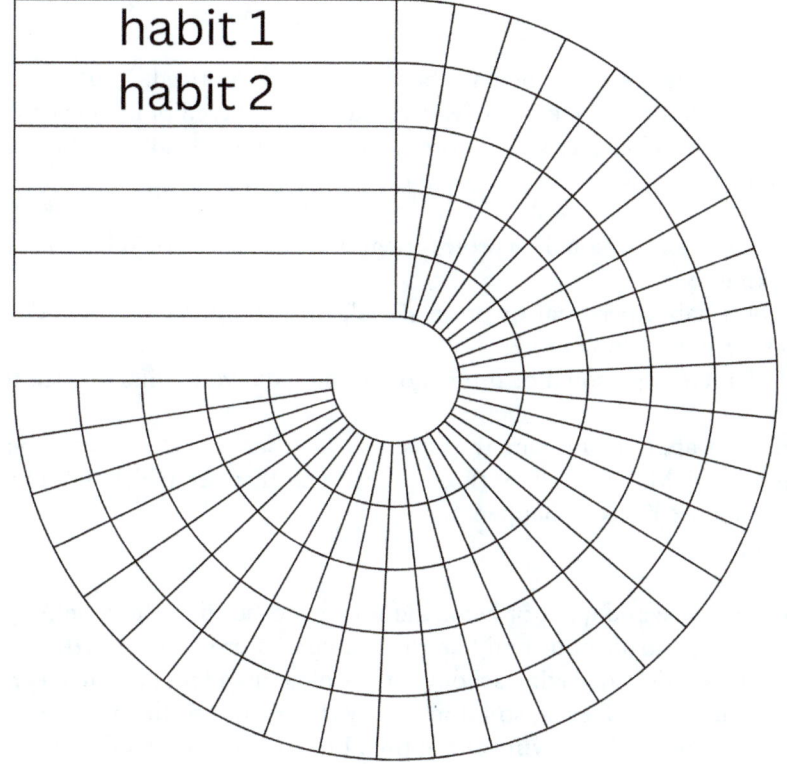

DOI: 10.4324/9781003571322-6

Theory versus practice

You're a bright individual. In a workplace quiz, you'd likely get top marks for knowing what's good for you, for your well-being, and your productivity. I'm guessing there may be a dissonance, though, between those quiz answers and your lifestyle. You find yourself working too long, missing the gym despite your paid-up membership, or eating quick food rather than the nutritious meals you've been promising yourself...

The issue isn't your knowledge; it's the gap between your knowledge and how you put it into practice. There's another gap too: the gap between knowing how to apply what you know and the attitude that fuels your commitment. It's tricky aligning all this even for one individual, let alone a whole school.

Inset days are a good example. They offer information and some experience, but then it's up to all the individuals to take what they've learnt and make the Inset day goals happen. How do you all keep things going until those intentions have become your regular behaviour and part of the school culture? This is key to actualising your vision.

Start with you

As a leader, your habits are important because they get noticed. You could choose to be a 'Do as I say, not as I do' kind of leader and risk your credibility. Or you could aim to lead by example. Whatever you choose, people will notice and be influenced by your example, so let's start with you:

1. Think of a habit, personal or professional, that you stick to. What are the reasons for sticking to it?
2. Think of a habit, personal or professional, that you don't stick to. What are the reasons for not sticking to it?
3. Think of a habit, personal or professional, that you would like to stick to.

What could you apply from your responses so far that would increase your chances of sticking to this? Make a note of those points, and then see which would make your intention even more likely to happen.

Some examples:

1. I enjoy the peace and quiet of being alone in my office first thing before the school day starts. I get loads done and like the feeling of a productive start.
2. I don't always stick to leaving school at the time I intend to. I like to clear things off my to-do list before I leave, so I don't carry things over to the next day.
3. I would like to stick to leaving at the time I intend. Then I would have more of an evening, which would have a positive impact on my relationships and well-being.

Notes:

- My determination and focus allow me to get work done within a limited time slot.
- I match the task to my energy.
- The schedule of the school day is immovable and constant.
- I shall make my cut-off time immovable at the end of the day and keep to it.

Share with others

It's one thing to decide on a change and another to make it happen, routinely and consistently, in ways that gradually improve performance and change the culture. The more people know about your intentions, the more likely you are to make them happen.

Here are some strategies for your use and for your people, so you can choose how to manage and minimise what gets in your way.

Choose a simple, easy, and achievable habit

The habits that tend to stick are those that take less than two minutes to accomplish. That's a great starting point. You'll build momentum and feel motivated by doing something that doesn't take long and is easy for you to do. You can build up to more challenging habits. For now, you want to build momentum and the success you feel when you keep a streak going. Here are some examples:

- Get outside and get fresh air every day.
- Note down what you're grateful for about each day before you leave work.
- Do some stretches before you go to bed.

Write it down

The process of writing down your intention means you revisit the purpose and the benefits it will bring. It enables you to be specific about your approach and how you'll make it happen. Writing it down brings more ownership as you hear your own voice behind the written words.

Keep a tracker

Keeping track of your progress can be a compelling reminder. Keep a tracker visible and tick off or tally every time you've managed to do the habit. This is quicker than a journal entry and gives you a progress check at a glance. It's not a competition, though; it's a log. It shows if or when you miss a day or two and prompts you back. It could be anything from a tally chart to a spreadsheet. You just need some system to record when you've completed your habit. You are in the world of recording progress, so simply select the tracking process that works for you. Diaries often have trackers. If yours doesn't, you can easily create a row of five or seven boxes each week that you can tick when your habit for the day is done.

You can download a series of simple, easy, and achievable Resilience Habits, complete with trackers, that contribute to the culture you hope to create, from www.routledge.com/9781032945392:

- Habits for taking care of yourself and managing your stress.
- Habits for keeping confident.
- Habits for keeping yourself organised.
- Habits for resilient relationships at work.

Know your triggers
Spot what might stop you and specify what you are going to do instead. Again, writing this down makes it more real and honest, so it may give your commitment that extra boost:

- Instead of channel hopping or scrolling through social media, I'll remember to follow my wind-down for bed routine so my mind and eyes are screen-free by the time my head hits the pillow.
- When I'm tired and fancy some chocolate or crisps, instead of going for carbs, I'll find a fruit snack and a glass of water, so I feel nourished and hydrated.

Be clear about 'yes' or 'no'
Clarity keeps things simple. What does your new habit mean saying 'yes' to? What will you say 'no' to? Again, writing this down helps you to adapt and manage your behaviour change gradually, and on your terms.

Practise the words you will use when saying 'no' so that you feel more confident when you need to turn something down or refuse a request:

- 'Right now, I need some air and headspace. If it's not urgent, I'll see you back here in fifteen minutes. Or I'll be in my office after 4.00.'
- 'Those birthday treats look yummy, thank you. I'm sticking with fruit though for my healthy habit, so thanks but no thanks!'

Manage your expectations
Habits that last tend to result from a gradual approach. It's disappointing if you start with the intention of a daily or weekday practice and realise you've missed a day or two. Contrast this with the intention of 'I'll do this at least three times a week.' Then you'll be pleased if you manage your new habit three times and super-pleased if you manage it five times. The more you get into your habit, the more your habit will get into you.

It's easy to feel demotivated if you miss a couple of days. When that happens, it's important to be kind and patient with yourself and not to beat yourself up. Stick to your baseline minimum, and you'll feel good and motivated when you see the other days adding up.

Once you are past the introductory stage of forming a new habit, there's likely to be a dip in attention and practice. Whether it's coaching, mindfulness, growth mindset, self-care, or resilience habits, no matter how committed you are at the start, you're human, and it's likely your attention will be drawn towards other priorities. When your new habit becomes not so new, when your enthusiasm fades, and your commitment wanes, you'll need some reminders to keep the momentum going.

Reminders
Visual cues
A sign on your door, an image on your notice board, or a sticky note on your diary or computer are the most common ones. Change these frequently so that they can prompt you anew.

You could create a card or find an image that inspires you to keep going. Or jot down a word or short phrase and keep it with you, in your pocket or attached to your phone. Notice it throughout the day and let it nudge you into action.

Reminder app
Set alerts to prompt you into action. Acting on the alerts is imperative here! Otherwise, they'll irritate you and become guilt alerts.

Choose proactivity over guilt
Whenever you feel annoyed or guilty about forgetting or not doing the habit, be proactive. Instead of accepting a flimsy excuse, do something that gets you back on track. Notice what you did or didn't do and put something in place that will remind you not to fall for that again.

Revisit why it's important – who benefits from your doing this?

Say it out loud
Tell someone. State your intention. Choose someone who will buddy you (hold you accountable in a friendly way), and who will notice or at least enquire when you have and haven't done what you intended. Saying your intentions out loud is a significant step towards making them happen. No matter how senior your position is in your school, it can add something to your relationships if you share and role-model changing a habit. The very best accountability buddies are likely to be your pupils! How about you announce your habit to them?

Link it to something you do anyway
There are some habits that can be done while you're doing something else, especially those thinking, reflective, and mindset-type habits. Short, reflective practices lend themselves well to having a shower, walking from your car to your office, or savouring your first cuppa of the day.

Remain consistent. The same time and same place can mean you get used to making this your routine.

Display success
What symbol or metaphor could you create to represent momentum and keep things going? Display this on the staff room notice board and ask everyone to contribute their successes to the display over time.

Look for opportunities
Keep an eye out for times each day or during the week when you can practise your habit, then you'll naturally reinforce your new behaviour patterns.

Finding it difficult?
Focus on one aspect of the habit. If there's a particular aspect of the habit where you seem to stumble, put more focus on that aspect so you can experience gradual progress.

Imagine the future
Imagine that you have embedded the habit, that it's a routine part of your (working) life. What would you say to others about how you got there, and what the benefits are?

Team talk
Generate ideas and suggestions for how to keep habits going when people are together. Your team members will share what worked for them, and this will revive interest and enthusiasm as well as ownership.

All the above points can be applied to anyone and everyone aiming to form new habits for cultural change. This means that when you introduce change, you can offer ways of making the different behaviour choices and new habits stick. You could diarise highlighting one of the reminders at team meetings over the year. That really would show your persistence and encouragement.

Now back to that personal or professional habit that you'd like to stick to? What's your plan for starting and keeping it going?

There are numerous good resources on habit building such as (Duhigg, 2013; Clear, 2018).

Coaching approaches
Coaching yourself
You know yourself best:

- What has worked for you to keep something going?
- What's interesting about that?
- What's affirming?
- How will you act on this to build in (and on) your success?
- How will you factor in some accountability?
- When will you start?
- When and how will you review progress?

Coaching others
- What one small and easy habit would make a difference in how you feel?
- What one small and easy habit would please you if you kept it going?
- What would this look like in practice?
- How might you make this happen?
- Who could you share this with in the spirit of friendly accountability?
- How would you summarise this discussion?

Coaching upwards
- In your role here, how do you demonstrate the habit(s) that we aim to embed across the school community?
- Which habit would you want to practise further?
- What's a good way of doing this so that others see you as a role model?
- What opportunities are there for you to demonstrate your commitment?
- How will you remind yourself to keep it going? For it to become a routine approach?

Perspectives

There are many, many factors to embedding behaviour change across a community. How we communicate and relate together is just one of those factors but a very significant one. Here are pointers you can consider when you want to embed gradual change among different individuals.

Innovators – are easily bored, and repetition will drag them down to a halt. How will you make this fun, different, and new?

Achievers – like tasks that are easy to tick off their to-do lists. How will you make this productive and pacey?

Perfectors – deliver well on consistency and thoroughness. How will you convince them this is (another) priority?

Harmonisers – enjoy the momentum and support offered through others. How will you enable a team approach to get them on board?

Keep in mind – if you're meeting with resistance to change, it *may* be a lack of commitment, but it may also be something else, something deeper, that is worth raising with the persons concerned.

References

Clear, J. (2018) *Atomic habits: An easy & proven way to build good habits & break bad ones: Tiny changes, remarkable results.* London: Random House Business.

Duhigg, C. (2013) *The power of habit: Why we do what we do and how to change.* New York: Random House Books.

SECTION 2

Wellness

Where Section 1 covers the guiding principles for *People Solutions for School Leaders* – respect, communicating, empowering, and embedding habits – the unifying focus for Section 2 is your well-being.

Whatever your role at work, keeping well is essential for doing your job well. School leaders routinely sacrifice their well-being in service to their pupils and to keep on top of their workload.

Well-being and workload are cited as common reasons for leaving the profession. Therefore, to remain in the profession, leaders need to know what works for them to stay well and to enjoy what they do.

This section is about keeping yourself well physically, mentally, and emotionally, and enabling your people to keep well physically, mentally, and emotionally too.

CHAPTER 5

The life-changing benefits of self-compassion

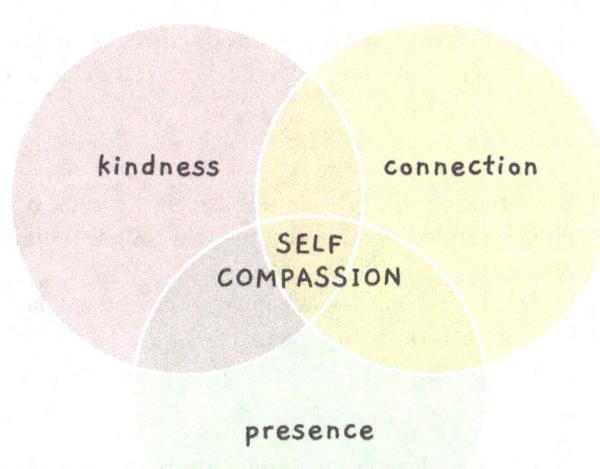

Emotional intelligence and self-compassion

I've been a student of applied emotional intelligence (EI) since 2005. Applied EI has shaped my values in life, underpinned my coaching practice, and influenced my relationships with myself and others.

Self-esteem is fundamental to applied EI, and I have duly given it a lot of importance while exploring ways to build and increase it.

In 2015, I came across Kristen Neff's (Neff, 2021) work on self-compassion. This added a new dimension to my work on applied EI in general, and on well-being and resilience in particular.

I had three lightbulb moments in quick succession on discovering Dr Neff's work that really changed my thinking. More than this, they changed my approach to life from the inside out:

1. I realised the difference between self-esteem and self-compassion when I read Kristen Neff's 'self-compassion steps in *precisely* where self-esteem lets us down' (Neff, 2021, p. 153).
2. Self-esteem is how you evaluate yourself whereas self-compassion is how you treat yourself.
3. Self-esteem increases when you become skilful in the process of comparing yourself with yourself (not others).

I just want to clarify that self-esteem, self-worth, and self-regard mean broadly the same thing – how you *value* yourself. Self-compassion is how you *behave towards* yourself.

When your self-esteem goes out the window

Transpose yourself to a situation when your self-esteem hit rock bottom. That awful place of isolation, feeling stranded, lost, and unworthy. What remained for you when you felt alone and wretched?

I'd never really considered what was left when your self-esteem had gone. Once I did, I got it – I got what self-compassion really means.

Self-compassion is how you treat yourself

Whether it's a dip or a pit, how do you pick yourself up and get going again? How do you survive loneliness or fear, shame, or embarrassment? Whether that's alone in a hospital bed, facing devastating news, or feelings of failure, you practise self-compassion.

Self-compassion is extending kindness, care, warmth, and understanding towards yourself when you're facing your shortcomings, inadequacies, mistakes, setbacks, and tragedies instead of criticising yourself, being hard on yourself, beating yourself up, or thinking 'Why me?' And it works.

You treat yourself *exactly* the way you would treat someone you love and care for. The only thing is it feels a bit weird because we're not used to doing this and it's deeply personal. While we've learnt from role models in our lives how to care for others, we haven't been taught how to transfer that care inwardly, how to apply that process to ourselves, so it feels awkward talking to ourselves in a comforting, loving way.

Would you push an exhausted child to keep going through the night with their schoolwork until they'd finished? More likely, you'd encourage them to stop, take a break, and return to it fresh. You'd be kind to them and problem solve with them. You can do that with yourself.

We're much more familiar with self-talk that is critical and unkind. How did we ever lose sight of our ability to turn kindness inwards and soothe ourselves better?

Comparison with yourself

Self-esteem grows when you compare yourself with yourself, and your progress today with yesterday, last week, or last year. Self-esteem is not about being better than others.

Kristen Neff highlights how, in our data-driven education system, we feel good about ourselves and our schools **IF** we feel equal to, or preferably better than, others. If we need better results than others to feel good, then we require other people's results not to be as good. That applies to a child in the classroom absorbing how well other children did. It applies to you as a leader, scrolling through other schools' results and grades in your cluster. Neff acknowledges this 'unwinnable' state of affairs:

> When we're deeply invested in seeing ourselves positively, we tend to feel threatened if others do better than we do. The very reason we want to succeed is because we want to feel accepted and worthy, to be close to others and belong. It's a classic Catch 22. The very act of competing with others for success sets up an unwinnable situation in which the feelings of connectedness we crave are forever out of reach.

(Neff, 2021)

I feel troubled about how important and significant these points are for life and how little focus is given in schools on intrinsic motivation that is not based on the pressures arising from comparison with others.

In my view, putting self-compassion into practice, learning how to make things better for yourself, may be the most personally empowering thing you can do. I've seen this happen with headteachers, their school culture, and their own families. Self-compassion strengthens you from the inside out. It develops the inner resource you need to get through the ups and downs of life. It certainly develops self-reliance, a much-needed skill for the future.

Imagine self-reliant young people knowing how to cope with peer pressure, distress from social media, shyness, not feeling good enough, bullying, exam stress, among other pressures.

In my view, the ultimate self-empowerment is accessing those inner resources. It's knowing how to make yourself feel a little bit better from the inside out when you're feeling down. Not reaching for alcohol, drugs, social media distraction, or harming yourself. It's knowing how to feel good about yourself through challenges and the ups and downs of living.

PEOPLE SOLUTIONS FOR SCHOOL LEADERS

Table 5.1 Explaining self-compassion

What self-compassion is not but what most people do	*What self-compassion is* but most people haven't yet learned how to do
judging yourself	accepting yourself
giving yourself a hard time when your struggling	giving yourself support
putting yourself down	valuing who you are
belittling or ignoring what you really feel	thinking kind thoughts about yourself
comparing yourself unkindly with others	believing you are good enough
isolating yourself when you feel embarrassed, guilty or ashamed	reaching out and connecting with other people you trust
catastrophising when things go wrong	reassuring yourself you will cope
neglecting to do what keeps you well	taking care of yourself to keep well

If you know, as a school leader, how to empower people in this way, if you share your interpretation of self-compassion with your people, and very gradually, they become more self-reliant, you will be part of a sea change in society.

So, how to do this?

Explain self-compassion

Self-compassion is simple and it's complex. Take a moment to think how you would define it.

It may be easier to understand by contrasting what self-compassion is *not* with what it *is*. Table 5.1 lists what self-compassion is *not* but what most people do, alongside what self-compassion *is* but most people haven't yet learned how to do.

If you think of self-compassion as a Venn diagram (Figure 5.1), the practice is the sweet spot in the middle, where the components of presence, kindness, and connection align:

Presence – being present for yourself so that you notice what's happening without being pulled into your feelings or tripped up by your thinking. Being mindfully aware

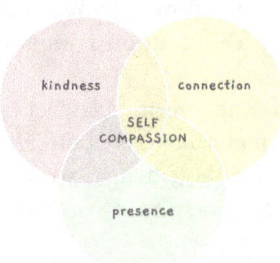

Figure 5.1 Self-compassion Venn diagram

so you can acknowledge and accept painful thoughts and feelings in a clear and detached way.
Kindness – at the same time showing kindness to yourself, allowing yourself warmth and understanding, especially through difficulties, stress, and setbacks. (Kindness reduces the cortisol stress response and increases oxytocin).
Connection – knowing you are not isolated in how you feel; realising your experience is shared by others; and recognising suffering is normal and part of being human.

Share simple techniques to practise self-compassion

- *Presence* = Notice – Pause – Breathe.
- *Kindness* = Reassure yourself with kind words – create your own oxytocin.
- *Connection* = Normalise, recognise it's not just you.

Raise awareness of how most people don't practise self-compassion

Table 5.2 highlights what many people do when facing difficulties or setbacks contrasted with a self-compassionate response. Instead of kindness, most people go straight to judgement; instead of connection, they isolate themselves; instead of being truly present, they take a distorted view of their reality.

Choose resources for practising self-compassion

The resources illustrated in Figure 5.2 are available for download from www.routledge.com/9781032945392. You can select the most useful downloads for the groups of people you are working with to match their levels of receptivity and pragmatism.

- Use the graphics from this chapter to explain and discuss self-compassion.
- Talk about self-compassion in three easy steps:
    Notice – Pause and breathe.
    Reassure yourself – Create your own oxytocin.
    Normalise – Recognise it's not just you.
- Share the self-compassion tracker for each individual's daily use that lists 30 self-compassion habits.

Table 5.2 Lack of self-compassion is a common response

When facing difficulties or setbacks

What many people do	Self-compassionate response
Judge and blame themselves, use critical harsh messages	Show warmth, kindness, and understanding to self
Self-isolate, feel alone and responsible	Reach out and connect with others
Self-absorbed, catastrophising, narrow perception on reality	Remain present and detached, moment by moment

Figure 5.2 Self-compassion resources

THE BENEFITS OF SELF-COMPASSION

- Share the blank self-compassion tracker for people to customise it for their personal self-compassion habits.
- ('When the Tension Goes' (no date)) is a website all about self-compassion. The downloads include a poster you can display and share with your school community.
- Explore how children learn self-compassion and how you teach self-compassion in your school. Start with *Reassuring Myself* for ideas, resources, and practices. It's a 30-page PDF booklet designed for children and is written for the inner child in you.
- Share the *Habits for Family Care and Compassion* within your school community (these resources can all be downloaded from www.routledge.com/9781032945392).

Too soft and fluffy?

I've experienced how difficult it is for headteachers to put self-compassion into practice for themselves, even though they agree with it. Why? Mainly because (at least in Western society) their family upbringing and their education have programmed them to believe it's selfish. They feel selfish putting their own needs first. Whatever metaphor they use for others (the oxygen mask on the aeroplane, the empty fuel tank in a car, the 1% battery in their phone), they struggle to role-model this kind of self-care or what Kristen Neff refers to as 'Tender Self-Compassion'.

This sense of 'soft and 'fluffy' was challenged in 2021 when Dr Neff published *Fierce Self-Compassion* which complemented the model by adding the dimension of courage:

- Add courage to presence and it becomes seeing and speaking the truth, empowered clarity. 'I see what's happening. This is not OK. This needs to change.'
- Add courage to kindness and it becomes bravely protecting ourselves through speaking up assertively and establishing boundaries. Standing up for ourselves.
- Add courage to connection and it becomes finding strength in numbers. No longer the bystander, standing up for others in similar situations.

Figure 5.3 includes fierce self-compassion in the self-compassion Venn diagram. Self-compassion is not soft and fluffy at all. Believe me, this work is tough.

There is increasing evidence now from Dr Neff's research at the Centre for Mindful Self-Compassion https://centerformsc.org/ to show how fierce and tender self-compassion enhance well-being. For example:

- They reduce depression, anxiety, and stress. They increase happiness and life satisfaction and improve physical health.
- They deactivate the threat-defence system and activate the care system helping us to feel safe.
- They transform negative states into positive ones. It feels good to open our hearts; it's a meaningful and rewarding experience.
- They counteract shame. We can easily confuse our behaviour (what we did) with who we are (I am a failure).
- They provide emotional resilience by helping us to get through painful times without being knocked flat.

Figure 5.3 Fierce and nurturing self-compassion Venn diagram

- They help people with health issues to stay emotionally balanced and get through the day.
- They improve how you relate to yourself (which is more important than the intensity of the challenges you face in life).

In Dr Neff's words:

> 'When we relate to ourselves with tender self-compassion, we care for and nurture ourselves.'
>
> 'When we relate to ourselves with fierce self-compassion, we assert our autonomy and stand up for our rights.'
>
> 'When fierce and tender self-compassion are balanced, we can be fair and just.'
>
> *(D. K. Neff, 2021)*

Imagine a staff team, a year group, a school community that cared for and nurtured themselves, who asserted their autonomy and stood up for their rights, who were enabled to be fair and just.

Imagine.

Shared experience

A primary school headteacher shares their personal growth from living and leading with self-compassion.

Understanding what self-compassion is has given me the tools to show kindness to myself – this is, I guess, the most obvious or direct impact of exploring the topic. But more significantly, over the months, and years now, of applying self-compassion practices, I realise the guilt has gone about actually being kind to myself. And that there is so much more…

For me, self-compassion practice has given me the overwhelming ability to be authentic in my leadership and completely at ease with this concept. Self-compassion has allowed me to accept myself as truly imperfect, but certainly good enough. It has halted the need to regularly compare myself as a leader with others; if I ever slip back into this pattern of thinking, I can quickly recognise what I am doing and the damage this causes. This recognition means that I am also able to pause the negative thinking and reframe my thoughts so I can move on more positively.

Being able to be 'authentically me' has taken away fear, helped me to find deeper resilience and empowered me to lead with increased confidence. This was even true when Ofsted visited. Naturally I felt apprehensive as I took the phone call, but I didn't feel 'fear.' I felt convinced that I was 'enough' and our school was 'enough.' Yes, I was prepared, having sat in an 'Ofsted window' for a while, but the internal feeling of strength was coming from something far more empowering than being prepared. I compassionately gave myself full permission to be authentic without trepidation of being judged for this or told I was 'wrong.'

Suddenly I know I'm not a copy of any other leader or any other school. There are so many great leaders and great schools out there and the world is richer for having so many variations of 'great'. This is not a negative tool of comparison for me, it is a genuine source of inspiration. On the Ofsted day, my self-compassion practice let me know that I should fearlessly celebrate the things we were doing well at the time and engage in professional dialogue without guilt or judgment about our next steps, or concerning myself with comparison of others.

Afterwards I initially wondered how the inspection had helped us to be any better than we had been before, however, after a longer period of quieter reflection, I realised that what I learnt was that I can be 'fearless, authentic and strong' as a leader and people are OK with this – even Ofsted inspectors! How much better can we continue to be as a school if we don't allow 'fear' to control us? I know that by being satisfied with my authentic self, I am more alive to the parts of the job I adore and the parts I find more challenging. This in turn helps me to seek help where I need to and enjoy the deep satisfaction of the parts that I like the most. We can keep on improving and enjoying this growth whole-heartedly.

This practice is spreading to others in the team too. By being authentic, regularly talking about my connection with self-compassionate practice, I find that others are drawn in and curious about using these tools in their own lives. The people who have joined this quiet movement, perform their jobs well and like me, find joyful satisfaction in what they do. When you know how to treat yourself with kindness, it is a pleasure to lead naturally with a genuine feeling of joy and growth.

References

Neff, D.K. (2021) *Fierce self compassion: How women can harness kindness to speak up claim their power & thrive*. Penguin Life.

Neff, K. (2021) *Self-compassion: The proven power of being kind to yourself.* 10th anniversary ed. London: Yellow Kite, an imprint of Hodder & Stoughton.

'Self-compassion practices' (no date) *Self-compassion*. Available at: https://self-compassion.org/self-compassion-practices/ (Accessed: 16 January 2025).

When the Tension Goes (no date) *When the tension goes*. Available at: https://whenthetensiongoes.com/ (Accessed: 12 January 2025).

CHAPTER 6

Choices for everyday well-being

Empowering habits for staying well

If you want to perform well in your leadership role, it matters that you keep well. This means that prioritising your well-being is not selfish – it's essential. And this is likely to mean allowing yourself to do less work. All of which takes quite a lot of un-learning, for you and for others around you too.

Another area that involves un-learning is allowing yourself to rest. Resting enables you to top up your energy reserves so your enthusiasm naturally returns. You become more at ease in yourself and easier to be around. My mentor asks the probing question: 'How can more ease create more impact?' Definitely one to contemplate.

This chapter offers quick-fire, ready-reference lists to scan whenever you or your people are feeling flat. You can choose what fits your needs in that moment and link self-care with motivation.

Neuroscience has shown that dopamine, oxytocin, serotonin, and endorphins are the four feel-good hormones. There are things you can do naturally to increase the action of these hormones and benefit your brain and body. Table 6.1, along with the infographic illustrated in Figure 6.1, show you what to be aware of.

You can download the infographic, complete with trackers, as illustrated in Figure 6.1, from www.routledge.com/9781032945392

Table 6.1 The four feel-good hormones

DOPAMINE	for energy, motivation, pleasure, and reward.
	· Dopamine affects learning, attention, concentration, and mood.
	· Be aware – patterns of addiction can result from the repeated dopamine rush (computer games, social media hits, drugs, sex, alcohol, shopping, overeating).
	· Gain dopamine's benefits through self-care activities – eat nourishing foods, complete a small task, dance until you sweat, sort your sleep hygiene.
OXYTOCIN	for belonging, trusting, and bonding.
	· Oxytocin affects feeling connected to others.
	· Be aware – low levels are linked to depression.
	· Gain oxytocin's benefits through socialising, physical touch (hugs, including hugging yourself), reassuring yourself with kind and honest words, massage, listening to relaxing music, singing in a group, stroking an animal.
SEROTONIN	for mood, well-being, and happiness.
	· Serotonin affects mood.
	· Be aware – low levels are linked to depression.
	· Gain serotonin's benefits through ensuring safety and respect, going outside in the sunshine, immersing yourself in nature, mindful movement, exercising, workouts, cycling, meditation.
ENDORPHINS	for releasing stress – the body's natural painkillers.
	· Endorphins affect determination and euphoria.
	· Gain the benefits of endorphins through dancing and exercise, listening to upbeat music, playing musical instruments, watching a film, playing and having fun, laughing, enjoying a hot bath.

CHOICES FOR EVERYDAY WELL-BEING

Figure 6.1 Twenty feel-good habits with trackers

Tables 6.2, 6.3, 6.4 and 6.5 are based on the infographic and offer quick ways to gain the benefits of each feel-good hormone:

As well as being useful personally, these prompts may be helpful to empower your people gradually towards more self-reliance. So, when you or they are feeling low, demotivated, and/or lonely, you can find a more natural way of shifting the mood.

It's easier to make lifestyle choices happen when others are joining in, so how about displaying these posters in the staff room and on the loo doors to get people talking and feeling part of something that shows well-being really matters? The trackers enable everyone to see, experience, and practise simple steps to feeling well.

Table 6.2 Quick ways to gain the benefits of dopamine

DOPAMINE – *energy, motivation, pleasure, reward*	
1. TIRED	· Allow yourself to take a nap.
	· Find what works for you to top up your sleep bank.
2. MOVE	· Walk around.
	· Use a standing workstation to change the way you work.
	· Stop your shoulders, stomach, and back slouching.
3. NOURISH	· Replace quick fix sugar and carbs with bananas, avocados, pumpkin seeds, soy, dark chocolate.
4. BE FIRM	· Give yourself a good and kind talking to. Focus on the facts.
	· Find some boundaries.
	· Take action to prioritise YOU.
5. RELAX	· Meditation, yoga, Pilates, mindfulness – find what works for you so you get life back into perspective.

Table 6.3 Quick ways to gain the benefits of oxytocin

OXYTOCIN – *belonging, connecting, bonding*

1. KINDNESS	• Be with kind people.
	• If your energy is low the harsh, the inconsiderate, and the drainers are not good company for you.
2. SOOTHE	• Tension gets stored in your body – your shoulders, neck, and back muscles. Find ways to release it. Gentle movement. Massage.
3. CONTACT	• Touch matters. Hugs are ideal.
	• Hold your hand, stroke your arm, pet an animal.
4. SOCIAL	• Do things you enjoy while being with others.
	• Walking, singing, dancing.
	• Get together for a cuppa.
5. CALM	• Be patient. Let go. Find calm. Trust that these difficulties will pass in time.

Table 6.4 Quick ways to gain the benefits of serotonin

SEROTONIN – *mood, well-being, happiness*

1. SATISFY	• Prepare yourself a healthy, satisfying meal and savour it.
2. OUTSIDE	• Breathe in some fresh air.
	• Go outside and sit in Mother Nature's lap.
3. RESPECT	• Choose where to go, and who to be with, so you can ensure safety and respect. And be at ease in yourself.
4. PRESENT	• Move away from the screens.
	• Turn off all devices that ping, buzz, and distract you away from being present.
5. CENTRE	• Relax so you find your centre. Focus your attention on the part of you that is calm, detached, and balanced.

Table 6.5 Quick ways to gain the benefits of endorphins

ENDORPHINS – *stress release*

1. LAUGH	• Find something, do something or watch something that makes you laugh out loud.
2. NEW	• Go somewhere different.
	• Have a change of scene.
	• Click refresh on your patterns, old habits, or routines.
3. FUN	• Be playful and let go.
	• Do something light-hearted.
	• Do whatever is fun for you.
4. CREATE	• Do something you enjoy – sketch, write, go for a run, make music, create something fun, or beautiful.
5. INSPIRE	• Discover something meaningful for you.
	• Reconnect with whatever nourishes your soul.
	• Take your thoughts somewhere else and find relief for a little while.

CHOICES FOR EVERYDAY WELL-BEING

Coaching approaches
Coaching yourself
- Using the ready reference guide or infographics, list the activities or actions that would work for you to raise your energy and/or prevent a low energy state from recurring.
- Select one or two that you are prepared to commit to.
- As well as being accountable to yourself, who can you share your intentions with, who would also hold you accountable to the practices you choose?
- When will you start doing this?
- When will you speak to your accountability partner?
- What will feel like progress?
- How will you record or chart your feel-good progress?

Coaching others
- Looking at the descriptions on the ready reference guides, what is the closest match to how you've been feeling and/or what you need to feel a bit better?
- What steps could you take to start to raise your energy a little at a time?
- What would you be prepared to do right away?
- Who could you talk to about your intention so that you can check in with them about how you're getting on – someone who would hold you accountable in a friendly way?
- What next steps will you take?
- How will you keep track of your progress and how you feel so that you can refer to what works well and what doesn't work so well for you over time?

Coaching upwards
- How aware are you of the four feel-good neurochemicals?
- To what extent do they inform your day-to-day living?
- What would be most useful for you to apply from the ready-reference guide or infographics?

Perspectives

Coaching Styles highlight the traits of people at work. Here, in the context of being a danger to your own health, some of those strengths are flipped into flaws. It may be useful to read them as alerts.

Innovators – enjoy taking risks and going fast. They are high-energy individuals and from a distance can seem foolish in how they fuel those high energy levels. Their speed and low attention to detail mean things come back and bite them. Eventually, it's their health. They don't go for reflective practices as they prefer thinking out loud to others – often the others surrounding the Innovator daren't hold the mirror up to reveal the more sobering truths.

Achievers – drive themselves so hard they crash and burn out. They won't *stop*, so are phenomenal in getting things done. They're likely to ignore or stifle any signs of deteriorating health because they really don't have time for such inconveniences. From a distance, there's a foolishness to this, but they are too close to see it and will disregard any concerns from others because they believe they know best. Hence the real need for self-awareness practices.

Perfectors – are risk averse and require time to reflect and consider. It really matters to them that they get things right, so, to this end, they carry the weight of overload and a backlog of tasks, which they conscientiously take home to complete. This causes different types of punishing health issues and relationship tensions. The cumulative strain of over-analysing, withdrawing from others, not letting out their fears, feelings, or concerns, and their reluctance to compromise on quality all take their toll. They remain stubbornly fixed and don't get a true perspective on what they are doing to themselves.

Harmonisers – are cautious about upsetting people because they are sensitive to the needs and feelings of others. They require harmony and that need often results in things remaining unresolved, decisions being delayed, workloads increasing and inevitably, what they most dread – people becoming unhappy with them. They don't easily see through how their conviction to help others becomes burdensome. They become overwhelmed emotionally because they can't please everyone and overloaded with work demands because they put their needs last.

Keep in mind – pressures outside the workplace, disability, recent recovery from an illness, or having different cultural beliefs can add pressures above and beyond those that go with the job.

CHAPTER 7

Personal organisation

First things first

Your workload is high, even before the many unexpected occurrences in any school day. It's easy to believe you will never get to the end of your to-do list because there really is always more to do. The sense of overload starts to become familiar but can easily lead to feeling overwhelmed and a growing concern about how long you can keep this going.

It's time to reframe what keeping on top of things means and to reset your approach. To keep well, perform well and enjoy your role, you need to do well and do less. You need to un-learn the societal and professional drivers that push you to do more and more.

This chapter has strategies to help you take charge and un-learn some of that programming.

But first, if your executive functioning is low, or your energy and attention dip when reading about organising yourself, just read and apply these three points:

- Follow your strategic vision.
- Identify your priority each day.
- Focus on accomplishing that priority.

And please remember that personal organisation is a particular skill set that highlights individual differences. It's easy to be inconvenienced by other people's lack of organisation and to judge them for that. (Beware the word 'lazy'.)

Working life would be much easier if the same time management system worked for everyone. There is no such system. How you manage your time must work for you. It doesn't matter whether it's high-tech or low-tech.

What works for you is unlikely to work for your team members, so it matters in leadership to share, and experiment with, different approaches, thereby, enabling each person to find their own way. You can start experimenting with *A Guide to Time Management Models* (*Virtual College*, no date).

Work will always fill the time you make available for it

- How much of your time are you prepared to make available for work?
- How do you keep within the time you allocate for work?
- How do you keep track of where your time is going?

Your well-being, the example you set for others, and your need to be focused, all require you to manage how you use the time you have available. In no small part, the quality of your life rests on your attitude towards, your decisions about, and your actions around time.

The first, and perhaps most difficult imperative, is to accept you won't get everything done.

This is a big one. It's not so much an action as a state of mind. You won't get everything done; there will always be more to do. The to-do list and the inbox will keep on filling. There is a cost that comes with constantly striving to clear your workload, a cost to your life choices, your relationships, and your well-being.

You set an example for everyone if you can show through your actions that you are serious about your time, your boundaries regarding how you use your time, and your willingness to accept that sometimes things don't get done.

Once you can accept you won't get everything done and let go of the professional and societal pressures upon you, you'll start to feel relieved.

Determine your priorities
Great minds in the world of individual effectiveness agree on this imperative – identify your priorities and work outwards from them. Priorities in this case are your priorities in life, not just work-related priorities.

By clarifying, returning to, and updating your priorities, you set the bedrock for how you use your time. If you can keep your focus on your top priorities, you'll have the peace of mind that you've dealt with the things that matter most.

What is a good use of your time?
- Eliminate tasks that are a waste of your time.
- Learn from tasks that take longer than you anticipated.
- Negotiate with people who take too much of your time so they start to take less.

    Include general interruptions here too. Clarify some simple criteria for when it's OK and not OK to disturb you. You don't always have to have an open door.

Clarify your boundaries then communicate your boundaries
In simple terms, identify where you need to set boundaries, let others know this, and then keep to the boundaries you've set.

Prompts for boundary setting:

- What are my boundaries to ensure I get a good night's sleep?
- What is my most productive time for meetings?
- How do I manage emails more effectively? How much time to give them? When to start and stop?
- When do I finish work?
- What are my boundaries around messaging and social media?

Give a clear explanation of your new approach: 'I've decided to take a different approach to how I manage my time for my well-being and my workload management. In order to have time and space to get on top of things, and to switch off after I've finished work, I've decided:

- I will be home by 6 p.m. three days a week.
- I won't reply to work texts after 8 p.m.

- I'm removing emails from my phone, and my cut off time for emails is 8 p.m. If something is urgent, and by urgent I mean (specify what you mean), it's OK to phone me. Otherwise, we wait until the next day.'

If other people access your diary, create and communicate some simple guidelines and agree on the process for adding or changing what's scheduled. For example, if another priority coincides with what you have in your schedule – and it will – make sure your original commitment is respected, not lost. Especially if that commitment is to your strategic time.

Plan backwards/around your priorities
This may seem like stating the obvious, but it's often overlooked. For example:

- You know the date for the Full Governing Board Meeting. You know what you'll be expected to deliver. Schedule preparation time the week before so you know you'll be ready. Then you won't be worrying about how you'll find the time to fit the preparation in, and you won't end up working late.
- You have booked a holiday over half-term and you know you'll be interviewing on the Monday and Tuesday when you return. Schedule time for your preparation the week before you leave and honour this time. Enjoy the peace of mind that it's pretty much all done before you set off, ready for you on your return.
- Most importantly, know yourself and how you are most productive. If you work best with tight deadlines, do block out time before the deadline to make sure you meet it. Don't waste your energy feeling guilty about not planning in advance.

Block out time for the unexpected
Things crop up every day in a headteacher's life. If there isn't any space to allow for that, those demands will take up time and you'll feel overwhelmed. Of course, the unexpected won't crop up conveniently at the times you've scheduled, but having some reserve space, even 30 minutes each day, will mean the priorities won't be completely displaced by the unexpected.

Avoid the trap of 'all or nothing'
There are three variables in your work – quality, time, and resource:

- To get home on time to fulfil your priority wish of putting your kids to bed yourself, you may have to compromise on the high quality of the report or document you're working on.
- To deliver a quality project with limited resources, you may have to ask for more time.
- To deliver on time and with good quality, you may have to do or include less than you'd originally thought.

PERSONAL ORGANISATION

WfH FGS!

You may feel guilty about working from home. Perhaps the headteachers you worked with earlier in your career would have frowned upon this, or you feel guilty about the freedom to do this when your people are bound by timetables and classroom-based activities.

You are not needed in the classroom, and there are times when working away from distraction is essential so you can set the school's direction. Instead of putting 'WfH' on the staff noticeboard, write instead 'Strategy Planning Day'. Back at work the next day, let people know how much you were able to get done, how much it benefited the school and the bigger picture.

To-do lists

What system works for you? Electronic, sticky notes, written to-do lists, marker board, notebook by your bed? Choose the most reliable for you.

Eat the frog

A popular time management technique, taken from an old Spanish story, is based on this question: If you had to eat a frog, medicinally, every day for the rest of your life, when would be the best time to do it? What if it was a big warty frog? Consider:

- How would you feel once that was out of the way for the day?
- What would be the worst thing to do?
- How can you apply the frog principle today, tomorrow, and this week?

There are so many benefits to getting the difficult things out of the way sooner rather than later in your day.

Structures for creating more work/life harmony

Using a structure to organise your priorities across the term will enable you to feel more in charge of your time. You can share the following suggestions with other team members so they feel more in charge of their time too.

Half-termly planner

Choose your preferred format to create a half-term planner: a blank page in your diary or one side of A4.

Divide the page into spaces or boxes – one for each seven-day week. Number them Week 1, Week 2, etc.

Determine your priorities for the next half-term – your priorities for home, work, family, yourself, and relationships.

Add each priority to the corresponding weekly space:

- Pizza night with the kids might occur every Saturday night.
- Your Pilates class meets every week.

- The School Improvement Plan might be in week 2.
- Performance Reviews: weeks 4 and 5.
- A weekend walk or date night with your partner every single week.

Weekly planner

Transfer each week's priorities into a weekly planner. This could be your week-to-view diary or a separate sheet of paper with a space for each day.

Where will each priority fit?

It won't be long before you realise you just can't fit everything in. You'll probably see a clash of meetings and tasks that may be occupying a lot of room in your diary. What to do with these?

- Delegate?
- Reschedule?
- Complete them and take less time doing so?
- Let them go? Acknowledge that they won't get done, but your priorities will.

As a headteacher, a key part of your role is strategic, so it's essential to delegate the operational tasks. A useful question to ask yourself – 'Am I the only person who can do this?' If the answer is 'no', reconsider who could do it.

Once you have scheduled your priorities, including free time, you are better positioned to decide on other tasks (while keeping in mind the time you have available and the need for some flexibility). Whether you say 'yes' to a given task, 'no,' or 'I'll think about it' (with a view to letting go of something you've already agreed to do, or negotiating), you'll be more confident that you are focusing on what truly matters.

Daily planner

Take a realistic look at each day:

- Schedule your priority tasks at times that match your energy levels (remember the frog).
- Sounds obvious, but be sure to schedule time for travelling to and from meetings. Then, schedule time to complete any actions from meetings that you agreed to do. Finally, allow yourself some time between meetings; back-to-back online meetings can be draining.

You can download the *PDF Keeping on Track - Creating Work/Life Harmony (Termly, Weekly, Daily Planner)* from www.routledge.com/9781032945392. You can print it off, share it with others, and use it as often as you like. These are particularly useful for people early in their careers.

Keeping on Track doesn't solve all your work overload and time management problems. It provides some structure to make your priorities feature first so that you reduce some of the overwhelm and overload you may be facing.

Coaching approaches
Coaching yourself
Get clear on the key priorities in your life. Follow the guidelines and fit them into your planner:

- What does this exercise clarify for you?
- What challenges does it raise for you?

Work/life harmony is different for everyone. How will you make the transition gradually from overload to work/life harmony?

- What needs to stop?
- What do you need to say 'no' to?
- What do you need to say 'yes' to?
- What boundaries need to be in place to achieve more work/life harmony?
- How do you feel about this?
- What do you need to develop?
- What's your plan?
- Who will support you through these decisions and actions to ensure you keep your priorities prioritised?

Coaching others
After working through the planner:

- What are your key priorities for the half-term/next six weeks?
- How do you intend to manage your workload to make sure the priorities are met?
- What do you need to communicate and assert to others?
- How will you stay well in doing so?
- Let's recap…

Coaching upwards
- How do you role-model work/life harmony to other people in school?
- How do you communicate your priorities?
- How do you demonstrate adaptability so that individuals who have competing demands on their time can follow your example?

Perceptions
Too much disharmony between work and home life impacts individual well-being. If this goes unaddressed, people tend to get ill. If it goes on for too long, people wear themselves thin, go off sick with stress, and sometimes face burnout. Here are some traits to be aware of in yourself and others:

Innovators – may tend to over-promise and then not be able to deliver. They *intend* to fit everything in but don't consider how they will do this. Stress, disappointment, and frustration follow for all concerned.

Achievers – are likely to commit to achieving everything work-related first. They don't mind giving others more to do. Their families and relationships tend to fit around or be displaced by work priorities.

Perfectors – tend to experience overwhelm and overload by taking longer over tasks than is often manageable. They struggle with just doing enough and find it hard to let go as they are concerned others won't do things well enough. The reality is that there isn't enough time for them to do everything to the standard they would like, so family, relationships, and personal time get impacted.

Harmonisers – aim to keep everyone happy and often put themselves last. This isn't sustainable and, as stress levels increase, it becomes apparent no one is happy with how things are. The chronic disharmony then takes its toll on the Harmoniser, who becomes overwhelmed.

Keep in mind – a discussion about the most useful strategies and reasonable adjustments may be useful with anyone who recognises the need to develop executive functioning (for example, people with ADD or ADHD).

Reference

A Guide to Time Management Models | Virtual College (no date). Available at: https://www.virtual-college.co.uk/resources/time-mangement-models (Accessed: 12 January 2025).

CHAPTER 8

Mental and emotional fitness

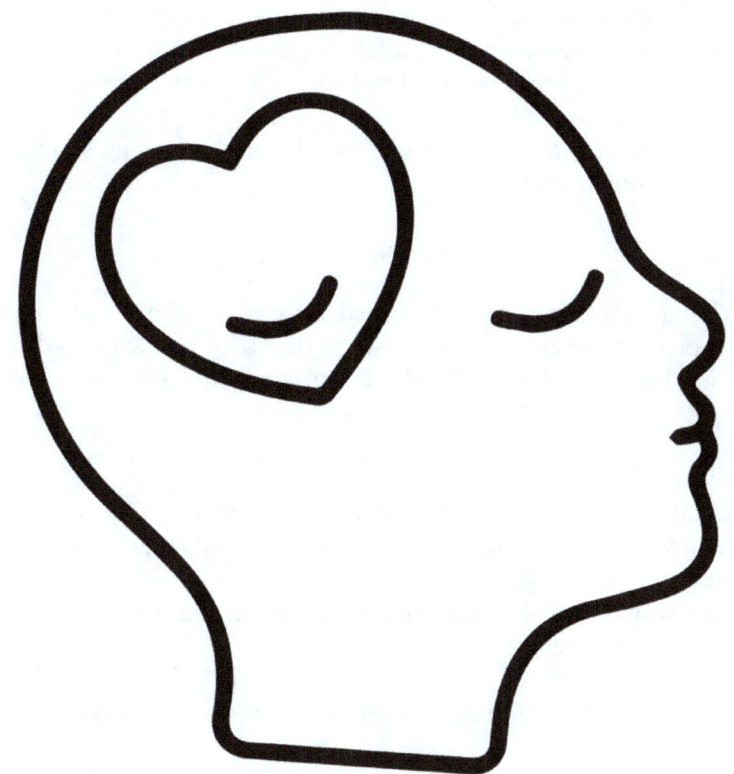

The importance of self-care

If you are to give your best as a leader, you need to keep well mentally, emotionally, and physically. There are many simple practices that make a lasting difference to your well-being if you choose to use them.

Here are ten clear steps to keep yourself fit, mentally and emotionally, so you prevent yourself from becoming eroded by the pressures, demands, and behaviours surrounding you.

Slow down

Note down what's going on in your head right now.

Empty out all the noisy thoughts competing for your attention. The next paragraph will wait for you, and you'll take more of it in if you've slowed down your thoughts – albeit briefly.

Brains never stop thinking. Let's face it, there will have been times when your thoughts were at a crescendo, where you felt your head was fit to burst because there was so much going on in there. Then the headaches follow: migraines, feeling nauseous, and sometimes panic attacks.

It's infinitely preferable to prevent these awful states. A strong starting point is to slow your thoughts down routinely.

Notice

You won't change anything until you listen to what your body is telling you. Interoception, or body awareness, is the sense that tells you when you're hungry, or stressed, or clenching muscles needlessly. By growing this awareness, you can make choices:

- Choose to stop.
- Choose to take a minute or two to slow down. Think of it like taking your foot off the accelerator because the speed you're driving at is dangerous.
- Breathe deeply.
- Breathe in a way that feels gentle and soothing for you. Keep going until you feel your muscles start to relax.

What you need to do next will become a little clearer from this space.

Deeply rest

I once worked with someone who said she was fine about having a minor operation as it was the only time she truly relaxed! Let's look at some options that don't involve anaesthetics or drugs!

If sitting in a chair and listening through headphones is your thing, find an app that allows you to sit back and be guided into deep relaxation. Search for relaxation apps or deep breathing apps so you can listen to soothing words and sounds that suit you. There are apps where you can create your own menu for Deep Sleep, Power Nap, Relaxation, or Meditation.

Try different apps until you find the one that works for you. The beauty of sitting back and listening is that you can let go and be the recipient for a while. This is a very effective habit to help you decompress after work. After fifteen minutes or so, you can face the evening ahead as the calmer you rather than the frazzled you. Once people see the different you emerge, they'll wait before bombarding you with their needs.

For immediate use, here's a tried and tested one for free. The Self-compassion break from Kristen Neff takes just over five minutes. ('Self-compassion practices,' no date)

Learning to rest within yourself, even for a few moments a day, can make a lasting difference in the long term.

Close your stress response cycle

If you don't fully rest, your body marinates in stress chemicals. And that's not good for you or anyone else around you. If you find it difficult to stop and allow yourself time to rest, familiarise yourself with the Nagoskis' Stress Response Cycle. (Nagoski and Nagoski, 2020). Or listen to Brené Brown's podcast with the Nagoskis. To complete the stress response cycle whenever you're stressed, implement one or some of the six evidence-based strategies and allow yourself some r-e-s-t:

Breathing

It always starts with breathing. Your brain and body need a good boost of oxygen to cope with stress. You can do it immediately, so a lack of time doesn't stack up as a reason why not.

Moving

Ideally, get your heart beating fast in whatever way is easy and works for you. Take a brisk walk or a run outside. Walk up and down the stairs a few times. Go to the gym. Shake it out – shake your body like you're trying to get rid of something sticking to you (you are!). Put on some dance music and dance until you sweat. Make that tension release enjoyable.

Crying

If you can, a good old blub is a natural way to release stress. Forget the stiff upper lip and the brave face, stand under a shower and sob. Use a sad film as an excuse. Have a massage and let the tears flow. You'll feel relieved afterwards and tired – in a good way – ready for sleep.

Laughing

This may be a preferable alternative to crying, especially if you can connect with others at the same time. If you can, aim for thigh-slapping, uncontrollable laughter. It is a brilliant form of stress release.

Affection

A twenty-second hug or snuggling up with a person or pet releases oxytocin, so your body and mind can relax and feel safe again. In this moment, the danger and tension you were holding onto fade away.

Creative expression

Writing, drawing, singing, knitting – something to express yourself through your hands and body – will keep you feeling safe and able to relax more.

> **Shared experience**
>
> A headteacher shares how she got back 'the old me' by closing the stress response cycle.
>
> Work was becoming incredibly stressful as a head of a school judged as 'requires improvement.' I was tired constantly with self-care a thing of the past. I was holding it together at work but taking it out on my family at home. My palpitations had returned, and I no longer had the energy for anything. I was low, cried a lot and felt like I had nothing to give. I was in a bad way and starting to feel concerned about my mental health, until one day I was reminded about the importance of closing the stress cycle. I had heard this message many times before but had stopped listening. I decided action was needed. Helping myself was important or I was going to burn out and then I would be no good to anyone. I knew physical activity was my go-to method of closing the stress cycle so I made a commitment to myself that I would do some form of exercise at the end of each day.
>
> There was no overnight fix, I didn't suddenly feel like the old me, no doubt because stress had been building inside me for some time. However, over a period of weeks I slowly started to heal. Every day after work I would go for a stomp or lift some weights, prioritising myself at the end of another day of anxiety, worry and stress. It almost felt like I was pushing all the stress out of my body.
>
> Closing that stress cycle really does work. The old me was returning. I no longer went to bed filled with anxiety about work. My heart palpitations were decreasing, and I was starting to find small sparks of joy in the job again. This was the start of my journey back to health. I was no longer running from the stress; I was tackling it head on. I even shared the theory behind the stress response cycle with my husband as he was showing signs of stress following an intense promotion process. Making music and playing golf was his method to close the cycle but the impact, if consistent, is the same. You can take back control. You can manage the stress. So my new mantra is: 'Close the stress cycle!'

Manage the way you think

When something someone has said or done is niggling away at you and keeps taking over your thoughts, try these:

MENTAL AND EMOTIONAL FITNESS

Not taking things personally

If you're prone to taking things personally or find yourself advising others not to, here's a structured approach you can take for yourself and share with others:

- Describe what happened – the situation, the context.
- What was actually said? Be objective and state: what are the facts of this situation?
- How do you feel about this?
- What is behind this? What is the person aiming to accomplish?
- How did the person communicate with you? Were they respectful? Was it in line with the school or team values?
- What was the impact on you?
- What do you need to feel a bit better?
- Go here: (*When the Tension Goes*, no date)
- What will you absorb yourself in next, or as soon as you can, to completely take your mind off what's happened?

Revisit the situation after a few days and do a reality check to consider the following:

- The neutral facts of what happened from your perspective and the other person's perspective.
- The impact on you.
- How to take ownership of your feelings and decide what options you have to progress or resolve the situation.
- What's your preferred option?
- How will you rise above a comment like this next time, or welcome constructive feedback?

You can download *Not taking things personally* from www.routledge.com/9781032945392.

Focus on something else instead

If I say, 'Don't think of an orange', the first thing you're likely to think about is an orange. Your brain hears 'orange' and takes you there; it likely goes citrus on you! Sometimes so powerfully that, before you know it, you get that refreshing zesty smell, and your mouth's watering with the prospect of juicy, freshly peeled segments. See what I mean?

Instead of telling yourself not to think of something, decide what to focus on instead. And take your attention there. What you'll have for dinner, what you'll say in assembly, or an activity you're looking forward to.

Concentrate hard on something else

Take some time to become absorbed in another topic or situation. Your focus takes you to another place and shuts out distractions. This allows some time to pass and means the niggle shrinks into a truer perspective.

Process your emotions

The following activity offers you a structure to alleviate any persistent irritations that are still preventing you from switching off. Allow about 30 minutes to complete the process.

Identify what you're feeling

Give yourself some space, or an opportunity, to check in with yourself and identify the emotions you are feeling. Label them: Anger, Disgust, Fear. This will immediately shift you to the more rational part of your brain and enable you to start to become a little more objective.

If you feel able, close your eyes, and notice where in your body you feel the emotion. It may be your stomach, your shoulders, or your heart – that 'pain in the neck'!

Find the cause behind the feeling

Ask yourself the following questions and write down your responses. Write them in free flow – this is important. No editing, no grammatical correctness – just let the unfiltered words pour out through your writing. There will be no real need for you to re-read this, so get all the emotion out of your system with any number of expletives and unreasonable statements that you wouldn't say out loud. Let yourself vent! No one else is going to read this. The paper isn't judging you:

- What's causing me to feel this way?
- How can this feeling serve me today?
- What can I learn from it?
- What is the situation showing me?
- What is there to learn or see from this?
- What's the truth of this experience?
- What is my personal development from this?

Decide what (if any) action you need to take to enable you to feel better and consolidate

Write down any insights or final points you want to retain going forward.

Park the situation or issue

Switch off from it by focusing your attention on something else. You'll have renewed energy from having offloaded, so direct that energy somewhere valuable to you.

Decide what to do with what you've written

Don't leave it lying around or in a place where others could easily find it. If you want to keep it, put it somewhere safe. Some people find it highly cathartic to burn what they've written. Others enjoy shredding it.

MENTAL AND EMOTIONAL FITNESS

Revisit – if appropriate
While you might have vented much of what you needed to vent, there may well be other emotions that come to the surface now that you've cleared the way. At a later point, you can reflect on how things feel from this different perspective and repeat the process for any different emotions that are surfacing.

There's evidence nowadays that writing routinely in this way builds resilience. Processing your emotions puts you back in charge. If you ignore them, it's likely the feelings will lurk below the surface and get triggered the next time you experience your values being violated, or something similar. Processing feelings in writing will move you on, calming and clearing some of the noise in your head and freeing you up to focus on what matters.

This process is my absolute go-to whenever difficulties start getting to me. After 30 minutes of structured offloading, I feel relieved and lighter, ready to take action and move on.

Sleep
You know sleep is important for well-being and performance. Let's just remind ourselves why:

- In sleep, we grow new brain cells. In sleep we lay down and rewire memories. No sleep, no new brain cells.
- Our reworked brains are literally different when we wake up, sort of like those science fiction stories where people awaken each day a whole new person. Every night we have rewired, rebuilt, reset, reconstructed, and redone our brains.
- Rest is the original transformative technology. Through rest we rebuild, rewire, and renew ourselves – literally.

For more resources on sleep, see Matthew Edlund, Director of the Center for Circadian Medicine and author of 'The Power of Rest' (*The Rest Doctor - Regeneration Health News*, no date) (Edlund, 2011).

Sleep isn't just important for well-being and performance; it's crucial. There are aspects of the job you do that keep you awake at night, and maybe your family life does too.

Because of its importance, much has been written and researched about sleep. Here are some simple points to consider so you can start making some adjustments.

What do you need to stop after a certain time?
- Consider no caffeine (or stimulants) beyond late afternoon. What will you drink instead? Hot water is my nurturing, cleansing, and hydrating drink of choice these evenings.
- When is your cut-off point for food so that you can let your body rest too? Twelve hours after your first food of the day is a common guideline.
- Have you noticed any foods that keep you awake? Or worse, that cause you indigestion which keeps you awake?

- What time will you switch off the beeps? When is the right time for your electronic devices to leave the room?
- Be selective about what you fill your head with before bedtime. You may want to be aware of what's happening in the world, but how does the news and its distressing images relax you into sleep? I make sure comedy is the last thing I watch before bed.

What do you need to do instead to unwind?
- Empty or quiet your busy brain – get all your to-dos noted somewhere so that you can trust you'll remember them tomorrow. Then you can go to bed feeling a little more on top of things for the day ahead.
- Do the things that can't wait or get help with the things that can't wait. How can you share the load with others? You're not the only person who can do the dishes.
- Burn up some physical energy so that your body gets tired, and you relieve some of the tension stored in your muscles.
- Wind down – adjust your pace and activity to match the time of day. Read, listen to music, or watch something that lightens you, engages you, or absorbs you. Bathe – include your favourite bath time concoction – bubbles, lavender oil, muscle soak.
- Fall asleep with gratitude – once you're comfortable in bed, reflect on what you are grateful for from your day:
  - I'm grateful that I started the day with a lovely, hot shower.
  - Mmm, that first cup of coffee in the quiet before the action started.
  - I'm glad I can breathe fresh air deeply as I leave home.
  - I'm grateful for the smiling faces in the playground.

Mindfulness

In Chapter 5, we saw how mindfulness is a component of practising self-compassion. When mindfulness becomes a routine, people notice gradual changes in their day-to-day life, like feeling calmer and less stressed. Headteachers know this and often invite people in to run mindfulness sessions for staff and pupils. It looks good, but it doesn't mean they practise it themselves though. Time is the number one reason why they don't. Think of all the emails they could clear in those ten minutes. If that sounds like you, here's a way to make mindfulness a routine practice without having to take time out.

Notice

Simply monologue what you are noticing as you walk around school. If the walk from your office to the car park takes two minutes, that's potentially two minutes of mindfulness.

Here's an example of the monologue in your head.

> I'm noticing…
> the very straight line of the bridge over the road
> the ladybird on the leaf

MENTAL AND EMOTIONAL FITNESS

my disappointment at the cans on the side of the path
that I'm grateful I can be doing this
the paint colours of the windows
the breeze on my neck
the cool, the warmth
the particular shade of orange in the rust
I notice I'm thinking about work and that I'm bringing my thoughts back to noticing.

I'm noticing...
the sound of my shoes on the pavement
birdsong
voices over the fence
the tone of irritation
my resistance to that conversation
a leaf being blown across the drive
dancing like it's in a performance.

I'm thinking about the conversation I just had.

I'm noticing I feel sad about the conversation I just had.
I'm noticing I'm trying not to feel sad, wishing I didn't feel sad, noticing I'm finding sadness really inconvenient right now.
I'm noticing myself feeling sad, watching myself feeling sad, knowing it's OK to feel sad.
Accepting it's OK to feel sad.
Relaxing into feeling sad.
Remembering to slow down for a few moments to breathe.
Reminding myself 'This will pass'.
I'm noticing I'm feeling a bit lighter.
Calmer.

Mindfulness, or being present, allows you to step outside of *being* your feelings to *watching* your feelings and thoughts. It allows you to ask, 'What am I experiencing right now?' This brings a very different perspective, which means you are more likely to respond kindly to yourself, with greater composure and care, as you would respond to a friend, instead of responding in ways that don't value who you are.

Mindfulness has the potential to quiet the noise for a while. It creates some space in your mind where you see the need for care and warmth more than judgement. With mindful awareness, you have choices, and this changes things.

A significant and very practical benefit of mindfulness is feeling calmer. This pays off at times of tiredness and low tolerance. If you have a level of calm you can draw on, you'll be able to manage your anger differently. Anger is a perfectly natural response in those times when your personal values are violated. It's good to know how to access calm and remain composed when you need to.

[Disclaimer – These suggestions are based on my experience of what headteachers in my coaching practice have found beneficial. If you have concerns about your health, please visit your GP or health professional.]

Coaching approaches
Coaching yourself
- How much do you want to be emotionally and mentally fit?
  Not very 1 — 2 — 3 — 4 — 5 Yes, absolutely.
- How much are you willing to commit to some practices for your emotional and mental fitness?
  Not very 1 — 2 — 3 — 4 — 5 It's imperative that I do.
- Which of the techniques seem to be what you need most right now?
- In what ways would you like the practices to make a difference for you over time?
- What would make them worthwhile for you?
- When will you start the practices you chose?
- How will you remind yourself to keep them going?

Coaching others
Which of the following describes how you are at the end of the term?

- Exhausted
- Bothered by thoughts you can't let go of
- Prone to negative thinking patterns
- Anxious about the future
- Foggy brain and frazzled
- Unable to switch off your noisy, worried mind
- Not in touch with yourself, how you really are
- Disturbed sleep
- Despair, feel like giving up
- Judging your feelings as bad ('I shouldn't feel this way')

- What would you most like to work on and change?
- How willing are you to practise some different approaches to build your emotional and mental fitness?
- Discuss the choices from the list with someone you trust.
- Arrange to check in next term and see how to keep things going.

Coaching upwards
- What do you know about the stress response cycle?
- Rest is a crucial part of the process. What does rest mean for you in your life?
- How can we make it OK to rest?
- How can we encourage and make it OK for our people to rest?

MENTAL AND EMOTIONAL FITNESS

Perspectives

When committing to an emotional and mental fitness practice,

Innovators – are likely to give it a go and not keep it going.

Achievers – are likely to prioritise other tasks over emotional and mental well-being strategies.

Perfectors – are likely to let scepticism get in the way of their practice.

Harmonisers – are likely to encourage others to do so more than applying them themselves.

Keep in mind – We are all different where stress is concerned, which means that something you find stressful may pass others by or vice versa. The crucial points are to recognise when you are stressed and to take action to lessen your stress. Mindfulness and other techniques work well, but they need time and persistence so they become habitual.

References

Brené with Emily and Amelia Nagoski on Burnout and How to Complete the Stress Cycle (no date) *Brené Brown*. Available at: https://brenebrown.com/podcast/brene-with-emily-and-amelia-nagoski-on-burnout-and-how-to-complete-the-stress-cycle/ (Accessed: 12 January 2025).

Edlund, M. (2011) *The power of rest: Why sleep alone is not enough. a 30-day plan to reset your body*. 1st ed. New York: HarperCollins Publishers.

'Exercise 2: Self-Compassion Break' (no date) *Self-compassion*. Available at: https://self-compassion.org/exercises/exercise-2-self-compassion-break/ (Accessed: 12 January 2025).

Nagoski, E. and Nagoski, A. (2020) *Burnout: Solve your stress cycle*. London: Vermilion.

'Self-compassion practices' (no date) *Self-compassion*. Available at: https://self-compassion.org/self-compassion-practices/ (Accessed: 16 January 2025).

The Rest Doctor - Regeneration Health News (no date). Available at: https://regenerationhealthnews.com/ (Accessed: 16 January 2025).

When the Tension Goes (no date) *When the tension goes*. Available at: https://whenthetensiongoes.com/ (Accessed: 12 January 2025).

CHAPTER 9

Responding to anxiety

Anxiety – an overview

Anxiety is a common and mainly unwelcome emotion. Anxious thoughts are thoughts about a future that we don't want to happen because we fear we won't cope, or we'll be worse off in some way that matters to us. We all differ in what makes us anxious.

It can help to differentiate anxiety into the particular and general. Particular anxieties have a narrow focus and concern things you can influence, at least a bit. Worrying about a difficult meeting with a parent or being nervous about introducing an unwelcome change in school are particular anxieties. General anxieties are wider and concern things you cannot easily influence. Fears about global warming or the impact of an increase in mortgage rates are general anxieties.

Anxiety can be a difficult emotion to manage. Here are some pointers for working with your anxiety and that of others.

Particular anxieties

The keys to managing your particular anxieties are:

- to understand your make-up
- to use that self-awareness as a spur to action
- to focus on your coping skills.

You will know if you are a natural worrier, and you will know that trying not to worry rarely works. It's more helpful to accept that you tend to worry and then do what you can to alleviate particular concerns.

Whether you worry a lot or a little, it's much easier to manage your anxiety if you focus on what is in your power to change and consider options. Thinking (just enough – not overthinking) and then taking appropriate action can go a long way toward reducing anxiety and empowering you to face difficulties.

However, measured consideration isn't always an option. There will be times as a leader when you'll have to act quickly, with too few facts, limited support, and maybe the wrong view of what you're trying to resolve – so things may go wrong. This is where coping skills are so important. If you can move on without becoming too judgemental and hard on yourself, then you'll know that you can continue to take action when facing future setbacks.

General anxieties

General anxieties are harder to deal with because they focus on events that are outside your control yet could be individually catastrophic (a serious health issue) or collectively catastrophic (a flood or a pandemic).

There is no surefire way to calm general anxieties. It helps to focus on where you have power, such as looking after your health or joining a pressure group to raise concerns about the environment. If you find that despite your best efforts, you struggle to cope with and are being badly affected by general anxieties, it is important to seek help and support.

Anxiety in others

Assuming you can manage your own anxieties, here are some ways you can work with your people.

It's useful to start with your own Coacting Style (see Chapter 2) and consider how to balance your style against the needs of another person whose style is different from yours.

Innovators – you are usually energised by change and new directions without realising your people may be very worried by them. While your positivity is an asset, you will also need to get down to the nitty-gritty of their concerns.

Achievers – you achieve because you make demands and push for results. This means you can be quite blunt in how you express your wishes. Some can find you intimidating, especially if you are in a position of authority. Similarly, in responding to another's anxiety, you may feel, and assert, that they should get a grip on themselves and get on with the job. This will leave them afraid of you and what you think of them.

Perfectors – you are comfortable with facts and a systematic approach to leadership. This can be calming, but it can also make you seem distant. You don't have to be inauthentic in how you show emotions, but taking others' emotions seriously and hearing them out can go far in building a bridge between you and them.

Harmonisers – you are likely to be keenly aware of others' well-being. You will naturally swing more towards feelings and helping the person than thinking about tasks and workload. In doing so, you risk feeling overwhelmed or taking on extra work rather than delegating ('because everyone else is working so hard').

Keep in mind – In addition to the different styles, when it comes to anxiety, people are affected by their cultural and family backgrounds, trauma, autism, attention-deficit, to name but a few. You can't expect to know what's happening for all your people, but it's important to keep in mind that other things may be going on for them. You may miss or misjudge emotional cues, and others may miss yours. There is no single way to get this right. Like all leaders, you will need to take time with others, check if they see things the way you do, and offer as much support as you are able.

Key tips for working with anxiety

Here are some key tips – some practical and some personal – that I've collected and shared with headteachers.

It can be helpful to see anxiety as a combination of uncertainty and powerlessness, so as a leader, you can use the following questions to enable individuals to find some certainty and to empower them.

1. What I know – list the facts, the definites, the black-and-white areas.
2. What I'm less sure about – note what's uncertain, unclear, the grey areas.
3. What I can influence – write down areas where you can make a difference, manage, or change things.
4. What I can't control – add whatever you can do nothing about.

Of the four, it's most constructive to focus on what you can influence.

Team activity for managing anxiety
You can use the same questions as a team activity, too.

Create four columns or quadrants for the four statements on a board or flip chart.

Taking each statement in turn, encourage your people to respond with as many points as they can think of.

Usually, people feel better for hearing one another's views, saying them out loud, focusing on what they can influence, and then specifying actions and next steps.

To reduce anxiety, focus on the facts, on what is certain, and on where you have some influence or control, where you can empower yourself to take charge.

In a hurry
Run through the best-case scenario, worst-case scenario, and likely scenario.

Cultivate calm
The following questions are useful to reflect on for yourself, and also to consider for those around you:

- What are your core strategies for calming?
- What soothes you?
- What centres you?
- What relieves you?
- What uplifts and inspires you?
- What heightens your self-belief?
- How will you be courageous?
- This is tough. You're not alone in this – who is there for you?

Strive to be the calm presence
Calmness – what a precious commodity for leaders and life generally. Whoever we are, whatever distressing circumstances we find ourselves in, that person who has a calm presence just makes us feel better by simply being there and being calm.

This is where everyone reaps the cumulative benefits of mindfulness practices.

Listen
Really listen, with your focus and attention on the anxious person, not with your thoughts elsewhere on how much you still have to do or how long this is taking.

If you feel you are not the most appropriate person to listen, find someone you think can offer the right listening presence and negotiate tasks and duties with them. Listening, without judgement, enables the person being heard to feel better and lighter through talking.

Be kind
It's almost magical how kindness can make a difference and enable someone to feel better. Think of when someone has shown you kindness and compassion in your worst

moments and how that lightened things. Weighing what people need alongside everything that has to be done is indeed a fine balance. Generally, people in need will appreciate kindness so much; they will feel better sooner, and they'll come back with more energy.

Reassure with facts
If you can, provide certainty, factual information, or genuine reassurances about what is going to happen. It's easy for people to magnify fears out of all proportion, so hearing someone they trust stating the truth can bring a great sense of relief. Don't assume. Sometimes stating the obvious is reassuring too.

Ditch perfection and encourage 'good enough'
When people are worried about the standards they and you would normally expect, encourage 'good enough' or, as I like to refer to it, 'just right'. Reassure an anxious person with phrases like 'What's manageable?', 'What's just right for this situation?', and 'That's good enough for me.' Make sure there is no tone of favour, inconvenience, or judgement. Flexibility can be a real kindness.

Common sense actions
When anyone is anxious, they usually feel better for one, some, or all of the following:

- A change of scenery – especially if it can be outside.
- Being active in some way – moving around as vigorously as is reasonable.
- Breathing deeply – especially fresh air, minimally via an open window.
- Nutritious food – that both nourishes and comforts.
- Reduced screen time – especially the images and messages beyond the news headlines and toxic social media responses.
- Water – to hydrate, cleanse, and relax the body's systems.
- Sleep – easier said than done, but there's nothing like snuggling somewhere safe and comfortable to soothe anxiety and give your body half a chance to rest.

Awareness of, and access to, resources
There is a wealth of self-help material out there on anxiety. This is a relevant site to start with.
   (*Guides, articles and videos on anxiety for teachers and education staff*, no date)

Awareness of, and access to, services
If someone needs more than you or your team can offer, what services do they have access to within your organisation? Do they know about them? What information can you provide?
   Education Support offers important services outside of your own organisation. https://www.educationsupport.org.uk/

Keep connecting

Anxiety is a scary and debilitating place. Once there, it gives people a little more peace of mind if they know they can reach out and connect with another person. Who do they have?

Anxiety is exhausting

It's likely the person is worn down, impatient, or tetchy so they may come across as snappy or even rude. They are not themselves at these times so don't take things personally or expect thanks.

> **Shared experience**
>
> A headteacher shares how they managed anxiety after an incident where a staff member was injured by a pupil.
>
> As a headteacher, I consider one of my most important roles is ensuring the safety and wellbeing of all in the school community. This is a great sense of responsibility, which at times can feel overwhelming. So, when a member of staff is deliberately hurt by a pupil in the school, it evokes a whole range of feelings and emotions.
>
> Dealing with the immediate situation at the time is the greatest priority; administering first aid, ensuring everyone is safe, calming the pupil, contacting parents, making difficult decisions about suspension and any further actions that may be needed. This is often then followed up with a debrief for the staff directly involved and supporting others who may have witnessed the incident.
>
> Throughout this time, you are in automatic mode, wearing your 'headteacher hat' and pushing your own emotions aside to enable you to do this. I found it vitally important that staff who had been injured or who had witnessed the incident were given the time to deal with their own thoughts and feelings, to allow the adrenaline to subside and to have a good cry if needed. They may need time to themselves in a private space in school, to go out for a walk or to go home to recover emotionally, as well as physically. Sometimes staff will tell you that they don't need this, as they are so used to putting the children first, so they may need encouragement and permission to focus on themselves in this situation.
>
> In the days and possibly even weeks following an incident, staff anxiety may be high and morale low. I learned how important action planning was for this stage so that everyone involved is absolutely clear on the steps to take should there be a repeat and/or the strategies we need to implement to reduce the chance of this. Staff feel reassured if they know exactly what to do and who to call if things start to escalate. Ideally the whole staff team need to be aware of this, as it empowers some to step in and support, at least in that time before a member of the leadership team arrives.

Being honest with the team, acknowledging the challenges and being really clear on the actions to be taken reassures them and subsequently improves morale. They need to know that you care and have confidence in your ability to reduce the chances of it happening again (even if you feel at a loss as to how to achieve this).

There is a temptation as headteacher to be the 'martyr,' who is always called upon when a pupil is extremely dysregulated and becoming dangerous. Whilst it is important that you are available to support, there is a danger that staff can become disempowered and over-reliant on the headteacher. It's important to involve the staff in action planning as many of them know the pupil better than you do. Also, to offer training where necessary and/or give opportunity for them to spend time learning from others in the school who can model what this looks like. This builds staff confidence and knowledge and shows that you have trust in their abilities. It also helps with staff retention as they naturally turn to one another for mutual support instead of feeling helpless.

It is only afterwards, when you have the time to reflect, that you really begin to feel the emotions. Witnessing a member of your staff, whose safety you feel personally responsible for, being hurt by a pupil is really hard. You feel that you should have done something more to prevent it, feel that it should have been you and not them who was hurt. You worry that you've made the right decisions, taken the correct actions, that you've given the support they needed at the time, and afterwards. You consider what the following day(s) will hold, how others will view the decisions you made and what the consequences will be if there is a repeat. It's these thoughts that keep you awake in the middle of the night.

There are times when the job of the headteacher feels lonely but this is perhaps one of the loneliest of these times. No one else can really know how you feel unless they have been there themselves, making difficult decisions, pushing aside their own thoughts and feelings at the time to maintain professionalism, and support others who are at their most vulnerable.

Knowing who, within your own circle of support, you can talk to is so important. You too will need opportunity to debrief, to offload, to be reassured that you made the right decisions at the time. Friends and family members are often great listeners and will be able to empathise with how you are feeling. They will also provide the much-needed distractions so that you don't overthink or dwell on things that were/are out of your control. Having another headteacher, who you trust and can confide in, is also important. Even if they have not experienced a similar situation, they will know that feeling of loneliness that sometimes comes with being a headteacher. They will be able to help you to rationalise your own thoughts and feelings and support you in identifying actions that you can take to move forward.

You may feel like you have failed but be reassured that you will have made decisions at the time which were in the best interests of your staff and children. Those decisions and the care and compassion you showed others will have been appreciated even though this may not have been vocalised to you.

Coaching approaches
Coaching yourself
Think of a time when you felt really anxious, worried, or not able to control what was happening. Remind yourself what that was like, how it took you over, what a strain it was to do quite ordinary things:

- What got you through?
- What did you need?
- What would have helped you?
- How can this inform your perspective and your approach for your ongoing self-care, and with others?

Coaching others
If you are with someone who is struggling with anxiety, a simple prompt for them to talk plus your willingness to listen is enough. Here are some prompts and phrases to consider (but don't use all of them!):

- What's on your mind?
- What's troubling you?
- Would it help to talk?
- What's worrying you?
- How do you feel about that?
- I'm all ears!

Coaching upwards
The same applies to people senior to you – anyone who is struggling with anxiety may welcome your concern, so a simple prompt for them to talk and your willingness to listen is enough. You can test the water with some prompts and phrases to consider:

- What's on your mind?
- You seem like something is troubling you?
- Would it help to talk?

Perspectives
We're all different, so it's hard to get your response right for others who are anxious, or when you are anxious. The following prompts will help your interactions during anxious times:

Innovators – like to talk so finding someone who they can offload to, and who is at ease with exaggerations and grandiose statements, can really help.

Achievers – like to get on and do stuff and don't like to 'waste time', so talking while doing an activity can help them. Walking somewhere with them gives good opportunities to talk. They may also enjoy going for a run and burning up some physical energy to get their thoughts and feelings in a different space.

Perfectors – often withdraw and may prefer to express things privately through writing, sketching, or music rather than talking. Any small steps to encourage and validate their private self-expression can help them through.

Harmonisers – really benefit from knowing people are there for them. They prefer to be the person who is there for others and tend to feel selfish if they take others' time. It helps to encourage them, or even to give them permission to put their self-care needs first during times of anxiety.

Keep in mind – we are all different in what provokes anxiety. People with a trauma background may find themselves anxious for no apparent reason, but it may be because a circumstance or place has reminded them of a buried experience. Similarly, neurodivergent staff members are coping all the time, with a largely neurotypical workplace and can find even ordinary 'busyness' stressful. This awareness means you can be prepared and respond calmly and flexibly to how people present.

References

Guides, articles and videos on anxiety for teachers and education staff (no date). Available at: https://www.educationsupport.org.uk/resources/for-individuals/?resourcetype=Anxiety (Accessed: 12 January 2025).

SECTION 3

Reducing workloads

Since the pandemic, two of the main reasons for people leaving education have been workload and well-being.

An obvious strategy to retain staff, and to keep you going in the profession you once loved, is to reduce workload and improve well-being .

Section 3 gives you ways to explore what collaborating, living team values, and managing expectations all mean in practice – for doing less, not more.

CHAPTER 10

Workloads for everyone's well-being

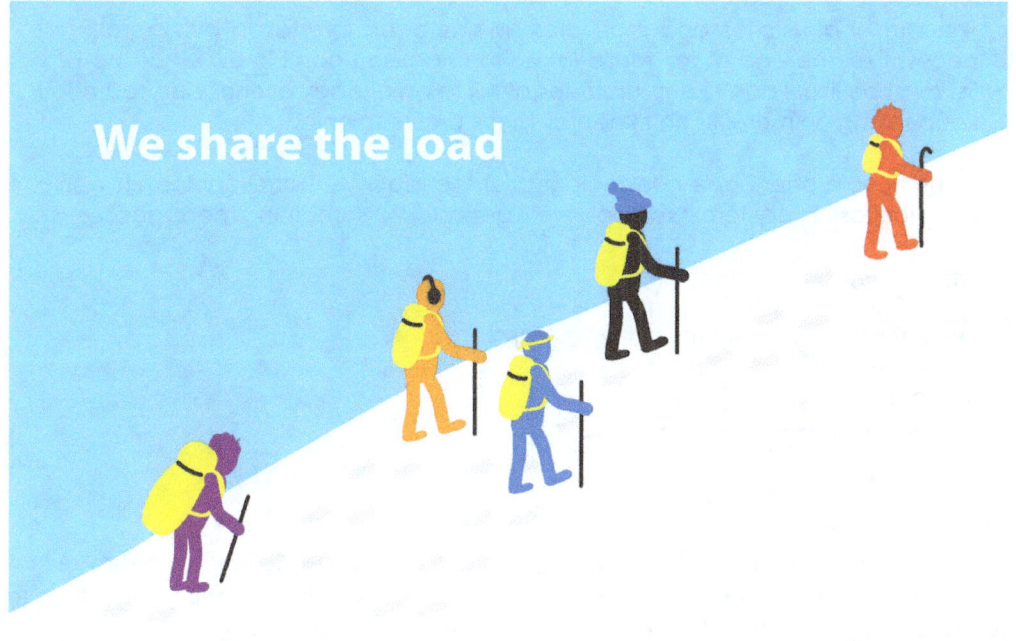

> **Shared experience**
>
> Notes from a school leader's reflective journal.
>
> 12th January 2021
>
> We've only been back a few days and again we're facing exhaustion and low morale. Everywhere, it seems people haven't returned rested from Xmas, but weary. Easily tipped off centre, tensions running high, natural resentment because of workload, and emotional overwhelm because of people's stories – children and adults, families and staff. We've had enough. We're all tired and flat. It seems impossible to find the energy and motivation required to get us through this term with so much uncertainty – Who will be in today? How will we cover? Where will extra support come from? This isn't fair – it's not fair on the children. It's not fair on staff who are overworked and worn down.
>
> The stuff that excites and motivates us has been overtaken by operational necessities. The end of my to-do list isn't in sight so I don't know what the HT's list must be like. I can't keep on delegating to an already overloaded team so I keep taking on more. I can't keep all these plates spinning.
>
> I wish I could offer hope convincingly but the reality is that every term is worse than the last. Every term we hope we'll get back to something manageable.
>
> Spring seems a long way off.
>
> NOTE TO SELF – REMEMBER THE PRIORITIES
> - Keep well
> - Children's safety
> - Teaching and learning.

We share the load

Here's an activity that will reduce your overload in five steps. It can be used to reduce other people's overload in five steps too. The aim is to enable you and your people to prioritise keeping well and to revisit the team value of collaborating.

Preparation
Timing:
15–30 minutes

Resources:

- Sticky notes for wall space/cards or sticky notes for a tabletop

Preparation:

- Write down, on sticky notes or cards, all the tasks on your to-do list – one task per note/card.

Activity
1. Spread your cards across the table in your meeting space (or sticky notes on the wall) and ask everyone to circulate and read your to-dos. The overload will be immediately apparent.
2. Ask team members to take the cards/tasks that they can do and are OK with doing or being responsible for doing.
3. Of the remaining cards, you take the ones ONLY YOU can do.
4. Agree, as a team, how to manage any cards/tasks that are left.

The team value here is collaboration, the focus is a fair distribution of workload, and the purpose that underpins the activity is well-being – yours and theirs. The goal is ensuring current priorities are met.

Concerns
If you're concerned about doing this kind of activity because you know how much your people have to do already and how overloaded they are, look at the image for this chapter and extend the visual metaphor to your situation:

- You're facing adverse conditions.
- Your people are drawing on reserves of energy to get through.
- It's vitally important that people keep well to keep going.
- To make the summit, people must even the load they are carrying, lighten it, or revise the route, or change the timescale.

Hopefully, your people are willing to adapt and are keen to make the best of the situation.
Keep in mind these points:

- This is an activity that leaders can do with their teams too – to re-evaluate and redistribute workloads for well-being.
- It's likely there will be too much to do in your current timescale. Together you can agree on what gets left behind, what doesn't get done, what parameters need to be in place, and when it's OK to stop.
- The activity may highlight someone who has 'sloping shoulders', someone who isn't pulling their weight, or someone who takes on more because they become uncomfortable with the process. If so, that needs to be addressed appropriately – either with the team or at a suitable time and place.

Criteria

You could suggest some simple criteria for fairness to check the final outcomes of the process:

- Have we got the current priorities covered?
- If not, what needs to happen?
- Do you see the redistribution as fair?
- If not, how can we make it so?
- Do you believe you can manage this load and feel in control (not overwhelmed)?
- If not, what needs to happen?

Benefits

The benefits of the process and the discussion are:

- Everyone becomes more aware of overloads and sharing the load.
- Priorities can be re-evaluated.
- Team members agree on action about what is necessary within manageable timescales.
- Each individual shares responsibility for a lighter or more manageable load.

It doesn't all have to be on your shoulders: teams find solutions together.

> **Shared experience**
>
> A headteacher of a large primary school offers an adaptive leadership approach to retaining valued staff.
>
> A casual conversation with two members of my team worried me. Both dropped the bombshell that they were considering leaving the profession to work with children in a setting without any of the administration, paperwork, and most tellingly, marking.
>
> Both were four years and five years into their career and are wonderful teachers. I didn't want to lose them.
>
> I decided it was time to think again about marking. To scrap it. Marking has to be meaningful and relevant to the child. The most important feedback that children receive is in the moment during the lesson, face to face. Why do teachers have to mark everything that children do? The perception of teachers is that they mark pupils' work, and have done since teaching began.
>
> We decided to trial no marking in one year group first.
>
> My message was that I want my teachers to spend more time talking to the children; discussing what went right and what went wrong with colleagues after the lesson; discussing the afternoon lessons instead of sat in the classroom whilst eating their lunch with a stack of 30 books in front of them; chatting to each

other at the end of the day about the next day, instead of worrying about the 60 books in the corner which they couldn't do at lunchtime because they were running a club or had staff meeting after school.

Most of all I wanted my teachers to feel energised again. I wanted them to be excited about their lessons and being with the children under their care. I wanted them to feel like they were making a difference.

I observed one of my teachers early on during the trial. In the lesson she was everywhere. She got around every child in the room, giving precise feedback to each and every one. It was a joy to watch. And most of all she didn't look like she had the weight of the world on her shoulders, or more to the point, the weight of 32 books that needed marking at the end of the lesson.

We have undertaken interviews with staff and children as the trial still goes on. The overwhelming message is that this has improved their well-being and re-ignited a love for the profession.

Marking still exists. At the end of an important unit of work teachers are still spending time assessing children's work. And at the start of the trial one of my stipulations was that I didn't expect to see a drop in quality. The quality has gone up.

I want my staff to love doing the job they trained to do. I want them to love coming to work every day. I want them to do the very best for the children in my school.

Twelve years ago, as a younger headteacher, there was no chance I would have scrapped marking. But times have changed, people are changing, and we need to keep teachers in the profession. With experience comes the willingness to take more risks and as leaders we have to adapt.

Coaching approaches
Coaching yourself
- How do you feel about sharing the load?
- If you feel resistance, note down your reasons.
- If you feel anxious about other people's workloads, consider the impact on your own health and well-being if your workload remains this high because of putting other people's needs above your own.
- If you feel stuck because your workload is too high and other people's workloads are too high, consider the consequences.
- What will happen if your workload remains this high?
    - And what will happen then?
    - And what will be the consequences of that?
    - Then what?
    - Anything else?
- What will happen if their workload remains this high?

- And what will happen then?
- And what will be the consequences of that?
- Then what?
- Anything else?
- Consider your responses from the perspective of well-being.
- Consider the potential of the activity.

Coaching others
- How can you manage your workload and keep well?
- What could you do differently?
- What could you do less of?
- What could you take less time over?
- What would make a useful difference?
- What will you say 'yes' to and what will you say 'no' to?
- If you feel overloaded, consider the consequences.
- What will happen if your workload remains this high?
  - And what will happen then?
  - And what will be the consequences of that?
  - Then what?
  - Anything else?
- What are your priorities?
- How will you ensure you keep well and ensure the priorities are met?
- How will you communicate this to others?
- In summary, what are the next steps?

Coaching upwards
- How do we 'keep well and carry on' through difficult times?
- How do we role-model keeping well while managing challenges?
- How do we enable our people to do the same?
- How can we communicate these priorities?
- How can we demonstrate these priorities in our actions?
- How to go forward with this?

Perspectives

When times are pressured, working relationships often become strained, which impacts people's well-being. Whatever your Coaching Style, to keep well as a leader, make sure you attend to your 'flip side', and make allowances for it.

Innovators – tend towards quick thinking and rapid solutions. They will share the load but may not think things through sufficiently to minimise mistakes that then cause more work. *Beware* making quick responses without double-checking.

Achievers – tend to be pragmatic and task-focused, so will be OK with sharing the load as long as they believe others will get the job done. *Beware* doing it all yourself 'to make sure it's done'. Also, beware of expecting others to achieve as much as you can – Achievers are the ace 'doers'!

Perfectors – like to ensure thoroughness. They will share the load as long as they believe others will do the job properly. *Beware* doing it all yourself 'to make sure it's done well'. 'Good enough' doesn't have to mean complacency or poor quality; sometimes it means a good compromise, sometimes it means survival.

Harmonisers – want people to be well and to get along well together. They struggle to share the load if it risks others working too long and feeling the strain. *Beware* constantly putting other people's needs above your own.

Keep in mind – a 'sense' of workload comes more naturally, and accurately, to some than others. It's important to recognise that the same tasks may take different amounts of time and effort for different people. It's easy to make assumptions about how long things take and how easy they are. I make mistakes with spreadsheets. Some people feel stressed about making phone calls and so procrastinate. I have a colleague who takes about three times as long as others to write, check, and send an email. People may have home lives you know nothing about, nor need to, but things outside of work may impact what they are able to take on. Solutions for sharing the load need to take account of what each person can manage.

CHAPTER 11

Living the school values

Shared experience

Extract from a coaching conversation.

Headteacher
It dawned on me in the team meeting how wound up I was feeling about one person's behaviour in particular and also how disappointing it felt to watch most of the team tolerating low level, unacceptable behaviours. It's not unusual for Jim to interrupt and talk over people so they give up over time until I ask them directly what they think. People routinely remain silent and look down when Elsie goes on about not seeing the point of change and how things won't work. Both of them make meetings uncomfortable. I can sense the awkwardness people feel but don't really know how to tackle it.

Coach
How would you like team meetings to be?

Headteacher
Energised, enthusiastic, focused, with everyone contributing. Team members sharing their views and challenging one another – creatively. Not awkward about what's really going on around the table. I'd like people to take more responsibility and speak up instead of sitting there quietly waiting for me to deal with it all.

Coach
Anything else?

Headteacher
I'd like Elsie to just be a bit more positive and be willing to give change a go sometimes instead of sitting there so stubbornly. And Jim to take a look at himself and see what a terrible role-model he is in these situations, especially to newer team members. But I don't see either of them changing.

Coach
What's really going on here – behind the tension and disappointment you feel?

Headteacher
It shouldn't be this way. We wouldn't put up with kids behaving like this in the classroom and yet here we are as adults not living by the standards we expect of our children. It seems hypocritical.

Coach
How would you expect teachers to deal with this in a classroom situation?

Headteacher
Well pupils soon learn there's a code of conduct in the classroom that they stick to...

> And teachers explore the school values with the children, why they are important and what these mean in practice, how they're expected to behave together...
>
> Coach
> Which of the school values are not being lived out in the team meetings?
>
> Headteacher
> Respect mainly ... disappointingly ... respect, responsibility, and courage.
>
> Coach
> How could you address this?

Values – spoken and demonstrable

Agreeing and presenting values in any organisation is a long process. Once they are finalised and displayed in the reception area and on the website, they represent an important announcement – this is who we are. This is how we are. This is the way we do things here. Those values serve the whole school community as a source of guidance and inspiration.

Something happens, though, when people get familiar with the values and start taking them for granted. It's as if agreeing with the school values means you can safely assume they are lived out.

Take respect as an example: you don't have to look far to see adults in schools not showing respect for one another – talking over others in meetings, not clearing things away in the staff room, blanking people in the corridor, and remaining silent when they need to address an issue rather than taking responsibility for doing so.

How do you extend the process of showcasing the values to embedding them so that everyone remembers to live them out in practice?

This applies especially to leaders. How do *you* live the school values naturally, actively role-model them, and consistently put them into practice? What does showing respect really look like?

Team activity for ensuring school values stick

This works equally well as a congruent process in a team meeting or as a whole school activity, including lunchtime staff and the site manager.
Timings:
   Determined by the number of people participating.
Resources:
- Estimate 2 stacks of 20 sticky notes for each small group. Each stack a different colour.
- Marker pens or bold pens.

Step 1

- Divide the participants into small groups of three or four so that you can be sure everyone has a voice and contributes.
- Give each small group a generous number of sticky notes – the same colour.
- Share the aim of the activity – to give everyday meaning to the school values.
- Allocate one value to each group. (If you have a large number of people, there will be multiple groups working on the same value.)
- Ask the groups to take the value and describe the behaviours that demonstrate it in action – one behaviour per sticky note. As many as possible. Minimally ten.

What would you look for to find this value in practice? What would you see that shows you, the adults, are living the value?

- Create a sticky note gallery with all the behaviours. Cluster the sticky notes under each 'VALUE' heading.
- Discuss what's there and share the findings of what this value looks like in action.

Step 2
- Repeat the process using different coloured sticky notes.
- Allocate a different value to the same groups.
- The task now is to describe what the value doesn't look like in practice – how you, the adults, would **not** behave if you were demonstrating this value.

For example, respect, in practice, doesn't look like derogatory comments in the staff room or gossiping.

- One behaviour per sticky note. As many as you can think of.
- Create a second sticky note gallery of the behaviours that you don't want adults to demonstrate around your school.
- Discuss what's there and share your findings.

What do you anticipate will happen? All too often, people start to recognise that even though they believe in them, they don't live the values consistently. Then, they're relieved to have a way of raising what's wrong, incongruent, or inconsistent.

The gift of this activity is that there's no finger-pointing or shaming, just the sobering reality that living the values goes way beyond the intellectual exercise of creating the list of values. This level of awareness is exactly what's required for each adult to realise the significance of their behaviour as role models.

Step 3

- Create an inspiring **Living our school values** document of the behaviours from the sticky note galleries and circulate to everyone.
- Display the behaviours in the staff room, loos, in meetings – encourage people to keep a copy in their most used notebook.

Awareness brings choices

Awareness of this sobering reality is a great starting point, but it isn't enough to embed the behaviours that demonstrate the values. This takes action, accountability, and commitment. An excellent conclusion for the activity is to get people in pairs or in their teams to note down and articulate a specific action they will commit to. For example:

'Rather than remain quiet, I will speak up more in meetings and contribute something to every meeting.'

'Instead of being grumpy and offloading my frustrations in the staff room, I will respect and contribute to the calmness we all need in there by being a bit more smiley and upbeat.'

'Instead of being absorbed in my own thoughts each morning when I arrive at school, I'll greet people with a smile and say "Good Morning."'

Shared experience

This primary headteacher describes how they embedded the value of respect with adults and children across the school community by using the Equal-II-se model and questions (Figure 11.1).

When I first became a headteacher, we didn't have a core mission or vision statement that people could just say off the top of their head, or feel, as a statement of intent. Within eighteen months though we had created a place with fundamental values, where we could say what guided all our decisions, our behaviours, our choices. RESPECT was one of the values.

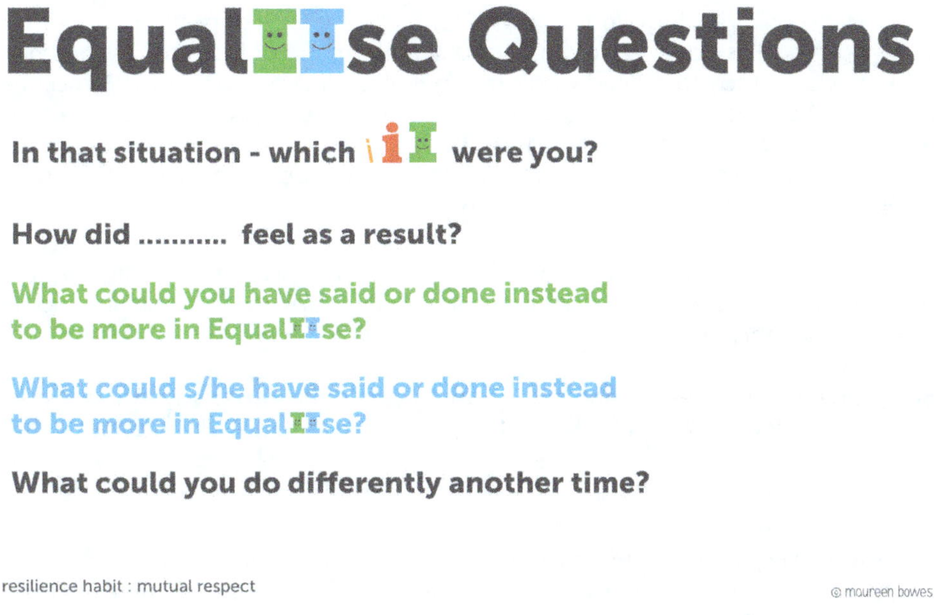

EqualIIse Questions

In that situation – which i I were you?

How did ………. feel as a result?

What could you have said or done instead to be more in EqualIIse?

What could s/he have said or done instead to be more in EqualIIse?

What could you do differently another time?

resilience habit : mutual respect

© maureen bowes

Figure 11.1 Equal-II-se – Children's version

It became apparent very quickly that we needed a vehicle for each of the values to make sense, to add community and to have a language around each one. We found the model of Equal-**II**-se gave us a way of using respect in action.

Straight away, even the youngest of children get the idea of **i** *i* **II**. It was so visual they understood exactly what we were talking about. They're different colours – no one needs to be the same. It's two people looking **I** to **I** at each other because both matter, both count. We can disagree and still get on.

The whole phrasing became like a mantra. When things had gone wrong you could hear children using the phrasing as an explanation.

'That person didn't let me do x, y, or z and then they called me this. That's not right is it? Because we can disagree about a game but we've got to disagree kindly haven't we? We've got to disagree with respect because we all count don't we?'

Big **i**, little *i* also became a way of talking about people that wasn't disrespectful. There wasn't the judgement and adults didn't fear difficult conversations anymore. There wasn't the fear with children talking about friendship issues because you weren't accusing anyone of anything. You were just saying 'I think you're being a bit Big **i**.' It wasn't saying 'I don't like you.' It was just observing that was a bit Big **i**. It was an awareness thing as opposed to a judgement thing, or telling off thing.

Among the children, it gave those who felt 'little *i*' a way of getting out of their shell. It gave us as adults a way to encourage them out of their shyness or timidity. How do you say to a child who's being timid, 'stop being timid'?! By nature, they are the quieter ones who don't want to cause a fuss. The conversation is counter-productive if you're suggesting they need to be more courageous. Actually saying 'I noticed you were a bit little *i*. I wonder what we can do to be more Equal-**II**-se?' was a whole different conversation.

The language of Equal-**II**-se gave everyone a voice. And for the adults, it meant every intervention was an investment in relationships rather than the adults resolving a friendship issue.

Being able to say, 'I feel equal to you,' and getting children to say that out loud, is just really empowering. **I feel equal to you** is such a powerful sentence.

Sharing responsibility
Even with the very best of intentions, it's natural as time goes by for these behaviours slide a little. That's where you really need each other to step up and share responsibility.

The final part of this activity is well suited to a follow-up meeting.

- Ask the group(s) how they would respond when they see their colleagues **not** living the school values. If it's useful, give them the following choices – Would you:
  1. address it
  2. ignore it, or
  3. go and let someone more senior know so they are aware of it?
- Explore the consequences of each choice until it becomes self-evident that most of the time, it's the responsibility of the person present to address it.

It's a shared responsibility to embed the values, and if you don't acknowledge when people are not living the values, then at some level, you're not living them either. The headteacher or senior leaders are not solely responsible for ensuring everyone lives the values. They can't be everywhere at any one time. Therefore, if you or anyone notices something that goes against what the school values are about, it's important to address it and reference it as soon as possible before it turns into a bigger tension or problem.

Encourage people to find an easy way in by saying, in a firm but friendly way, something like, 'Remember those discussions on the school values? What you said just then/the way you behaved at that time wasn't in line with that. Remember, we agreed we'd all take responsibility, so I'm reminding you as part of that agreement.'

Better still, agree on a phrase or a shorthand message that you can say to one another at those times of forgetting, to keep the discussion alive and to de-personalise the comment. You could, for example, agree to say the acronym 'RTV!' (Remember The Values!) That way, you'll ensure the values become embedded across the school.

Coaching approaches
Coaching yourself
- Gain clarity for yourself about how you role-model the school values (and your personal values). Find specific examples of how you routinely demonstrate each of your school's values with your staff.
- And examples of when you haven't.
- Rate yourself from 1 to 5 (where 1 is low and 5 is high) on how consistently your behaviour is aligned with the school values.
- What will you do differently to increase your rating?
- How will you keep track of how you're doing?

Coaching others
- What examples can you think of that show how you demonstrate the school values? What can people see that shows you are living the values in your day-to-day school life?
- How do you know?/How can you find out?
- What do you sometimes do that isn't in line with the school values?
- How do you know?/How can you find out?
- What aspects would you like to change so you are naturally demonstrating the school values?
- What action will you take to change these?

- What would work for you to keep track and embed these behaviours?
- What could we agree on going forward to make this work?

Coaching upwards
- Raise the topic of school values with the person(s) in authority and discuss how each of you may be perceived in this context. For example, the school may have courage as a value, but you know people are reluctant to challenge those in authority here because they know their responses can be patronising.
- How important is it to invite feedback on living the school values?
- Explore opportunities for giving and receiving feedback on the behaviours that represent the values.
- How best to develop one another in this feedback process?
- How can we make this feedback routine?

Perspectives
People with different styles can struggle with various aspects of living the school's values and their own values. These examples show what they may or may not know but tend to do anyway:

Innovators – It's not considerate to let others down.
Achievers – It's not respectful to routinely put your needs first.
Perfectors – It's not motivating to feel scrutinised.
Harmonisers – It's not caring to avoid conflict.
Keep in mind – Values may not change, but their interpretation does. Not very long ago, it was considered rude if a man didn't open a door for a woman. Now I feel I'm quite capable of opening my own door, or opening a door for a man who's struggling because he's carrying something heavy! Also, someone who's depressed, anxious, or caught up in the moment may *seem* to act thoughtlessly without intending to do so. You don't want the values police; you do want genuine respect between people.

CHAPTER 12

Clarifying expectations

The importance of ground rules

Whenever I facilitate a course with a group, the starting point is always the same: establishing a group contract (ground rules) together and managing expectations. As a facilitator, I believe these are absolutely essential for enabling individuals to form well as a group. Here's an activity that is important for your leadership team. Once they have experienced this process, they can repeat it with their teams.

Managing expectations

In the context of a course, I usually have three groups discussing and providing feedback on their agreed points on the following (one point per group):

1. What are your expectations of me as a facilitator?
2. What are your expectations of each other?
3. What are your expectations of the programme?
4. And I contribute with – What are my expectations of you as participants?

Once the whole group agrees that we can each deliver and meet the expectations, we are ready to start the programme.

I believe clarifying and agreeing on expectations is imperative not only for individuals on courses but especially for people working together as a team. It is a valuable process that leaders often omit. While values remain the same in navigating towards your school vision, expectations may well change.

If you assume expectations of one another rather than discuss them, you have a recipe for tension and conflict. It's well worth starting the year with an honest team discussion to agree on expectations. That way, as fallible human beings, you can be confident you'll avoid letting one another down.

Team activity to support managing expectations
Preparation
Timing:
Given the stage your team is at, you determine how long you need to discuss these points effectively.

Resources:

- Note taking materials

Preparation:

- Plan how to manage the time to allow for effective discussions.

Activity
- Clarify the context and the parameters of the discussion.
- Divide the team into two groups, with you as the third group.

- No more than three people in each group. If you are a team of three, then it's one person per group!
- Divide the three topics among the three groups allowing ten minutes for discussion and reflection.

1. What are your expectations of me (team leader/headteacher)?
2. What are your expectations of each other?
3. What are my expectations of you (team members/leadership team)?

- Allow five minutes per group to provide feedback on the key points. One person summarises, and another person captures the bullet point summary in writing or typing to share with the team.
- After each small group has provided feedback, determine whether the remaining group members agree. Is there anything they disagree with or want to change?
- Explore this further with the whole group, clarifying the following points:
  - What does this look like, e.g., on a day-to-day basis?
  - How do we demonstrate accountability?
  - What do we need to communicate? When? Through what channel?
- Decide what the team can act upon and what needs further discussion.

Agree on when the next discussion will take place. Make sure to keep the ongoing discussion a priority.

Coaching approaches
Coaching yourself
- What situations have left you feeling disappointed over the past year?
- In what ways were your expectations too high?
- How will you adjust your expectations to manage the reality of what's ahead?
- What does that mean in practice?
- What do you need to communicate to others?
- What do others need to communicate to you?
- What do you need from them?
- What do they need from you?
- What simple strategies will you discuss to find workable solutions?
- With whom?
- When?

Coaching others
Take your situation and explore:

- What are your expectations?
- What is the reality?
- How can you manage your expectations to be realistically optimistic?

Coaching upwards

In the context of morale, how do we minimise disappointment and keep expectations realistic:

- Governor expectations?
- Teacher expectations?
- Parent expectations?
- Pupil expectations?
- Local authority expectations?

Perspectives

When it comes to expectations and disappointment:

- *Innovators* – tend to be over-optimistic, trusting things will work out OK without having enough actual evidence to convince others.
- *Achievers* – are driven to make their expectations happen, without realising the harsh impact this can have on the people around them.
- *Perfectors* – tend to take disappointment very personally and see it as a sign of personal inadequacy if they don't meet expectations.
- *Harmonisers* – tend to become overwhelmed when others are disappointed and risk not addressing the problems by wanting others to feel better.
- *Keep in mind* – people who come from a different culture, or who are coping with broader difficulties elsewhere, or are neurodivergent may not follow agreed-upon ground rules for reasons other than unwillingness. It's important to keep an open mind when members of staff are not adhering to agreed ways of working and to check assumptions about what is the norm. It may seem inconvenient to take everyone's needs into account, especially when they are not what you anticipate. Clarity is all-important to prevent misunderstandings.

SECTION 4

It's all about relationships

Leaders get things done with, and through, people. Managing relationships effectively across a whole school community is imperative, and requires a high level of personal awareness and interpersonal skills.

Schools are great places to work, but tensions arise through not valuing or accepting differences. Unattended, these tensions can soon become conflicts which, if not addressed, feed into a toxic culture.

Section 4 equips leaders well for communicating appropriately, co-operating, and collaborating so that everyone has a better chance of fulfilling their role in educating the children.

CHAPTER 13

Sharing responsibility

I'm not OK. You're OK. passive	I'm OK. You're OK. assertive
I'm not OK. You're not OK. passive aggressive	I'm OK. You're not OK. aggressive

Rights, responsibilities, and generational awareness
We are all products of our times and circumstances

There are many factors that make each of us uniquely different. One key factor is the time we were born into. This simple timeline exercise is a useful reminder of this factor.

- Draw a timeline of a hundred years and populate it with significant life changes for you, your parents, and grandparents. Historical events like wars and pandemics; societal changes like healthcare advances and technology; major political influences; and then key stages and events that are personal to your life.
- Reflect for a while from your birth year onwards and the circumstances that have influenced your life perspective.
- Then consider the parents and carers in your school community across this timeline, and the societal changes that have influenced their life perspective.
- And of course, your pupils and their evolving perspectives on life.

I first did this timeline exercise in a moment of exasperation to help me understand and process the feelings I have about what's going on in today's society. I found it useful to contrast, for example, what the teaching experience might be like for a young, earlycareer teacher alongside teachers and support assistants who are approaching retirement; for secondary school teachers working with teenagers through and post the isolation of the pandemic; for parents who have never been without a mobile phone or social media.

It's an interesting exercise on many levels and is likely to highlight some relevant points about your school community that may be hiding in plain sight for you.

What was striking for me was the stage in my career where rights, respect, and responsibility influenced society in general and education in particular. 'The Bill of Rights' became a reference point for adults on assertiveness programmes and for school charters from the 1970s. The aim was to support people who might have been marginalised to voice their wishes without feeling repressed or ashamed about them. At the same time, writers advocating rights also advocated responsibilities.

I considered how the 1990s and 2000s progressed, and it seemed to me that something sinister happened, that the responsibilities part of the assertiveness equation got trampled. Programmes on TV reinforced aggressive behaviour and disrespectful comments as being acceptable. Programmes like 'The Apprentice' and other reality game shows, hostile interviewing (You're not OK), and UK Prime Minister's questions hardly exemplified respectful interactions, no matter how often the term 'honourable' was used.

Interactions became fraught as rights-based expectations were not met. Many became more blaming, looking for fault in others as opposed to recognising the part they too play in the situation and the resolution.

As a result of my timeline exercise, I found myself questioning what happened to taking responsibility and sharing responsibility.

You may have the word 'responsibility' written into your school or classroom charters, but like values, just because people are in agreement about responsibility, it doesn't mean they are actually taking responsibility, particularly in those trickier situations and when they feel under pressure.

It's worth reconsidering what responsibility means in practice across the whole school community:

- What does taking responsibility look like?
- What behaviour does responsibility necessitate?
- How do you enable your people to take responsibility – for themselves, their workload, their well-being, their relationships at work?

My hope is that these questions empower you to reconsider the boundaries of rights, respect, and responsibility so that you get the respect you merit as a human being and school leader.

Team activity – What's your responsibility here?
One to two sessions

Suitable for most groups, Inset Day activity, or team meeting. It's a thought-provoking activity, so consider what's needed for team members to contribute openly. The activity benefits from a follow-up session.

Timings: 1 hour per session
Resources
- Screen or board and pens
- Paper and something to write with.

Step 1

- Ask people to work in pairs. (Pairs discussions enable people to clarify their thinking.)
- Ensure everyone has some paper and something to write with.
- Share the aim of the activity – To explore rights and responsibilities.
- On the flip chart/board/screen, display the title 'I have the right to…'
- Take 5 minutes for group members to discuss in pairs: 'What rights are reasonable to expect as part of this school community?' Provide an example to get people started, perhaps: 'I have the right to feel safe.'
- Where possible, go around the pairs in turn. Ask them to share with the whole group one of the rights they discussed by finishing the sentence 'I have the right to…'
- Make a list of these rights so the whole group can see. There are likely to be similarities between some of the rights, so aim to create simple statements that capture the main points.
- Depending on the time, either go around until all the rights have been listed or until you have a list of six to ten rights to display.

Step 2

- Ask group members to choose the right(s) that are most important to them and write them on their paper, allowing some space to write underneath each one.

- Then, under each right, complete the sentence 'I have the responsibility to…' Extend your example to demonstrate.
  'I have the right to feel safe.'
  'I have the responsibility to take care of myself and address anything I believe to be unsafe.'
- Where possible, go around the pairs in turn. Ask them to share with the whole group the responsibilities they discussed by finishing the sentence 'I have the responsibility to…'
- When the list has the corresponding responsibilities for each right, discuss any areas where people feel conflicted in living out that responsibility and/or enabling others to have their rights.
- Agree on what action you can all take for team members to be able to demonstrate their rights, show respect, and fulfil their responsibilities.
- Agree on how to share responsibility for making this happen.

You can revisit and adapt this approach to exploring responsibility at any point. It's a good companion exercise to those in Chapter 12: Clarifying Expectations.

Coaching approaches
Coaching yourself
- How is responsibility communicated in your school:
  - Across teams?
  - In performance management?
  - With pupils?
  - With parents/families?
- What ways are there for you to communicate responsibility more effectively (in addition to the written word) across your school community?
- How can you raise awareness of responsibility:
  - Alongside respect?
  - Within the school's ethos?
  - Demonstrated in daily practice?
- Boundaries and consequences can be tough. What assertiveness practices do you and your people need in order to restore respectful and responsible relationships?

Coaching others
In this partnership or working relationship:

- What are your rights and what are your responsibilities?
- What are my/the other person's rights and what are their responsibilities?
- What can you be pleased about?
- What needs work, what needs to be addressed, and what needs to be said?
- How will you do this respectfully?
- Specify out loud what needs to be said (to me and/or others).
- Keep rehearsing these points until you feel more articulate when making them.

Coaching upwards

- In your view, what are the main rights and the accompanying responsibilities within your role?
- How can demonstrating responsibility become more overt for our people and parents?
- How do we ensure the principles of respect when discussing rights and responsibilities?

Perspectives

Consistent and effective practice of rights, responsibilities, and respect can be hard work, especially when you are under pressure or attack from others about things that matter to you. In worst-case scenarios, be aware:

Innovators – may put their needs first, make big statements, and be less concerned about their responsibilities.

Achievers – may use aggressive and curt responses, belittle others, or scare people into submission.

Perfectors – may find fault in others and undermine people through evidence-seeking questions.

Harmonisers – may manipulate others and/or procrastinate in addressing issues in the hope of preventing or avoiding conflict. Both behaviours contribute to a toxic culture.

Keep in mind – the aim of this chapter is to encourage acceptance and inclusion within the setting of Equal-II-se. Some of your people may be struggling with the effects of discrimination because of, for example, poor health, gender orientation, or their beliefs. It can take considerable time to create an atmosphere of safety and mutual care so that everyone in the school community feels empowered both to assert their rights and to practise their responsibilities to others.

CHAPTER 14

Resilient relationships

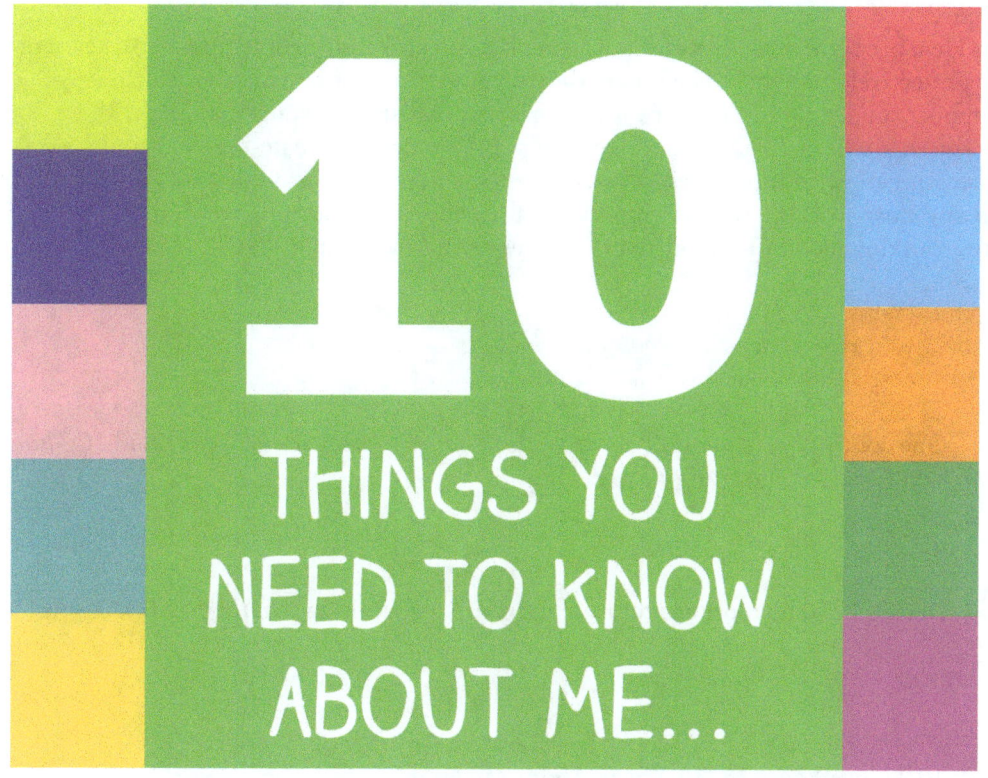

Resilient relationships

Part 1: It matters that people work well together

A working relationship is an essential partnership that often determines your effectiveness and the quality of your experience at work. It's very much like a dance where you must learn the steps, move with co-ordinated ease, and enjoy performing together. Imagine the learning support assistant and class teacher who are of one mind in the classroom; the office staff who appreciate their complementary skill sets and manage the different dynamics at the reception desk; governors or trustees who engage well with teachers.

Unfortunately, relationships at work can be a real strain on people and significantly affect their well-being. Unspoken tensions can lead to individuals feeling demotivated and not looking forward to coming to work, sometimes dreading it because of personalities, attitudes, and behaviour. It matters that people work well together. It matters that tensions and differences are resolved before things become conflictual and then toxic.

Here are some activities and resources for you and your people that fast-track working effectively together. They increase your awareness of one another so that you can support, understand, and care for each other. Most importantly, though, these conversations will enable you to adapt the way you communicate together and be more accepting of your differences. You can use them across teams, with year leaders, and/or in any close working relationship like headteacher and chair of governors.

You can download the resources from www.routledge.com/9781032945392

Activity – Colleagues, not mind readers

Resources:

- One copy per person of the downloads *What Are You Like at Work?* and *10 Things You Need to Know About Me.*

Preparation:

- Decide who the most appropriate pairs are for working together on this.

Timing:

- *What Are You Like at Work?* 20–30 minutes
- *10 Things You Need to Know About Me* 60 minutes

Part 1

Put people into appropriate pairings. This could be the people who are already working together, have been working together, or are about to work together.

Give each person a copy of *What Are You Like at Work?*

Take 10 minutes for each individual to respond to the questions.

In pairs, discuss together:

- How do you see yourself at work?
- How do you think others may see you?

Take 20 minutes for the pairs to discuss:

- How they are different.
- How their differences can be complementary strengths.
- What will work well with their similarities.
- What might not work so well with their similarities.

Part 2

Give each person *10 Things You Need to Know about Me*.

The pairs then work through each of the *10 Things You Need to Know about Me* statements, informed by and extending their discussion from *What Are You Like at Work?*

It works well if each person in the pair takes each statement in turn.

Allow at least an hour for this discussion so each individual can share important points about themselves and learn important points about their colleague.

Consolidate the discussion by asking the pairs to agree on three things they want to remember, routinely, to keep working well together.

Encourage everyone to schedule a time each term when they will revisit the sheets to remember what they've shared and learnt about each other since. That way, they will keep strengthening – not straining – their working relationship, communicating well, and minimising tensions.

Remember

We don't see things the way they are, we see things the way we are.

Here are some key points to see things the way each of the styles sees them. You need to know that:

Innovators – like fun, energy, and enthusiasm. They get bored and demotivated with too much detail, pessimism, and criticism.

Achievers – like action, pace, and progress. They get wound up and impatient when things go slowly or don't happen.

Perfectors – like thoroughness, quality, and clarity of understanding. They don't do well with unclear communication or a hurried approach.

Harmonisers – like team spirit, co-operation, and people feeling good. They find selfishness and disrespect hard to work with.

Keep in mind – not everyone fits the styles and not everyone reads emotions in the same way. Our cultural context, neurotype, levels of sensitivity, and life experiences may impact the way we interpret and therefore trust others. The more you understand your people, the more understanding and trust will be created.

Part 2: A different workplace relationship – relating to people in authority

In addition to regular workplace relationships, you also have visitors who monitor and inspect how the school is doing against their criteria and standards.

The role of moderators and inspectors is a combination of auditor and interviewer. They represent authority, and this adds a power dynamic to relationships:

- They come into your school to check if standards are being, and have been, met; that there is nothing faulty; and that nothing is illegal.
- Their interpersonal relations with you and your people – within respectful parameters – are secondary to the task at hand. This is a very different workplace relationship which, inevitably, puts you and your people under pressure.
- They assess you but you don't (usually) assess them. Their assessment has implications for you, your school, and the school community.
- When auditors/inspectors are competent, the strain on people is high. It's higher still if they are less competent. Lack of competence can be technical; for example, they don't understand your school, or the guidance, or how to ask the right questions. Lack of competence can also be relational; they may come across to you as rude, overbearing, or indifferent.
- They might also reflect a top-down 'agenda' following a particular brief. (Remember 'Covid is no longer an excuse'?)

The impact of power dynamics and conflicting views is often surprising. Assertive, even respectful, communication can go out of the window. When faced with an authority figure, it's easy to feel under pressure. Then, what you intend to say can often come out all wrong, especially if you're nervous. You and the individuals you work with might talk for too long; remain too surface-level when depth is needed; go blank; seem clunky in what you say; and not realise the implications of what you are saying. None of which inspires confidence in the inspector. None of which makes you or your people feel good afterwards.

The inspection process is not just about what you know and how you evidence what you know; it's also about how confidently you communicate what you know. It can be helpful to have reminders for yourself to keep your thoughts on track and to keep self-doubt at bay.

Writing the reminders down serves to reinforce the messages to yourself. The simple presence of a slip of paper in your pocket with the reminders you want to give yourself can be empowering.

Affirming thoughts:

- 'You are a visitor in my school.'
- 'I am an expert at my school.'
- 'I will show you what is great about this school.'
- 'I will provide evidence and challenge any misconceptions you may have.'
- 'I will not allow you to make inaccurate judgements about what you are seeing.'
- 'I will ensure the wording of your report is a true reflection of our school.'

RESILIENT RELATIONSHIPS

Activities – Presenting confidently with people in authority
You can adapt the following three activities to get yourself and your people ready for talking to people in authority, whether that's an inspection, an interview, or a panel.
Timing: 30 minutes
Resources:

- *What Are You Like at Work?*
- *How to adapt your Coacting Style.*

Activity 1 – Team discussion to raise awareness of Coacting Styles.
Context
It's important that you and your people are familiar with how you all come across to others at work. If you haven't covered this already, now is the time to have the *What Are You Like at Work*? discussion as outlined above.
Based on this simple overview, what do your people think moderators and inspectors are like at work?
Use the remaining 20 minutes to discuss:

- What does the visitor need from you to make their visit go well?
- How can you adapt the way you communicate to match the moderation process?
- What do you need from them to make the visit go well?

The role of an auditor or inspector is Achiever/Perfector. It's natural then that Harmonisers and Innovators are likely to experience more tension when communicating with an inspector unless, of course, the inspector knows how to adapt their style appropriately.
The ready-reference sheet 'How to Adapt your Coacting Style' (see Chapter 2) outlines the traits you will be able to spot in the inspector/moderator role with prompts for how to adapt your dialogue and make the interactions go more smoothly.
The following activities get close to making the dialogue with authority real for people. Instead of you telling, advising, or reassuring your people on how to be with a visitor, they can get closer to the experience through practising what they want to say and hearing how others articulate themselves.

Activity 2 – Rehearsal circles
Timing: 30 minutes
Resources:

- Your list of key questions to ask the group.
- Enough chairs for all the group members.

Preparation:

- The key questions you want to group to practise answering.
- Create two circles of chairs where each person seated on the inside faces a person seated on the outside circle. (This can also be done standing.)

Explain the process

You will read out a range of questions that the visitor is likely to ask. The inner circle people go first and respond to the questions with the person facing them in the outer circle. Allocate a very short amount of time (be specific – two minutes?).

At the end of two minutes, the people in the outer circle move around one seat (to their right).

You repeat the question, and the people in the outer circle have their chance to respond to the same question with a different person in the inside circle. Time them again and shout out when two minutes are up.

Repeat the process with the next question and keep moving the people in the outer circle one place to the right each time until you have gone through enough of the questions.

The aim is for people to experience the pressure while knowing they are safe. It's not a real inspection, so although it might be stressful, it benefits everyone as it brings them a little closer to the feelings they may experience. This means you need to be OK with other people's discomfort because most people will be out of their comfort zone when they focus and articulate important responses in an artificial setting.

This isn't role-play; it's rehearsal. It's much more about practising than it is about receiving feedback. It's more about becoming familiar with what happens in your body when you feel pressure and learning some coping strategies for this. It's a great exercise to encourage interoception and self-reliance.

If people reflect on what happens to their bodies under pressure and how they feel, they can be better equipped to deal with what their bodies need at those times and feel more confident. Some people get headaches, some have dry mouths, or their voices go croaky while others feel itchy and twitchy. It helps to know what your body does and, therefore, what to provide to keep it soothed and reassured. This helps you feel more confident and less worried on the day.

Activity 3 – Role-play the dialogue

Timing: 15 minutes per person. Include some time to debrief at the end of the activity.

Resources: Notes on the key questions to cover.

Preparation:

- Agree who will role-play the inspector.
- Discuss the approach you want people to observe.
- Position two chairs at the front where everyone can see and hear the dialogue. One chair for the inspector role and one for the teacher/leader.
- Have water available throughout. People may feel drained, so be sure to have refreshments and energising snacks ready at the end.

Adapt this practice to whatever time you have available. It could be one role-play every team meeting or a whole afternoon of rehearsing:

- Select some key questions that a moderator/inspector is likely to ask.
- Decide who will be in the role as the moderator/inspector.

- Team members take turns, individually, to be at the front of the group with the 'inspector' directly asking them questions. The individual responds to their questions in real time, with all the other team members watching.
- Encourage everyone to take notes for their own reference.
- The other team members give feedback on what the individual did well and what they could do differently.
- Debrief.

In my experience, most people in a school setting don't like role-play, and even more so when you're role-playing yourself in what may well feel like a test. It's hard to ensure psychological safety here because part of the process is to familiarise people with the potential scariness of the situation so it becomes less of an unknown and, therefore, a little less feared. Give everyone the choice whether to take part and encourage a growth mindset approach.

Everyone learns from taking part in this, either as a role-player or as an observer. Everyone gets ideas for what to do and what not to do, what to say and what not to say. Everyone can support each other with useful suggestions and supportive feedback. It's scary and very empowering. People usually feel much better for having tried this, even when they feel they didn't do as well as they'd hoped to. It means they know what to do and say differently with the actual inspector/moderator.

This whole process is impactful because it comes closest to creating the pressure and fear individuals feel during an inspection, but with the knowledge that this is a rehearsal and each person has the support of colleagues in a safe environment.

Just like an auditor, an inspector will see right through any distractions or waffly responses because they are laser-focused on finding the information they need to do their job well. The more you and your people engage efficiently and effectively with them, the more confidence they will have in you, and that they can achieve everything they need in the time they have with you. You will manage a professional rapport, build trust and inspire confidence that you and your people are sharply focused on the efficiency and overall effectiveness of the inspection process too.

Coaching approaches
Coaching yourself

- Check your self-awareness – when you are under pressure, communicating with a person in authority, how do you usually come across?
- How would you like to come across? What would you like to be different?
- What are an inspector's communication needs?
- How can you adapt the way you communicate to match those needs?
- What will enable you to do this – to be that way?
- How will you prepare for this – for yourself?
- How will you prepare your people for this?

Coaching others

- How do you want the inspector to perceive you?
- What first impression do you want to give?

- How do you want the inspector to feel at the end of their time with you?
- What do you need to prepare and have in place to achieve the above?
- Make a list of things to do that demonstrate these points.
- Make a list of prompts for yourself – reminders for how to be from the inside out – to get yourself in a good space for any interaction with the inspector(s).
- Keep these close at hand in the run-up to, and during, the inspection process.

Coaching upwards

- What do you perceive as your strengths when in dialogue with inspector(s)?
- What do you believe the inspector(s) needs from you?
- Within the limited time you have together, what could go wrong?
- How can you prevent that?
- How will you prepare for the visit?

Perspectives

Increase individual awareness of how each style under pressure might irritate an inspector/moderator so everyone can remember how to communicate well and what to say (and what not to say) when it really matters. Under pressure:

Innovators – may deflect, distract, be too chummy, and talk for way too long, giving the impression they are bluffing.

Achievers – may bristle within the dynamic of their role and the inspector's role, coming across as too competitive, pushy, intolerant.

Perfectors – may over-provide, offering too much initial explanation. Go for bullet points first, and have paragraphs easily within reach – verbally and on paper.

Harmonisers – may be too soft and general in their initial approach and feel unsettled by the directness and brevity of the person in authority.

Keep in mind – the very nature of these activities is challenging and may be too stressful for some. There are many reasons why people may refuse to take part. Be prepared to accept their non-participation or preference to simply observe. You may want to offer alternative approaches.

Shared experience

A junior school headteacher decompresses after Ofsted – reflecting, consolidating and venting.

We wouldn't have got 'Outstanding' if it wasn't for me!

The Ofsted inspection process is a hard and demanding challenge. It's designed to be rigorous, but sometimes it doesn't feel like a true reflection of the work you're doing. It feels like a set of hoops to jump through, a game of perceptions, and one where the rules are made by people who don't always understand the nuances of your context. And after that two-day inspection, I was convinced of one thing: if it hadn't been for me pushing back, challenging, and asserting what we knew to be right, we wouldn't have received the judgement we deserved. The inspection felt like a test of endurance. It was certainly a test of my resolve, pressuring me to contest with justice in mind.

What I felt during the Ofsted process:
- Disappointment: The flawed evidence-gathering process made me question how accurately we were being assessed.
- Frustration: Both inspectors have secondary backgrounds (with the Lead Inspector not having Senior Leadership experience), and both missed the nuances of a primary phase school.
- Concern: The inspection could go one of two ways, and I feared it wouldn't reflect the fantastic school we are.
- Empowerment: The need to stand firm and assert our school's achievements

Context: Ten Years in the Making
We'd waited ten years for Ofsted to show up. Ten years of hard work, planning, reflecting, and improving. In that time, we had invested so much into the school – shaping its culture, refining our teaching, and ensuring we were doing the very best for the children in our care. Ofsted had been coming for years. I'd been told "soon" time and time again. But there's something about the moment when the call finally comes, the moment when you're actually under the microscope, that changes everything. The pressure is real.

End of Day 1: Disappointment and frustration
At the end of Day 1, I needed to vent. I wrestled with the gaps and what felt like injustices. The more I reflected, the more it became clear that the inspection wasn't capturing the reality of our school. There were several things that I just couldn't let slide.

- We are a Junior school. The inspectors were both secondary leads in an Ofsted randomised pairing. One had no comprehensive understanding of how we differentiated and adapted the learning in mathematics in our school.
- At the end of the first day's inspection, the inspectors had seen two 15-minute drop-ins of maths and one where an inspector observed an ITT student. That's not enough to gain a proper understanding of our approach, and I knew it.
- During the feedback session, where you observe the HMIs review the day's evidence-gathering, the lead inspector was insistent that children should be writing in depth across foundation subjects. And that didn't sit right with me.
- The inspectors seemed to have a personal belief – after seeing some English books – that our children should be writing extensively across all areas of the curriculum.

I started to realise we would be saddled with an inaccurate judgement of the school. We weren't being seen for the school I knew we were. I wasn't having that!

Challenging the inspectors: standing up for what's right

I challenged both inspectors. First, I pointed out that this was their opinion and therefore subjective. Secondly, this was not something in the inspection handbook, and I wasn't going to let personal beliefs dictate the way we ran our curriculum. I made it clear that I wouldn't be turning my curriculum into a writing curriculum for the sake of appeasing their expectations.

But more importantly, I reminded them of the context we were working in. I explained that, at the time of the inspection, our Year 3 cohort had less than 50% combined ARE (Age-Related Expectation). There were far more relevant and challenging targets than making young children write at length across foundation subjects when they hadn't even attained the basic knowledge to do so.

I wasn't just standing up for our school; I was standing up for the children who needed a curriculum that suited their developmental needs, not one dictated by arbitrary external standards. The inspectors had missed the mark, and I wasn't going to let that happen.

Halfway point: Gaining clarity

By the time Day Two was approaching, I felt a sense of clarity and purpose that hadn't been there on Day One. I knew what I had to do. I couldn't let this inspection be a reflection of anything less than the best of what our school was. I began to map out my approach.

Steps I took after Day 1:

- Evaluated strengths and concerns with my Deputy Headteacher (DHT). We reviewed what the inspectors had seen, what had been missed, and where we could still make an impact.
- Formulated a clear plan for Day 2. I needed to be direct with my staff: what had happened, what to expect, and how to approach the day. It wasn't about waiting for the inspectors to notice us – it was about showing them.
- Clarified what we needed to push back on. The writing issue was the biggest concern. I was not going to let that shape their perception of us.

I also reached out to trusted advisors – colleagues who had been through similar inspections. I needed external validation and a reminder that I wasn't alone in this. Their feedback was invaluable in reinforcing my strategy.

Day 2: Standing firm

By the time Day 2 rolled around, I was more determined than ever. I gathered the staff early that morning and addressed them head-on.

What I said to my staff:
- We hadn't been seen for who we are. I told them openly: Day 1 wasn't a true reflection of us. We had to take ownership of this inspection.
- I shared my conversations with the lead inspector. I wanted them to know the challenges I had raised and how I intended to make sure our strengths were represented.
- I gave clear directions. Maths had to be shown as the well-planned and carefully thought-out subject it was. Writing in foundation subjects wasn't the priority for Year 3 children; we had more pressing academic goals to meet.

I needed my team to feel empowered, confident, and ready to show our best. We had **one day** to change the course of the inspection, and I knew they had it in them.

The final push

The rest of Day 2 was a whirlwind. My team rose to the occasion, showing the inspectors everything they had missed on Day 1. The maths lessons were observed with clarity and understanding. Writing was showcased through rich learning journeys that highlighted progress over time, not just the final product. We made sure the inspectors saw the full picture.

When the final feedback came, it was emotional. The inspectors acknowledged the depth and impact of our work. For that, I was grateful. They saw us for who we really were.

However, the final report that followed was another story. It came two months later, and when I read it, I was disappointed. It didn't capture the full depth of what had been shared in the feedback session. The report was underwhelming and lacked the detail and understanding the inspectors had shown during their final feedback. But at the end of the day, it didn't matter. We had been seen. We had been recognised for the hard work we had put in and the incredible school we are.

On reflection

Reflecting on the whole process, I'm still not sure where the courage to push back came from. I'd heard of people challenging Ofsted before, but I never imagined I would be the one doing it. It's not easy standing up to an institution that holds so much weight, but when you know what's right, you have to find the strength to ensure justice.

Without my resilience, inner strength, and moral purpose, I wouldn't have been able to protect my school's integrity. Without the response from my staff, who supported the cause and rose to the challenge, we would never have received the recognition we deserved.

In the end, we got the judgement we felt we deserved, and I am proud of that. We proved that, when you stand firm in what you believe, it's possible to reshape the narrative – no matter how entrenched the system might seem.

CHAPTER 15

When parents get angry

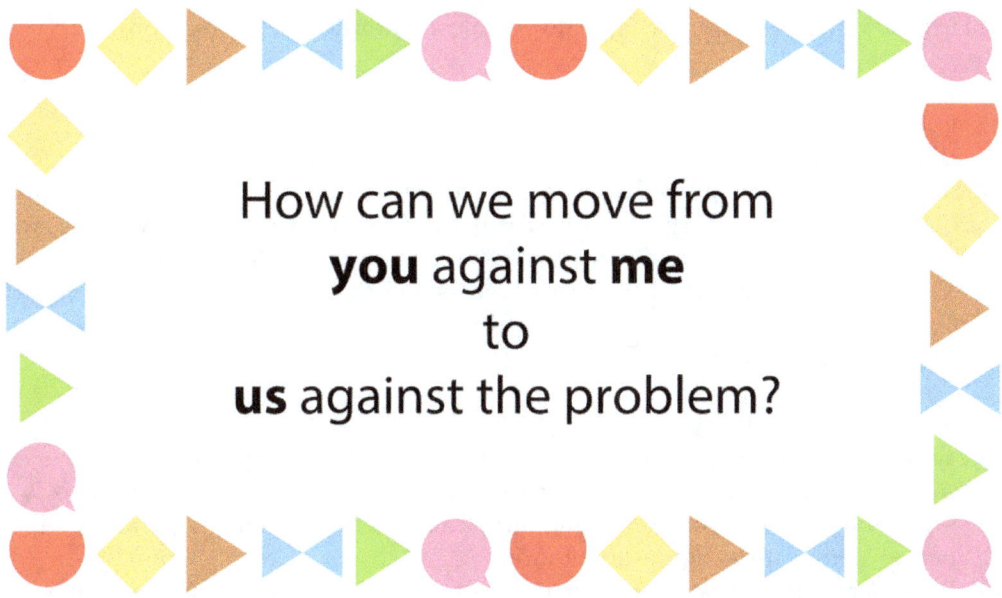

When parents get angry
Part 1 – It's emotive

When it comes to their own children, parents can struggle to keep things in perspective. They may accept that rules are necessary – until their child is adversely affected by them. They may acknowledge that every child should be included in the school community – until their child comes home with a black eye following an incident with another child who is given to emotional outbursts. They may acknowledge that teachers are in charge of the curriculum – until their child struggles to make sense of a new approach to spelling and isn't happy.

To make matters even more challenging, some parents and carers will express themselves in ways that cut across your values and the school's values. Some parents may insult you, provoke you, or feel it acceptable to unleash their emotions on you.

Some parents may use social media or other platforms to attack you and your school so that you come to dread seeing them and, when you do, you experience first-hand what fight, flight, or freeze reflexes feel like.

You may worry that, under enough pressure, you will lose your temper with them, or that you'll roll over and submit, only to regret your behaviour afterwards.

How do you move forward? How do you move towards a better relationship?

It's all about relationships

It's all about relationships and relating. These situations and dynamics make the relationship layered and complex. There you are, the human being carrying the authority of your position, and there they are with their backstory, their personal perspective, and their interpretation, angry and upset with you for not giving them what they believe you should. For now at least, connecting, understanding, and working things out isn't happening.

Key points to keep in mind:

- They may not be angry with YOU personally. It's often the headteacher role, or the system you represent, and the decision-making they are angry with.
- As a teacher, you know how to separate the child from the behaviour. This is a grown-up version of the same thing turned around for yourself – separate you-the-person from you-the-figure-of-authority.
- It's about protecting yourself from their comments instead of letting the comments in and denting you-the-person. You're OK, it's what's happening that they are angry about.
- It helps if you adapt your approach to match their communication needs (see Chapter 2) and the needs of the situation.
- It's not that you can't be yourself, it's more that they need you to talk their language, not the language of policies. Think about what will strike a chord with them and translate the key points into words that speak to their head and heart.
- In order to talk their language, it helps if you can understand where they are coming from. What's really going on behind this behaviour?
- It's about managing the process so that the parent feels heard when you respond.

WHEN PARENTS GET ANGRY

Here's how

In the early stages of a conflict, it helps to invite the parent(s) into the school in a way that sounds and feels informal. They don't want to feel summoned or in trouble 'going to the headteacher's office'. Try something like 'If you come to school for 2 o'clock, we can have a cup of tea together and talk through some possibilities before pick up.'

For the most part, face-to-face communication is the preferred option because you can both see, hear, and sense one another. You can clarify any misunderstanding in the moment as you have the significant advantage of being able to notice their non-verbal communication in ways that are not possible over the phone. You might hear what the parent is saying as anger, then realise it's more like anxiety as you notice they are wringing their hands. Trust more what the body is saying over what the words are telling you.

Be sure you sit at the same level together, around a table, rather than you behind your desk. In certain more volatile situations, you may want to sit in such a way that the door is easy to access, and that your office manager is briefed appropriately of what they need to be aware.

If being in the same room isn't possible, you can apply the same process outlined in the Vent Diagram (Figure 15.1) over the phone.

Offload

People feel better once they've got the pressing issue off their chest. So let them. Give them space and time to offload the awfulness of what they are experiencing. It defuses. It takes some of the heat out of the situation. They feel lighter. They are unlikely to say this, but they appreciate the relief of the opportunity you've given them.

Invite them to offload with questions like: 'Talk me through what's happened…' Or 'What do we need to talk about?' Or 'What's on your mind?'

Simply listen. Don't interrupt. Don't be defensive.

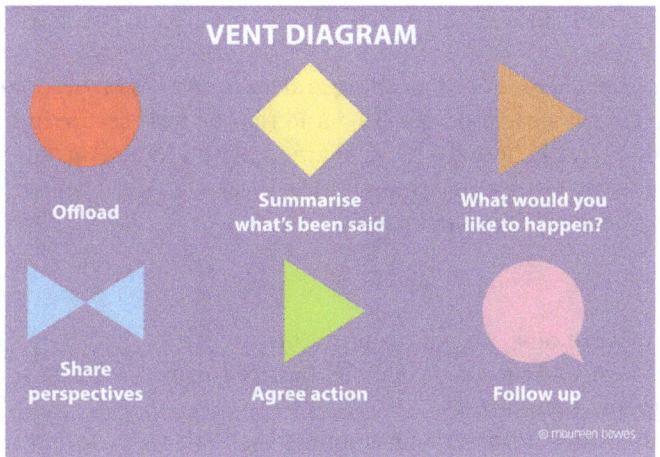

Figure 15.1 Vent diagram

Summarise what's been said

Summarising *proves* you've been listening. Keep it neutral and representative of what they've said. Summarising is powerfully affirming. How often does someone listen in that way, valuing the other human being by giving them all their attention?

'So, if I've understood you correctly Mr(s) Taylor…' [summary points]

It's impactful because it may be the first time they've heard their situation outlined objectively. Thus far, it's been an extremely subjective experience. Listening to your neutral summarising offers them a slightly different perspective.

They may want to add more. They may want to correct or clarify what you have said. Mainly, they want to feel heard.

Ask them 'What would you like to happen?'

Now things are defusing, you'll get a more reasoned, or at least calmer, response here.

Again, listen without interrupting, and summarise back their main points without sounding judgemental.

'If I've understood you correctly, you want Aaron to be on a full timetable, to have lunch in the main hall with the other children, and to have a different support assistant working with him.'

Share perspectives

Explain the situation in terms you are sure they will understand. Make it meaningful for them. Your goal here is empathy for the others involved. It's your chance for your reasoning to be met with more receptivity.

Get them to stand for a few minutes in your shoes so they start to realise more about the complexity of what's involved. Ask them, 'What would you do if you were me/headteacher/teacher?' and 'And if I did that, what would be the impact on the other people involved?'

Then start to negotiate. Look at what you can both agree on.

'We both want Aaron to feel safe and enjoy being at school. We both want the other pupils to feel safe and enjoy being at school. We both want the staff to feel safe and enjoy working here.'

'My job as headteacher is about teaching and learning. It's my responsibility to make sure we provide Aaron with good teaching and that he feels secure in his learning.'

'In order to do this, I believe we need to gradually build up Aaron's time here so he, and everyone, gets used to the patterns and ways of each day. Then we can all manage things together whenever things get tricky.'

Agree action

You can move forward now, even if it's just a few steps.

'What works best to help Aaron get the best out of his learning is when we work together and support each other.'

'We both want Aaron to be OK in school. In school, we've found that what works best for pupils is when parents and teachers work together on this and share some responsibility. So what can we do between us to share responsibility and give Aaron as good a chance as we can for his learning?'

WHEN PARENTS GET ANGRY

Agree what action you can each take, even if it's as simple as 'Let's go sleep on this and talk again tomorrow.'

Summarise
Ideally, ask the parent to recap what they've understood.

'Just to be certain we know what we've agreed to, let's recap what we're going to do.'

Make sure you are both saying the same things. Allow some time for this to prevent any misunderstanding or misinterpretation going forward. You both want to keep your word so it's important to summarise things out loud.

Follow up
They've offloaded, been listened to, seen the bigger picture, become more proactively involved, and time has passed to reflect on the situation.

Make sure you follow things up directly with them. Build the bridges so again they feel valued, not avoided, not tracked down. So that you feel respected, not put down.

Here's an example of a situation where you can apply the process of the Vent Diagram to restore the relationship with the parent by taking time to listen and talk through the situation towards a resolution.

Shared experience

A primary headteacher provides the context behind the email sent by a parent:

It's the autumn term 2020. Government (and therefore county) guidelines to schools are to get children back in school after the lapse in education and socialising. People ranged from unsettled to frightened to existentially anxious. Headteachers had to make decisions through all the different realities for different individuals and different families, and ultimately for the greater good.

In 2023, three years later, this example illustrates a parent's concerns that if her child attended school, they may get Covid and pass it on to their pregnant sister living in the same house.

The headteacher tried to contact the parent by phone, left a message, and then sent an email to explain that the pupil's absence from school would be unauthorised. They invited the parent to get in touch to discuss things further.

The parent emailed this response:

'Hi xxxxxxx

Thanks for that clearly empathetic and understanding email, the eagerness and willingness to try help a parent to one of your students under such distressing conditions is magical! Your concern is overwhelming! Sammy is doing great! I appreciate you have put these absences as unauthorised, being the stand up person that you are! But as her parent I have authorised them for good and

> genuine reasons and you can keep your judgmental, condescending, narcissistic opinions and judgments to yourself. I have bigger things to concern myself with than the opinion of a fat c*** who holds nothing but disdain for me! The feelings mutual a***hole! U know Sammy has been diagnosed as autistic now! You deemed her just a naughty kid and refused to accept something else was wrong. You were wrong!!! You failed her! You failed me! You failed in your duty as a teacher, a leader and a role model. Do not bother to contact me again! Find another means to communicate with me, go through another teacher, one less full of themselves, gods gift to us all you are not! No matter what u believe!
>
> Every word sincerely!
>
> Xxxxxxxxx'

Consider

- How would you have felt on receiving an email like this?
- What do you imagine is really behind these words?
- How would you respond after reading this chapter?

Part 2 – It's complicated

There are many, many reasons why home–school communications can become strained. It's not uncommon for teaching staff to dread meeting with some parents, nor is it uncommon for some parents/carers to dread meeting teaching staff. It's certainly not uncommon for headteachers to dread receiving emails from some people. Most know that sinking feeling when you see a particular name in the inbox.

The reasons why are often complicated but with an increased awareness of trauma informed practice, you stand a much better chance of understanding what might be behind the tensions or dread and how you might adapt your thinking and your approach (see Figure 15.2).

Alongside "The book's backdrop" in the Introduction, the following pieces may throw some light on your own school situations.

Ways to keep people feeling safe

- Provide staff training to increase knowledge and raise awareness of the impact of trauma across families and in the classroom.
- Raise awareness and facilitate the practice of self-compassion (see Chapter 5). When applied, these practices reduce isolation, guilt and shame, and support self-regulating processes.
- Explore well-being – especially with staff who are facing stressful interactions with parents.
- Use straightforward, everyday language to explain decisions and the reasons behind the decisions, involving the parent(s) as far as possible.
- Provide information for people to pick up – leaflets, posters on notice boards, free resources, helplines.

Cameo – Two truths

Teacher's thoughts

I've never found school life this tough. Coming back from maternity leave, I don't think I have the same level of resilience as before. The situation with Billy is getting to me. He's exactly the reason I went into teaching, yet I feel defeated. And scared.

I can tell his mum thinks I'm judging her when I'm simply trying to be empathic. I just want to co-operate with her and work things out but I can't reach her. She avoids me so then it's phone calls and she's immediately defensive or accusatory. She mishears sometimes because her baby is crying in the background and then she cuts short the call.

I'm so tired. Billy's homelife is keeping me awake at night. Not sleeping isn't helping me cope. My husband says I'm not who I used to be. Even when I'm home he says I'm not there because I'm thinking about school. Things have been difficult between us for a while. I'm weepy. I need to spend more time with mum since dad died. I'm feeling guilty as a working mum.

Managing how I react to Billy's mum is taking my energy, which is depleted anyway after a day in the classroom. I'm frightened I'll snap or burst into tears with her. She thinks I'm useless anyway. I'm scared she'll complain to the headteacher and beyond. I'm scared how angry she is with the world. What we're asking isn't unreasonable. I wish she'd co-operate a bit more and then we could work things out better.

My head is full of these thoughts. I can't switch off. I'm comfort eating again. Too much. I'm so tired.

Parent's thoughts

I know what others think of me. That I'm a rubbish mother, I can't control my own son... They don't know the effort it takes to get him to school on time. By 9.00 am I'm emotionally exhausted. When other parents are going home for a coffee, or a run, or me-time, I'm facing a disaster zone.

They're so patronising. I'm not telling them what happened with the dad this weekend. It's like my mum and dad all over again. I never thought it would come to that in my life.

It's none of their business anyway. It will just add to their reasons to take him out of school, just like my headteacher got rid of me. I could not cope with him being home all day. I'd go mad.

They judged me for forgetting his PE kit, today it was his packed lunch. Home life is chaotic enough, how do they expect me to sit down and read with him?

I wish someone would invite Billy to a party or to play. But that won't happen.

I wonder if he will ever leave home. When will I have some kind of life for me again.

I'm so tired.

If Miss Goody-Two-Shoes makes a beeline for me in the playground later, I'll just lose it.

Figure 15.2 Cameo

Handle with care

There are statements, observations, and phrases you can use to reassure, connect, and help people feel safe with you BUT it's important to say them sincerely and authentically, not in an automatic or scripted way.

For example, when someone tells you of a bereavement, it's easy to say automatically 'I'm sorry for your loss.' The words are honest and you mean them but it's worth considering how you convey that meaning authentically and in a way that matches and supports how the other person is at that time.

Applied to other emotional workplace interactions, you could familiarise yourself with how to make core statements your own so you can show more empathy.

There is a short video from Brené Brown that offers great guidance highlighting the difference between empathy and sympathy (*Brené Brown on Empathy*, 2013).

The podcast 'Pop Culture Parenting' is another useful resource. Two Australian men share the ups and downs of real life parenting (*Pop Culture Parenting*, no date).

Coaching approaches
Coaching yourself
- List the facts.
- Separate the person from the problem.
- How can you move from 'you against me' to 'us against this problem'?
- What's the real challenge for you here?
- How will you deal with that challenge?
- What are your trigger points – how can you manage yourself on the inside to prevent an anger outburst or tears on the outside? What strategies would enable you to remain calm and assertive?
- Note down your key actions and your reminders to self.

Coaching others
- What are your concerns in this situation?
- What are the facts?
- What ways can you most effectively communicate the facts to Mr/Mrs/Ms...?
- What will you actually say?
- Go through the dialogue and enable the coachee to practise saying out loud their responses.
- Ask the coachee to summarise the action they will take for reducing their concerns and for addressing the situation with the parent or caregiver.
- Remember to check in afterwards and see how it went.

Coaching upwards
- Explore the situation from different perspectives as appropriate – yours, the teacher's, the parent's, the child's, the school's etc.
- Brief the manager on the imperatives.
- What's the best-case scenario? The worst-case scenario? The likely scenario?
- How do we/you prepare for each?
- Clarify their level of support and offer your support.
- Agree action and follow up.

WHEN PARENTS GET ANGRY

Perspectives

When dealing with others' anger, it is useful to keep in mind your own style:

- *Innovators* – Your humour is an asset but it is important to give the other person a chance to express what they are feeling and to listen before speaking.
- *Achievers* – You may be tempted to retaliate or be confrontational. Neither will help to get to the bottom of the situation. Again it's important to listen and defuse the situation.
- *Perfectors* – You may feel intimidated and squashed by another's anger. It is useful to keep in mind that it is rarely YOU that is the problem: it's more your role and your fixity in maintaining a position that the other person is angered by. If you can, keep calm and allow people space to vent before you return to the task at hand.
- *Harmonisers* – Harmonisers are often extremely capable at working with others' distress. However, it's important to remember that you are not there to placate but rather to arrive at a joint solution to an issue.
- *Keep in mind* – Anger is a difficult emotion to work with, and for some people it is especially difficult. Those with a trauma background or with oppositional defiant disorder, for example, can find anger extremely quick to arise and extremely difficult to work with. These same groupings can also find it anxiety and even depression-provoking when on the receiving end of anger. No one size fits all.

Shared experience

A primary headteacher describes the processes involved for 'school and home' to work together and achieve 'us against the problem'.

Context and background

An anxious child started her Year 4 journey with a newly qualified teacher at the start of his career. A range of factors meant that the term did not begin well.

- The child was diagnosed with epilepsy during the summer holidays. This had an impact on the medication that she was already taking for her additional needs. She was hospitalised which made her, and her family, distressed.
- There were other children in the class who had additional needs, which added to the demands on the adults in the room.
- The teacher was inexperienced and struggled from the start to form a meaningful relationship with the child, despite being supported by a passionate and experienced mentor. Even with the intervention of the local authority behaviour team, the teacher struggled to implement strategies that would support the child in a whole class setting.
- An experienced member of support staff who is quiet, caring, and kind, quickly became overwhelmed with the needs of the children in the class and requested to move to another class in the school.

Behaviour patterns

The child's anxious behaviour was shown in a variety of ways. Walking into the classroom was tough for her, as the noise, hustle and bustle, lights, and the number of other children and adults was overwhelming. The immediate demands of the child were often triggers for shouting out, making noises, and unwanted physical contact with other children; mostly, it was loud. The child would struggle to settle and immediately refuse to complete tasks that were designed to calm and settle the class whilst the register was taken.

The child displayed negative behaviours, and her low self-esteem meant that she felt as though she would always fail and never meet the expectations placed upon her. This caused disruption for the class and their learning, often resulting in a member of the senior leadership team being called to support. Additionally, the teacher was failing their teacher training programme, putting all their efforts into managing the behaviour demands of one child, rather than evaluating the needs of all.

Support from home

The child's family were supportive and fiercely protective of their daughter and her needs. They were shaken by this diagnosis as well as wanting her to be successful in school.

As the weeks went on, they were receiving a lot of negative feedback from the class teacher. These messages were clearly taking their toll, and they were left feeling frustrated that her needs were not being met well enough. The family cooperated fully with the local authority behaviour team, welcoming them into their home and being honest in their thoughts and feelings of the school's performance in relation to their child. By Christmas though, the relationship between home and school was breaking down.

This situation was making everyone involved unhappy. The child was often dysregulated; the class-based staff were struggling to manage the behaviour and feeling stressed by the strain that this was putting on the children in the classroom; the family were witnessing their daughter coming out of school saying how much she hated everything; and the Leadership Team were trying to keep it all together and move forward.

This situation at school was the biggest problem and as headteacher, I was keen to find a way forward. I felt frustrated with the teacher for not being open to support and for not actioning strategies that were proven to work. Frustrated with the family who were often openly rude and aggressive when discussing their daughter and her needs and/or lack of support.

This is how we turned things around.

The first action was to REFRAME. To change the way I was thinking about all the people involved.

1. The child – she had a number of behavioural and medical needs. She did not come to school wanting to be 'naughty.' It is our primary role to reframe our

thoughts about her, look for the positives, and celebrate the wins rather than get pulled down by the negatives.
2. The teacher – he was inexperienced. He did not have the strategies in his teacher toolkit to meet the needs of this challenging child. Despite the support of his wonderful mentor, his colleagues, the Leadership and Local Authority Behaviour Teams – this was not enough. This professional did not come to work to purposefully fail, he was not equipped.
3. The family – they were scared. They were lashing out, due to embarrassment, frustration, and worry. Mum's perceived aggression on the playground was because she was constantly on edge, waiting for the phone call to come and collect her daughter, due to her behaviour or worse, a seizure.

Once the empathy and understanding were clearly in place, next came a strategy to move forward.

Preparation

We agreed the way to build a more meaningful relationship between school and the family was to create a sense of togetherness. This would be constructed by the headteacher and assistant headteacher through increased positive phone calls and regular face-to-face meetings.

We role-played how the meetings would go and provided important feedback on language choices, confidence, and body language.

We agreed what we would focus on:

- Listening
- Clarify what we can both agree on – *'We both want the best for your daughter – how do we achieve this?'*
- Outline everyone's responsibilities – *What are your responsibilities? These are mine...these are yours...Are we in agreement with this?*
- Clarity of boundaries – *'If your daughter sees you behave in a certain way, then she may behave like that with us...'*
- Providing examples that caused offence.
- Clarity of responsibilities – *'Our responsibility as a school is...' 'Your responsibility as his Mum is...'*
- Expectations for the future – *'Are we agreed on...' 'As a school we want to collaborate with you, in line with our school values. We are learning for life.'*

'One thing that would really help us as a school would be if...'
'We want to work with you to...but this will only work if...'
When you spoke to me in that way, while I understand that you were frustrated, I thought what you said was rude and I found it offensive.'

Once the focus areas for the meeting were agreed, we created a script for the meeting. Along with the assistant headteacher, we equipped ourselves with some sentence starters and areas for conversation.

1. 'Where are you with the appeal hearing for the EHCP?' (Education, Health and Care Plan)
   This allows the family to share their goals, frustrations, and ways forward providing common ground and agreement, allowing the meeting to begin with a shared approach.
2. Talk about progress and successes of the child in school.
   This allowed school staff to share positives and anecdotes from the classroom.
3. Strategies that were working to support behavioural needs.
   How these would evolve as they became customary practice in the classroom.
4. Boundaries and responsibilities.
   The challenging part of the conversation, using the sentence starters to guide this.
5. Schedule the next meeting
   The intention was to continue meeting to share progress and successes.
6. Close the meeting by repeating that the school wants to work with the family.
   Reinforcing that we are all invested in the child's future and well-being.

Success!

The meeting was a success. Having created appropriate boundaries for all stakeholders, reframing opinions, and spending time listening so that the family felt heard meant that the relationship between the family and school has significantly improved.

I now feel empowered to have challenging conversations when required with confidence. Ultimately, this has helped the child to know that we care, support her, and want her to be successful. All adults in school have taken time to get to know her, spend time with her, and most importantly begin to understand her. For this reason, the family are fully supportive and praise the effort and care that we all provide for their child.

References

Brené Brown on Empathy (2013) *The RSA*. Available at: https://www.thersa.org/video/shorts/2013/12/brene-brown-on-empathy (Accessed: 12 January 2025).

Pop Culture Parenting (no date) *Guiding growing minds*. Available at: https://www.guidinggrowingminds.com/popcultureparenting (Accessed: 22 January 2025).

CHAPTER 16

Necessary conversations

Necessary conversations

Most people dread 'difficult conversations.' They have become a regular topic in leadership and management programmes. One of the reasons a difficult conversation is difficult is because it has the potential to induce both fear and shame – emotions most people want to avoid in the workplace – leaving the recipient very vulnerable.

Any conversation that impacts on someone's sense of worth, identity, job security, or professional competence is likely to be met with emotive reactions that range from upset and anger to defensiveness and withdrawal. It's tough being on the receiving end of these reactions. There is always the possibility that your handling of the conversation will result in a complaint or grievance…

Here are some guidelines to increase your confidence in managing – let's reframe these as – necessary conversations.

Prepare yourself
- What is the purpose of the conversation?
- What are the main points to be covered?
- How do you ensure you have all the information you need?
- What must you say – spell out – make clear?
- What, if any, are the legal, policy, or procedural requirements that you must follow?

Self-awareness
- How do you want to come across to the other person?
- How do you need to come across?
- Consider the way the other person communicates – their Coacting Style. How do you think they would prefer you to come across? If you aren't attentive to this, they may interpret you as patronising, aggressive, lenient, or forbidding, not how you want to come across.
- Make sure you adapt your style appropriately to match theirs – as opposed to putting your style on them (see Perspectives below). This can make a big difference for the start and the end of the meeting.
- If you are nervous or anxious about the interaction, think through:
  - What do you need to do to reassure yourself?
  - How can you regulate yourself to feel calmer?

Other awareness
Whether the necessary conversation is a performance management issue with a staff member or a meeting with a parent, you do not know the full extent of what is really going on for that person. Nor can you know. You can only do your best with the information you have. You're only human, and it's easy to miss significant points and/or make assumptions. Keep in mind:

- Confirmation bias.
- Psychological safety.
- Past or present trauma in an individual's life.

NECESSARY CONVERSATIONS

- History, previous patterns of issues playing out in school interactions.
- Neurodiverse alongside neurotypical (see Shared Experience).

Get clear on your intention
- What is your intention for this conversation?
- How do you want the other person to be feeling by the end of the conversation?
- How do you want to feel by the end of the conversation?
- What do you need to do to achieve the above?

Preparing the other person(s)
- How will you let the person know that the conversation needs to happen?
- Given your relationship with them, what is the best method or medium to communicate with them – verbally, electronically, and/or in writing?
- Precisely what do you need to communicate in advance?
- If it's an email or text format, ask a trusted colleague to read it before you send it to help ensure you get the tone right.
- What, specifically, do they need to do ahead of the meeting or bring to it?

Emotional intelligence – your self-awareness, your awareness of the other person, and your awareness of what the situation needs
- What are the possible reactions to the specific points you need to communicate?
- How will you respond to these? (It's useful to have some considered phrases to draw upon.)
- What will you do to reduce any misinterpretation or misunderstanding?
- What are the likely points of contention?
- What are your vulnerabilities in this situation?
- How will you manage these vulnerabilities?
- How could the situation be sabotaged?
- What are your contingency plans?
- What will you do to ensure you keep your focus?

Think about the meeting itself
- What is the most appropriate time and place for the discussion?
- What is the best environment?
- Consider the seating arrangement, lighting, and room temperature.
- Provide water.

After the necessary conversation
It's likely you'll feel drained, so do what you need to restore your energy and recalibrate for whatever is happening next in your day. Here are some suggestions:

- Take some space and time to re-energise and rehydrate. You may need some fresh air. If it's not possible to go outside, open a window and take some deep breaths.
- Offload – you may feel better for talking to someone you trust about how it went. You may want to offload your feelings in writing to vent them out of your system or simply as a kind of debrief. This can help you to consolidate and unburden your mind, leaving you better able to move on and focus. Be sure to keep anything you've written out of the reach or gaze of others.

Review and reflect
- Review what happened by revisiting your pre-meeting goals and intentions.
- Keep in mind the change curve (see Chapter 20). The passage of time helps.
- Identify your learning – what did you do well, and what would you do differently next time?

In summary
Here's a basic structure for you to reference that uses an example of a situation when enough is enough, when someone continues with unacceptable or ineffective behaviour:

- Create the right environment.
- Set the context.
- Describe the behaviour using facts and being specific.
- Explain the impact of what has happened.
- Say what you expect going forward – specifically.
- State the consequences of what will happen if not, and what you would prefer to happen.
- Check their understanding – ask them to summarise what they've understood.
- Agree on a follow up to review progress.

How the process might look in practice
A teacher continues to arrive later than her colleagues. It doesn't inspire confidence in others, and people are annoyed. You've raised the issue with the teacher before.

The context
'Jen, we've had discussions before about the time you arrive at school. You said there are no real reasons why you arrive later than the other teaching staff. I want to check in with you: is that still the case?'

'Is there anything else it would be helpful for me to know?'

The facts
'Four days last week and three days the week before, you arrived just in time for registration – and only just ahead of the pupils.'

Impact/feelings
'We've discussed how being late and not being prepared well enough impacts on the children's learning and the effect it has on staff morale.'

'The children are not going into an environment that is fully conducive to learning.'

'Other staff commit to being ready and prepared for their pupils.'

'We've discussed lateness and how we might accommodate flexible working where possible. You agreed that you'd arrive by 8:00. It's disappointing because you've not kept to that agreement and it's part of your contract.'

'We need to work this out.'

Specify expectations
'My expectation is that all teachers are in the classroom at least 15 minutes before registration and are ready and prepared for the children arriving for registration. I also expect that if there is a legitimate reason why you are going to be late, you will tell me so we can accommodate that.'

State the consequences
'I would prefer not to do this and I'm sure you would prefer it too, but if you continue to arrive late without good reason, I will take more formal action. So would you ensure that, from tomorrow, you will arrive at the same time as the other teachers or by 8:00 a.m. so we won't need to have this conversation again?'

Check understanding
'Please, would you summarise what you've understood from this discussion so that we're both completely clear and in full agreement?'

Follow up
'Let's meet again after school on Friday to see how it's going and to check in on progress.'

Conclusion
The last two steps make a big difference. It's easy to overlook these in the relief of communicating the difficult message. To prevent misunderstandings, it's important that everyone is clear about the consequences. The only way you will know for sure how much the other person has understood is to hear it in their own words. There's a chance they may catastrophise or be sarcastic, so you may need to reinforce the main points once again and put them in writing. Get a follow-up in the diary. This ensures some accountability and reinforces your intentions.

While this feels like a lot of effort for a short conversation, the repercussions of missing any of the steps can steal large amounts of your time from your diary in the future. This, in turn, may drain you of your energy, impact your well-being, and prolong those awkward feelings and tensions for everyone. You may still be in for a difficult journey, but you'll have more confidence that you have what you need to get through it.

Coaching yourself
Before
- What makes this conversation so difficult for you?
- Anything else?
- Anything else?
- What are the real reasons for your discomfort?
- How can you reduce your discomfort so that you can be a stable and objective presence?
- How can you ensure a level of psychological safety?

Note down your strategy for before, during, and after the meeting.

After
- What went well?
- What could have been better?
- What would I do differently?
- Anything that made me uneasy?
- How do I feel about that?
- What does that tell me about me?
- What do I need to develop from this?
- How will I start?
- How will I keep this development going?

Coaching others
- What are your main concerns ahead of conducting the necessary conversation?
- What else?
- Anything else?
- How can you address and manage your concerns?
- How can you reduce feelings of anxiety or awkwardness?
- What would make you feel more confident about the conversation?
- How will you accomplish that?
- What are your key actions so you can feel less anxious and increase your confidence?
- Rehearse the necessary conversation.
  'Let's summarise your actions and approach.'
  'When shall we meet to discuss how it went?'

Coaching upwards
- What are your hopes and intentions for the meeting?
- Any concerns?
- (Select and share the appropriate sections from the guidelines.)
- How can we work together to ensure a fair and respectful process with good outcomes?

NECESSARY CONVERSATIONS

Perspectives

Self-awareness is all-important in necessary conversations, along with managing yourself from the inside out. Be sure to adapt your style to fit the person and the situation. For you, as:

Innovator – put some time and energy into thoroughness. Make sure you provide enough specific information for the person concerned and that you don't talk too much.

Achiever – prepare yourself for some emotion and be ready to listen.

Perfector – work on being concise and getting to the point. People zone out and stop listening when they realise the truth of a difficult message.

Harmoniser – don't soften or sugar-coat a difficult message, as this ambiguity will cause confusion. Acknowledge for yourself that you won't be able to fix the person's emotional state.

Keep in mind – necessary conversations can trigger responses from earlier times in your life, especially if the response to what you are saying is challenging. If you have reason to believe you may struggle, take extra care with preparation and, if need be, take extra time and engage extra support.

Have in mind the style of the person you're talking to:

Innovator – keep it fast-paced and direct. Make sure you hear their summary of what they've understood from the meeting. Get them to clarify their actions from the meeting in their words, out loud.

Achiever – cut to the chase – don't give a long preamble or be too 'nice' about things. They will respect you for saying it like it is. To be sure there is no misunderstanding, ask them to summarise the meeting and any actions.

Perfector – be thorough. Have the facts at your fingertips. Don't use general phrases like 'always' or 'never' – provide specifics. Listen to their summary of the meeting and agree on the main points in writing.

Harmoniser – although tension may be high, aim to reduce it and make the setting as comfortable as possible to establish some rapport – tea, preamble, empathy, tissues. Their summary is likely to be more emotional, so if necessary, encourage them to summarise again to clarify the facts.

Keep in mind – many of us would struggle to work through the content of a necessary conversation, but some may struggle more than most. For example, a peri-menopausal woman experiencing brain fog may find organising thoughts and readily remembering facts especially difficult. Someone may be struggling with depression without telling you. It's important to leave yourself sufficient time and emotional resources to cope with the unexpected.

Assertiveness techniques

Here are some simple assertiveness techniques and phrases that can be useful in necessary conversations.

When you're not sure how to respond

- Repeat what the person has just said: 'If I've understood you correctly...' This both clarifies and buys you time to formulate your response.

- 'I'll need more time to think this through.'
- 'Let me think about those points and get back to you when I have the information I need.'

When they keep interrupting
- 'I need to make some important points and be sure you've understood them.'
- 'We can discuss each point in turn after I've outlined them.'

When they persist
- 'It's important you have the full picture. Then we can discuss the points you want to make.'
- 'You'll see how all these points affect how we come to an agreement today. Let's get through them and then discuss.'
- 'I appreciate that you think this is ['outrageous']. We can talk this through and work things out once we're clear of everything that's come up.'

When it matters to say 'no'
Make sure you say the word 'no' within a concise explanation.

'This school functions well because of the values we live by and clear procedures, so my answer here is "no."'

When you disagree

'My experience is different here…'

'I see this differently …' 'I appreciate you see this differently from me…'

'I can see a difficulty here. Let's discuss how we might work this out?'

> **Shared experience**
>
> Reflections from two headteachers on accommodating neurodivergent narratives.
>
> How do we develop a neuro-affirming, humanistic approach where unconditional positive regard is the culture and practice among colleagues?
>
> As ethical leaders, how do we promote curiosity – not judgement, as a way of promoting diversity, equity, and inclusion?
>
> In the role of headteacher, it's all too easy for us to lose sight of the whole person behind the job description. We don't intend this; it's a direct consequence of workload pressures and demands on our time. While we may be diligent in noticing neurodivergence in our pupils, it seems we are much less so with our adults. When we're particularly frustrated with what a colleague has or hasn't done, it's so easy to think blaming thoughts like 'Why don't they just get on with their job?' or 'Just do as I've asked.' It's easy to judge individuals as 'lazy'.
>
> Typically, we do not recognise neurodiversity among adults until they are in crisis. Think about how many people in your school are in crisis or show signs of

being overwhelmed, where they require another person's support to regulate them, or sometimes a team effort.

As leaders trying to fathom aspects of a colleague's performance, we discussed exactly these issues and questioned what our part was in the behaviours that were frustrating us.

In their leadership role, our colleague was perceived as underperforming, with other leaders expressing frustration at their perceived inability to work effectively. Previous performance conversations hadn't resulted in any tangible change. These meetings were formal, disproportionately verbal in style, and were evidenced as ineffective through the lack of any change in behaviour. In these meetings, our colleague was visibly shutting down and unable to hear what was being said, offering rebuttals or remarks that looked to blame others rather than explore accountability solutions.

This is how we progressed:

- As joint leaders, we needed a safe space and dedicated time to discuss things that frustrated us. Initiating these conversations was integral for us to be able to explore more deeply our own responses in those conversations.
- These conversations led us to explore and identify our communication needs, which communication styles we preferred, and why.
- This stimulated discussions about how we process information, and we became more curious about how our colleague might process information.
- We began to unpick how such formal conversations provoke nervous system responses that reduce a person's capacity to process spoken language. We decided to explore this angle more openly with our colleague.
- It also made us think about what they are trying to communicate to us and why.
- Together, we explored how we might best communicate with each other in a way that enabled everybody's needs to be met, and ultimately the needs of the team to be better fulfilled.

A breakthrough moment came when our colleague was able to express the impact on them of the question that we often used, "How are you feeling?/How do you feel about that?' Questions related to feelings triggered a sense of vulnerability in our colleague that they recognised as activating a withdraw and defend sensation.

With further exploration, we were able to develop a collective understanding of what this question sought to achieve and reframed it as, 'What do you see as the challenges in this?' This was less personal, less triggering of emotions, more factual, and more rational for our colleague, making it much easier for them to engage and respond.

Together, we were able to create a more effective dialogue around the key issues that we all felt challenged by.

A simple change in the semantic choices we made, underpinned by a developing culture of positive regard for others, enabled us to have deeper discussions. This resulted in everyone being better understood, and more effective support being put in place.

Crucially, though, there was an unyielding sense that demonstrably respecting fundamental differences resulted in higher outcomes all-round. We see things differently, we communicate things differently, so instead of trying to change another person, we're finding ways to work together:

- Creating a neuro-affirming environment, including one-to-one walking meetings.
- Offering options for written, visual, and audio formats of meetings. Some colleagues may want to record and then re-listen for greater retention and understanding of information.
- Awareness of fonts in written communication.
- Multi-faceted approaches for delivery and follow-up.
- Space and time to process and consider questions.
- Clarifying what's been said through summarising – yourself or others.
- Visuals to reinforce meaning.
- Choice of language – for example, are you communicating deficit and danger through terms like risk assessment, support plan, safe space, mental health? What terms would your community choose?

Key consolidation points

Neuro-affirming practice encouraged our colleague to reflect on and identify their own thinking patterns and how they work best. This self-awareness led us to more effective communication, collaboration, and problem solving.

- Rather than focusing on what they are not doing, we validate their strengths.
- We ask them, 'How do you prefer to receive communication?' and we adapt how we communicate to meet those needs.
- We keep these points at the forefront of our minds:
    - What are they communicating to us?
    - How is our communication being received?
    - How do they process information?
    - What questions can we ask in a supportive way so they understand the expectations?
    - What does their journey tell us about how they show up?

SECTION 5

A sense of belonging

As a workplace, your school brings together people who may not otherwise meet. It can be hard to get to know people at work, but as social beings, it's important we feel connected.

We do our jobs better when we feel seen, heard, and connected as individuals within our roles. We do our jobs exceptionally well when we connect with people who share our passion, when we create with colleagues, and when we feel proud and purposeful together.

Section 5 focuses on connecting your people and getting them buzzing.

CHAPTER 17

Adding the human element to Inset Days

Adding the human element to Inset days

What an important audience you have before you. All your staff – familiar faces and new faces, different personalities, different approaches – working together to make a difference to pupils' education and lives. Your warm, welcoming words and gestures, plus a practical plan for the day, will reduce nervousness and ensure people feel valued and oriented in the first few minutes of being together again.

Those first minutes count a lot for making a great first impression and hooking your audience's interest. Whether it's your whole school staff on a training day or an open evening for parents, you can put people at ease and inspire confidence in the first couple of minutes if you apply what you know from the following.

Head and facilitator

Your audience is a combination of Coacting Styles (see Chapter 2) and their engagement naturally reflects this. You will have Innovators who want you to be funny, spontaneous, and entertaining; Achievers who want you to start on time, hurry up, and get on with things; Perfectors who need you to go into detail; and Harmonisers who want you to be warm and friendly. Your own Coacting Style will enable you to meet some of these audience demands quite naturally, but it's well worth being aware of these simple techniques to accelerate that all-important initial engagement.

Show warmth with a genuine smile and eye contact. If you can sweep your gaze gently across the faces of the audience while smiling and offering words of welcome, you will have won over the Harmonisers. Innovators will similarly be hooked if you can add a dash of humour to that welcome. Ideally, something spontaneous and funny – something that just happened, or has gone wrong, or is topical. This will put the room at ease and endear the audience to you.

Now you're just a few seconds in and you've already won over about half of your average audience. Your next point of focus is the Achievers who will be relieved once you've said – very concisely – what's going to happen and how long it will take. You really don't want them to be sitting there wondering and clock-watching. (If it's a parents' evening, reassure them they'll be back home by the time [something popular on TV] is about to start.) Perfectors are patient and will be happy for you to explain when and how you'll provide more detail – clear aims, a structural overview, and what the protocol is for questions.

That's it. All your audience is on board within the first minute. Then you can relax into the agenda; expectations have been managed, and people are at ease and ready for you to show your knowledge, expertise, and experience, ready to hear your pride and sense your passion. And trusting you'll keep to time.

30 minutes to reset

After a long break, it can take a little while for you and your people to move on from that end-of-the-holiday feeling and to feel glad to be back at work. Here are some ways to ease that process:

- welcome back
- inspire
- connect

ADDING THE HUMAN ELEMENT TO INSET DAYS

Welcome your people back!

It's an obvious thing to state. So obvious, it's easy to overlook it or to think people just know it. Be sure the 'welcome back' words are heard and appreciated because you mean them sincerely.

Inspire

Share three very different moments from the last academic year or term that inspired you and that represent 'what this is all about'. People, pupils, learning, and/or examples of the school values being lived out.

Talk from the heart because there will be plenty of 'head' talking throughout the day.

Connect

Ask each of your people to turn to the person next to them and share one of last year's moments that inspired them or that was meaningful to them. Following your authentic example, this will connect your people with ease. Importantly, it will also reconnect them with their core purpose, values, and the impact they have.

Repeat two more times, requesting that each person finds a different person to share and connect with.

Then you'll all be renewed and ready to start the new academic year, significantly more together than you were thirty minutes ago.

Ten Inset activities

Here are ten Inset activities for you to select to suit your goals, the time available, the mix of people, the time of year, and energy levels.

You can access all the downloadable resources from www.routledge.com/9781032945392.

I'm this…not this…

Timing:
10 – 15 minutes.
Resources:

- Visual prompts for example images on the screen or actual items for you to explain the activity.

Activity:

- People work in pairs for 2–3 minutes, then change pairs. Three changes are usually enough.
- To demonstrate this activity, I show these images on screen and explain how I'm 'smoothie' not 'fizzy drink' (Figure 17.1).

Figure 17.1 Two drinks

[At one level I can discuss this as my preferred drink, but at another level, I like to explain it as my preferred approach. I like to nourish and sustain people's learning through my work; I don't like to be a fizzy, happy-clappy, high-energy 'drink' that soon goes flat.]

Here are some other suggestions for these warm-up conversations in pairs between your people:

- Savouries or cakes, Wordle or sudoku, cats or dogs, spring or autumn, beach or woods, early bird or night owl?
- The warmup questions to ask are:
  - Which is you?
  - Which is not you?
  - What does that say about you?

Getting to know you questions

Timing:
10–15 minutes.
Resources:

- One copy of the Icebreaker questions list for each person.

Activity:

- Where possible, put combinations of people together who don't know each other very well.
- Ask the group members to pick three questions they would like to respond to.
- Go around three times so that each person takes a turn to share one response at a time.
- *Alternatively*, take 20 minutes and task the group to get through as many questions as they can with each person responding. It's OK to 'pass' if they don't have a ready answer.

ADDING THE HUMAN ELEMENT TO INSET DAYS

Icebreaker questions
1. Ever wanted to be in a band? What would your band be called?
2. What was your first ever job?
3. What would the film title be for the story of your life?
4. Have you ever had a poem or song written about you? Give the context.
5. What superpower would you choose?
6. Any unusual talents or skills?
7. If you could host a talk show or podcast, who would be your first guest?
8. If you ruled the world, what would you change on Day 1
9. Which comedian makes you laugh the most?
10. Have you ever won a prize or an award? What was it for?
11. Who would you love to see perform live (present or past)?
12. If your name was your choice, what would you change it to?
13. What's the furthest place you've ever travelled to?
14. What possession would you not even consider parting with?
15. Which book from your childhood made an impact on you?

Warm-up conversations
Timing:
5 - 20 minutes – timing is dependent on the group size.
Activity:
These topics have a gentle and positive focus that gets people talking together with greater ease. Ask each person to share with another, or with a few, their holiday experiences.

- Your funniest moment.
- Best thing you watched.
- Most delicious food you savoured.
- A significant holiday photo from your phone.

Jigsaw metaphor
Timing:
15 – 20 minutes to get the activity started. Continue through the half-term.
Resources:

- Jigsaw sheet.

Preparation:

- Create a jigsaw puzzle template where the number of pieces matches the number of people involved in this activity. Include everyone's name either as a list/key to the puzzle or one name on each equal-sized piece (see Figure 17.2).
- Add a header: 'People Points of Interest'.

Figure 17.2 Jigsaw

Activity:

- Explain the process: each person has a jigsaw puzzle with all their colleagues' names included. The aim is to start asking and sharing interesting points about one another within the time available.
- Give some examples of what you might learn about your colleagues.

Brian ran the London marathon. The most famous person Jenny met was Bez from the Happy Mondays. Malik used to live in Spain and can still speak some Spanish. Angie won a pub karaoke competition singing Bohemian Rhapsody.

- Suggest each person thinks up some questions, things they would really like to know about the people they work with.
- Distribute one sheet per person.
- Involve everyone in the goal of getting to know one another again, to reconnect in person over the next half-term, and add something interesting about each person to the puzzle pieces.

Wouldn't it be great if, one warm and sunny twilight, you find a way to bring your people together to smile and laugh and share some highlights of what they've learnt about one another and about themselves, collectively, through 'People Points of Interest'?

My birthday hits

Timing: 30 minutes – It could easily be longer depending on the group size.
Resources:

- Note paper and something to write with.

ADDING THE HUMAN ELEMENT TO INSET DAYS

Preparation:

- This involves a few minutes of preparation which could be done ahead of the day or during one of the breaks.
- Give everyone the link https://www.mybirthdayhits.co.uk/ Ask each group member to go online and enter their details to find out the song that was number one in the charts on their day of birth. *The number one on my actual birth date was 'Singing the Blues' by Guy Mitchell (groan) but on my tenth birthday it was 'I'm a Believer' by the Monkees (great song).*
- Note the song title down and the group or singer.
- Next look through your birth date each year and select one more number one hit single you really liked. Note this song title down and the group or singer.

Activity:

- Go around the group sharing their birthday hits. You could even add a spark and get people singing along to some of them.
- And, for a bit of fun, why not compile a Top 20 Birthday Hits list from your group members' birthdays. Maybe even a playlist.

Playlist
Timing:
20 – 30 minutes.
Resources:

- Note taking equipment.

Activity:

- Get people who will be working together into groups of four to eight.
- Request one simple ground rule – 'No judgemental comments about individual choices please!'
- Ask each person to think of any songs that immediately make them feel good.

The songs don't have to be their all-time favourites or have great lyrics, just the ones that when they hear them, they feel energised and uplifted, and life feels good. The ones that when they hear them, they turn up the volume or say out loud, 'I *love* this song!'

- If people are stuck, encourage them to think of songs that get them singing out loud or dancing. What song gets them on the dance floor?
- Each group compiles a list of about 10 – 12 song titles.
- Collect the lists.
- Create a playlist including all the songs to use as an energiser, morale booster, or for celebrating in the future.

This activity is very simple and just needs adapting appropriately to group size and teams. If you're in a small school, you could create a whole school playlist; a large school could have year group playlists.

The playlists will be on your preferred playlist provider in no time.

My proudest moments from last year
Timing:
20–30 minutes
Preparation:

- Plan the group size and timings. For example, allow five minutes for the brief introduction plus two minutes talking for each person in the groups.
- Decide the right combinations of individuals for the group dynamics.
- Decide on the most appropriate group size for sharing these personal moments within the time you have available.

Activity:

- Introduce the activity by acknowledging to the whole group that whenever times have been tough, there have been moments to be proud of.
- Share some of your experiences from last term or last year and what caused you to feel proud. When you go first and role-model this type of sharing, you are contributing to a level of psychological safety in the group.
- Ask the small groups to discuss:
  However simple – what are your moments to be proud of?
  What contributed to that sense of pride?
- Be the timekeeper and announce every few minutes how much time is left so that people keep the pace and everyone has a turn to speak.

You can extend this further, and go deeper, by asking people to share to the whole group some key moments. It's stating the obvious, I know, but allow extra time for this.

As facilitator, you can listen behind the words and note the qualities those moments represent across the whole school. Then reveal how the qualities demonstrate your school values in action.

Communicating!
Timing:
20–30 minutes

- 5 minutes for people to sit in pairs and for you to explain the task.
- 2 - 5 minutes for each person to have a go.
- 5 minutes to debrief.

ADDING THE HUMAN ELEMENT TO INSET DAYS

Figure 17.3 Shape sets

Resources:

- Pens/pencils.
- One blank sheet of paper per pair.
- Two sheets with the different shape combinations per pair (see Figure 17.3 for ideas).

Preparation:

- Create your own simple shape combinations on some A4 sheets along these lines.

Activity:

- Ask everyone to work in pairs (if you're left with a group of three, two of them can draw while the other instructs).
- Agree who will be the first person to communicate the instructions and who will be the person drawing as instructed.
- Give each pair blank paper and pens.
- Ask the pairs to sit back-to-back.
- Person 1 has the piece of paper with one of the shape sets. Person 2 cannot see this sheet.
- Person 1 gives instructions so Person 2 can draw what's on the paper as instructed.
- Person 1 can't look at what Person 2 is doing. Person 2 can't look at the piece of paper with the shapes on.
- Ensure everyone understands the rules – no peeking at what the person is drawing or what any other pair is drawing.
- Give the communicator/Person 1 the first sheet of shapes.
- Explain that Person 2 has five minutes to create an accurate copy of the shapes by following the instructions from Person 1.
- After five minutes, the pair can compare the accuracy of Person 2's drawing with the instruction of the original shapes given by Person 1.

- When the time is up, discuss the experience. The results are usually quite surprising.
- Give the second set of shapes to Person 2 and repeat the activity so both people experience giving and receiving the instructions.
- Debrief.
- Discuss what you learnt from the activity and what you can all learn from this for working together generally.

This activity amazes me in how something apparently simple becomes so complex. I love what it reveals about how we know what we mean versus what the other person hears!

Five ways to have a laugh together

This is great for returning to school after the winter holidays when the mornings are dark.
Timing: 10 – 15 minutes
Resources:

- For yourself – some funny material after researching your preferences from the following sources.
- For everyone else – note paper and pens to jot down the things that made them laugh.

Activity:
 Set the scene. We're different in what we find funny but when we laugh, we are connected. Laughter connects people like nothing else.

- Give people five minutes to come up with one of the following that they are happy to share. It can be from memory, or they can look things up. It's your choice how high-tech or low tech you go with this (YouTube clips, TikTok, etc.).

Give examples of what they might do:

- Share a one liner.
- Share your favourite Xmas cracker joke, for example: 'Why was Cinderella late for the ball? Because she had a pumpkin for a coach'. (No prizes for guessing why I like that one.)
- Classic Knock Knock joke – Remember the interrupting cow?
- Exam howlers.

Great sources for jokes:
 Edinburgh Fringe best jokes
 https://inews.co.uk/light-relief/jokes/edinburgh-fringe-one-liners-best-jokes-170356
 Tim Vine
 https://inews.co.uk/light-relief/jokes/tim-vine-best-jokes-and-one-liners-88044

"I said to the gym instructor: 'Can you teach me to do the splits?' He said: 'How flexible are you?' I said: 'I can't make Tuesdays.'"
Dad jokes
https://www.countryliving.com/life/a27452412/best-dad-jokes/

One for the album – create a fun photo
Timing: Varies according to setting and numbers. The most time-consuming part is likely to be rounding everyone up.
Resources:
A mobile phone camera and either someone who is willing and able to take good photos or someone who can set up an auto-timer on a camera.
Preparation:
Decide on the best setting for the photo, taking into account space, numbers of people, lighting and shade, and sitting and standing arrangements.
People have mixed views about being in photos, but most seem to be increasingly OK with having their photo taken since every mobile has a camera.
A group photo can be a great memento from the first day back. If you take a photo when the energy is right, when people are relaxed and participative, they'll remember the mood and the moment for many years to come.
Scenes from the day can be fun too, with less posing and waiting.
Tips

- Agree and reassure the photo will not appear on social media.
- Make sure everyone who wants to be included is included – don't miss anyone out.
- Be as spontaneous as possible – not too much posing or adjusting.
- Think of a word that will make people laugh to use instead of 'cheeeeeeese'.
- If someone really doesn't want to be in the photo, maybe they could be the photographer.
- Take a lot of the same photo in quick succession so you can choose the pic that most people will be happy/OK with.
- Ask who would like a copy. If you agree to the boundary of 'no sharing on social media,' you can be sure no one is worried by the prospect.

Coaching approaches
Coaching yourself
Before the Inset

- What is your goal?
- What do you want to achieve through the Inset activity?
- How will you facilitate this? For example, how will you ensure the right mix of people get together for new patterns to emerge and for everyone to feel included?
- How will you create psychological safety for people to feel comfortable enough to share?

- What is the best timing for this activity? To put people at ease first thing, to boost energy after lunch, to inspire at the end of the day?
- What could go wrong? How will you accommodate this?
- Think through these plans, especially the back-up plans: Plan A – things go to plan. Plan B – it's going well and people would benefit from more time than you've scheduled. Plan C – they finished much sooner than you expected

After the Inset

The following reflective questions enable you to take stock of the session and alert you to any areas you need to keep on your radar and/or respond to:

- What went well?
- What were the highlights?
- How did I feel and what were my reactions?
- What were the low points?
- How did I feel and what were my reactions?
- What insights or conclusions can I draw from the experience?
- What actions can I take based on what I learned about myself and others?
- Where are confidence levels high?
- Where do confidence levels need attention?
- How will I/we go forward with this?
- What can we improve in the way we work together?
- What works well?
- What are the next steps?

Coaching others

Through these activities:

- How can you learn from one another and learn about one another?
- How does this type of learning benefit your working relationships?
- How does strengthening team relationships improve your performance as a team?
- And ultimately, what are the benefits in the classroom for the children, if on the first day back we dedicate time for team focus?
- What opportunities do Inset activities bring – for example warm-ups, icebreakers, fun tasks, team building exercises?
- How do they add value?
- To what extent are they worth the time?

Coaching upwards
- In what ways do team activities enable leaders to be more authentic?
- How will dedicated team time add value for the first day back after a holiday?
- What types of Inset activities are important to prioritise at this stage?
- What will we gain from them?
- How will they save time, grief, and money going forward?

Perspectives

You can rely on the different facets of Coacting Styles to bring energy and balance to your reunion. With awareness of these dynamics, you can play to everyone's strengths.

Innovators – bring a sense of fun, and a lively and uplifting energy. They'll help get things started and be willing to give things a go.

Achievers – take action, keep the pace, and ensure things progress. They enjoy an element of competition. They'll help and make sure things get done.

Perfectors – attend to detail and work to prevent mistakes or things going wrong. They will ask questions to make sure everyone understands what to do.

Harmonisers – enjoy people being together and co-operating. They'll notice if something isn't right, or if someone isn't feeling OK. They'll put people at ease and make sure everyone feels included.

Keep in mind – even in schools that pay close attention to inclusion, it can sometimes happen they overlook their own people. Inset days give you the opportunity to celebrate diversity.

CHAPTER 18

I, me, or we? Criteria for being a team player

Team cohesion

At some point in your career, you've hopefully experienced how fantastic it is when team members trust one another and work productively together. When team members are on the same wavelength, work is much more satisfying, and there is a buzz to the team. You've probably also experienced how frustrating and disappointing it is when team life is flat or fraught, and work doesn't flow.

Leadership development courses usually cover some theories of team effectiveness, team types, stages of team growth, the importance of co-operation, collaboration, interpersonal effectiveness, and more. Yet frequently, two areas get overlooked in leadership practice:

- establishing ground rules for team cohesion.
- developing competencies for being a team player.

Overview

I dedicate time upfront in every single course I run to agreeing ground rules for the group. The longer the course, the more time I spend on this. Call them what you will – ground rules, terms of reference, or group contract – but please agree on them and apply them as early as you can in your group life together.

Creating ground rules is a process that may cause some resistance in an already established team. Some will think, 'Why take up time creating rules when we've got agenda items to discuss?' Truthfully, creating and using ground rules within a team will prevent hours of tension further down the line and eliminate frustrations like, 'She's always so negative…' 'He goes on too long…' 'We never get started on time…'

Rules are important for groups to ensure clarity, fairness, trust, and consistency. They provide a reference point to 'the way we do things here', a shared agreement for what's acceptable and what isn't, and an expectation of accountability. Team ground rules maximise the amount of team energy that is channelled into outcomes for children in your school rather than interpersonal tensions or conflicts between adults. With ground rules come credibility and a good reputation.

In short, ground rules:

- set the tone.
- create a climate.
- facilitate shared ownership and shared responsibility through co-constructing (this is important).
- reassure group members of safety, security, and belonging.
- serve as a compass to keep people in the right direction.

It's always best if group members come up with their own terms, but you may not have enough time to do so. You can accelerate the process by condensing the activity below into 15 minutes. Ask the participants to work in pairs and work quickly through the questions so they are co-creating their ground rules. Make sure you have two or three rules you want to be sure are included towards the end.

CRITERIA FOR BEING A TEAM PLAYER

Activity to determine ground rules
Timing:
Up to 1 hour of team participation.
Resources:

- Equipment for taking and displaying group points – a screen or board.

Preparation:
Know what you want to contribute to the discussion.

1. Ask team members to respond to the following questions and capture the significant points for everyone to see.
    - What do you look forward to about these meetings?
    - What irritates you about them?
    - How could our meetings be improved?
2. Agree on the main points and summarise them into a visible list of five or six ground rules for working cohesively as a team.

Frequently suggested ground rules
- Confidentiality
- Respect
- One person speaks at a time
- Non-judgemental
- Time keeping
- Mobiles off
- Honesty
- Challenge

Beware
The same danger applies to ground rules as to values; you don't want them to just be a set of words that people agree to and then forget about. You do want them to have meaning, and you also want each group member to behave in alignment with them in your meetings. Rather than just a word list, extend each one with an additional phrase. This reinforces and clarifies what you all mean. It helps team members operationalise each rule.

- Confidentiality – what's said in the room stays in the room.
- Respect – we don't talk down to each other, nor do we avoid challenging if we believe something is important.
- Communicate in a non-judgemental way – we value and accept each other's contributions.
- One person speaks at a time – we don't talk over each other, nor do we stay quiet if we have something to add.
- Time-keeping – we share the responsibility to arrive and finish on time.
- Mobiles off – no distractions during the meeting so we maximise our focus on the task.

- Honesty – we tell the truth in our views and responses.
- Constructive challenge – we value the important part this plays in our decision-making.

Airtime as a ground rule

A ground rule that I usually include is airtime: everyone has a chance to contribute.

If everyone applies this in practice, they manage the amount they say and speak up without having to compete to be heard. The airtime ground rule enables you to say, 'Thanks Kim. I'm conscious of airtime. What other views are there?'

Agreeing ground rules is just the start

After the meeting, create a version of the ground rules so that each group member can have a copy and it can be on display in your meetings from now on.

Explain how the document copy will work. It allows anyone to address comments or behaviours that go against what you've all agreed on together. With the group contract visible, you can easily remind team members of your joint agreement as appropriate. The brilliant thing about agreed ground rules is that they enable you all to address tricky behaviour as it arises.

'Hi everyone. Before we start, a reminder please to have your phones on silent.'

'There was talk in the staff room about the interviewees. People were saying things that were similar to our discussion at last week's meeting. So, a reminder to everyone, please, about the importance of confidentiality – what's said in this room stays in this room.'

'Good afternoon, Danni. We're on agenda item two.' Please note, this is said without sarcasm. It's a neutral statement that quickly brings Danni up to date and reinforces that they were late and that you didn't wait, as per the agreement.

Creating ground rules together, and ensuring they are applied in practice, ensures transparency of process and prevents tensions from rising. They save you heaps of time further down the line, and they make the group-forming process so much easier.

Team player competencies for one-to-one meetings

Reviewing an individual's competence in the roles and responsibilities of their job covers some parts of the performance puzzle. Discussing how effectively that person performs within a team can enhance the review process and make a real difference to the quality of team life and ultimately the school culture.

Here are some ways to raise awareness of, and improve practice in, being a team player. You can select any of the following team competencies for each team member to review how effective they are as a team player. They can rate themselves on a continuum from 1-5 where 1 is poor, 3 is OK and 5 is excellent.

Rate the extent to which you:

1. Include others (sharing information and solutions).
2. Treat others respectfully.

3. Demonstrate an understanding of diversity and the school values.
4. Contribute open and honest feedback.
5. Remain open to receiving feedback.
6. Speak up and challenge when necessary.
7. Ensure colleagues understand your words and intentions.
8. Support and implement decisions.
9. Proactively support others.
10. Show awareness of well-being.
11. Co-operate and encourage team co-operation.
12. Encourage realistic optimism.
13. Take pride in others' achievements.
14. Admit when you're wrong and take action to put things right.
15. Make a positive and effective team contribution.
16. Look for and create synergy within the team.
17. Recognise and value good teamwork.
18. Value individual contributions.
19. Have fun.
20. Celebrate success.

It can be useful, for clarity, to state the opposite of each competency so that there is more breadth to consider with each rating. For example:

- To what extent are you willing to contribute open and honest feedback, or are you more likely to hesitate about being truthful with others?
- How readily do you include others (sharing information and solutions), or are you more likely to think 'self' than 'team'?
- How frequently do you value contributions from team members, and how frequently do you dismiss new ideas?

Requesting actual examples from them can usefully highlight any discrepancies between their perceptions and the reality as perceived by others.

Teamwork as a leader

Leaders create the organisational environment that encourages good teamwork. Here are some additional competencies for you to rate yourself against as a leader (1-5) and give examples.
  To what extent do you:

- Set a positive example of being a team player within your leadership?
- Notice, label, and praise good teamwork and its impact?
- Explain and explore team roles and objectives to staff?
- Encourage positive, supportive team behaviours through precise feedback?
- Discourage negative, unhelpful team behaviours?
- Challenge team behaviours where necessary?
- Encourage co-operation and synergy?
- Recognise and reward positive team behaviour and success?

Take a moment to recognise your areas of natural aptitude where you can go from strength to strength. Then turn your lowest self-ratings into some simple and actionable development points.

Coaching approaches
Coaching yourself
- What is your starting point for creating, encouraging, and maintaining team players across your school?
- How does the climate in your school help or hinder teamwork?
- How do you enable psychological safety in your team(s)?
- What could you change in the environment or organisation to facilitate more effective team working?
- What processes could you use to bring teams together to get to know one another better, share ideas and ways of working?

Coaching others
- What does being a team player mean to you?
- To what extent do you perceive yourself to be a team player?
- What examples can you give to illustrate your being a team player?
- What more could you do to contribute to overall team effectiveness?
- What do you need to do less of in your team to contribute to overall team effectiveness?
- How will you approach and manage this?
- When will you start?

Coaching upwards
- To what extent do you consider yourself as part of the team here/'Team [name of school]'?
- To what extent are you, or could you be, more of a team player here?
- How would that benefit the school?
- How would you like to start?

Perspectives
Each Coaching Style makes a valuable contribution to team effectiveness, particularly when individuals can adapt to the demands and needs of a situation.

Innovators – bring a fresh perspective and valuable new ideas to a team. Be aware they can be difficult to hold to account and may be more focused on their own gains than team success.

Achievers – are big on action and getting things done. Be aware they are more task-focused than people-focused, so while they will bring success for the team, they may be less effective at bringing the team with them.

- *Perfectors* – contribute to team success through their keen attention to detail and ability to prevent mistakes. Be aware, they choose perfect over good enough; therefore, they may be reluctant to move on. Also, because of their very rational approach, they may miss what people are feeling and not know how to motivate or engage team members.
- *Harmonisers* – are natural team players. They are inclusive and connect well with others. It matters to Harmonisers that team members get along. Be aware they are likely to avoid rather than resolve conflict, so team tensions may remain unaddressed.
- *Keep in mind* – ground rules can play a crucial role in affirming the status of staff members who experience being marginalised for reasons like race, gender orientation, and/or disability. Finding language to suit everyone is time well spent.

CHAPTER 19

Buzzing

Emotional intelligence in teams

The importance of vitality in teams

Think of a time when you looked forward to going to work. What was going on then? What made it enjoyable?

Now, think of a time when you didn't look forward to work. What was going on at that time? What made it not enjoyable?

The key themes emerging from these questions tend to be the degree to which you were good at that job, the degree to which your job was meaningful to you, and the degree to which you got along with the people you worked with.

You can be great at your job and have a strong sense of purpose, but if there are unhealthy tensions with the people around you, it means you don't look forward to work as much as you might. The spark and the buzz fade, which impacts performance, well-being, and your happiness while doing your work. All of these impact staff retention.

How to cultivate 'buzz'

As a leader, how do you create that sense of belonging and camaraderie across your teams? How do you get people to gel and feel they are part of a great bunch?

As with most people-related issues and challenges, there are many ways in, but the 'buzz' questionnaire is especially effective. The questionnaire enables you to address the topic in a light way and to raise awareness without finger-pointing.

You can download the *BUZZ Team Questionnaire* from www.routledge.com /9781032945392 to give you that starting point. It's not too heavyweight, not too analytical, but just right for raising awareness. It has 20 very simple suggestions for creating a climate where people feel they belong and are part of an internal culture they can trust.

You know your people. You know how best to use the 20 questions and suggestions. Do what fits and feels right. You could, for example:

1. Pick the one *statement* and *suggestion* that you believe needs attention.

   You might start with the statement: *We co-operate. We help each other out.*

   Then combine it with the corresponding suggestion(s): *Share what you're stuck on (or with). Offer help. Remember to empower and enable.*

   Discuss the suggestion(s) with your team(s) and ask everyone to commit to the suggestion(s) – demonstrably – over the next few weeks.

   Check in on progress and what they're noticing. Recognise how it's making a difference.

2. Raise awareness by getting everyone to complete the 20 questions individually and, if it seems appropriate, anonymously. Collect them. Feed back the findings about the buzz, or the lack of it, at the right time, in the right setting, through the right medium.

   Agree which of the corresponding suggestions to start with and ask everyone to commit to that – demonstrably – over the next few weeks.

   Schedule in your diary how you will routinely check in on progress – what they're noticing and how it's making a difference.

3. Have each team complete the 20 questions and agree on what suggestion(s) is the key one for their team.

> They take ownership, they commit to the suggestion(s) – demonstrably – over the next few weeks.
> They build in ways to check in on progress, what they're noticing and how it's making a difference.

Why buzz matters
You'll find that the points raised from the *Buzz Team Questionnaire* surface issues by looking at how people are working together. Each of the suggestions impacts a team's dynamic and supports you and your people in living out the school values more closely and congruently.

Keep it going
The BUZZ Team questionnaire isn't just for one-time use. It's designed to gauge team emotional intelligence (EI). The twenty questions and suggestions all correspond to facets of EI so you can explore, revisit, and renew any facet at any time as the need arises, or ideally, to prevent the need from arising. Once you become aware someone feels a bit left out, or when morale or motivation dips, or when people are resistant to change, you've got somewhere to go for ideas. It makes a big difference.

Coaching approaches
Coaching yourself
Draw a timeline of the academic year and ask yourself, strategically:

- What are the times in the year when the energy in school starts to dip?
- Start with you. How will you role model your self-care and well-being to your teams?
- What are the signs that a dip in energy is starting to happen?
- How could awareness and practice of team emotional intelligence prevent and/or manage this?
- When would it be timely to introduce?
- And continue?
- If you believe this is important for your people's sense of belonging, is there anything that stops you from doing this?
- Anything else?
- What's the real reason that's stopping you?
- How will you overcome this, or get around this, to go forward?
- Note down your intentions and steps to action. Then add them to your timeline.

Coaching others
- What is the current climate like in the team?
- From this list of 20 statements, which three describe team strengths and which three would boost the energy in the team?

- Looking at the suggestions, which could you apply most readily?
- What ideas do you have for doing this?
- Any more ideas?
- Any other options?
- What do you need to stop doing to enable you to start doing this?
- What are your next steps?
- How will you know what difference it's making? What will you look out for?
- When would be a good time for us to update on how it's going?

Coaching upwards

In the relevant team context:

- How cohesive is the team/group/board?
- Which of these 20 statements describes team strengths and which are in need of attention?
- What suggestion(s) would be most useful?
- What suggestion would be good to start with?
- What options do you have for approaching this?
- Any other options?
- How will you go forward?

Perspectives

When it comes to generating buzz in teams:

Innovators – are upbeat and naturally bring a lot of buzz to a team. However, watch out for how well they listen and how well they communicate on detail that others may need.

Achievers – energise by making things happen and bringing action to a team. But they can leave more sensitive team members feeling squashed as they hurry things through.

Perfectors – 'go the extra mile' and generate reassurance that if they say it's alright, then they'll have gone through all the details. Watch out for how aloof or exacting they may seem to others, and ensure that their caution doesn't become nitpicking or deflate others' enthusiasm.

Harmonisers – bring a warm and friendly buzz to a team. They can be cliquey, though, which may mean people feel the need to keep in with them. They tend to avoid difficult conversations and giving critical feedback.

Keep in mind – you may have members of your team who are neurodivergent, LGBTQIA+, or disabled, or others who do not have general acceptance in the school community. The suggestions in the questionnaire provide a great opportunity to allow those who experience less acceptance in the school community (and society in general) to raise their needs, show their value to the team, and show that the team values them in return.

SECTION 6

Raising morale

This section looks at how to remain authentic when the truth is bleak, find inspiration, and keep your people hopeful.

In challenging times, leaders need to be able to act authentically and with integrity so their people can trust them to face the reality ahead.

Section 6 offers ways for leaders to dig deep so they can find their own truth and security within and bring people with them.

CHAPTER 20

Getting real about low morale

Maintaining morale

Morale is a frequent topic in leadership coaching. There's rarely a simple, or single, reason for low morale and there is no quick fix to make it go away. That's why, as a leader, it's important to keep alert to levels of morale and not take it for granted, so you can address it before it takes hold.

The following activity offers a comprehensive approach to tackling low morale. It can be adapted to an Inset Day or a dedicated team meeting. As always, you can modify it to suit your circumstances. As the person facilitating the activity, it's important to know that for this activity to work, the culture needs to be such that people can openly and honestly express themselves and their concerns. (If that isn't the case for the people in your school, I offer an alternative option at the end of the whole activity.)

Four stage process

As the facilitator of the activity, it's important you are aware of the process that happens, that you recognise the four stages you are taking your people through.

1. Reinforcing the reality of the times.
   The initial stage of the process means energy is likely to dip. Prepare yourself for this because the starting point, the current reality, is tough. You are acknowledging the reasons that are contributing to low morale.
2. Seeking ways to broaden acceptance.
   People can be agitated and grumpy in the second stage because they don't believe they can influence much, if anything. Prepare yourself for resistance and possibly facing rebellious or disillusioned comments. At this point, no one wants to accept the reality, people don't realise what they can influence and/or how this might make a difference.
3. Increasing awareness of the process of change.
   This stage is straightforward and easy to explain. People get this. They will all have experienced, and therefore will relate to, how change works.
4. Shifting perspectives to facilitate more of a thriving culture.
   This stage has three components. The first explores feeling proud and feeling grateful; the second enables people to feel valued; and the third focuses on action. The combined overall effect is empowering and moves you towards raising morale.

The following activity walks you through all four stages.

The first exercise focuses everyone on what they *can* change, rather than what they *can't*.

Current reality

Timing:
   Ideally 90 minutes in total to fully explore and process each part. Work out the right amount of time to allocate for each part to make the most of the whole activity.

GETTING REAL ABOUT LOW MORALE

Preparation:

- Packs of sticky notes – ideally two different colours.
- People will be working in small groups. Ensure the right combinations of people work together given the topics they will be discussing.
- Enough cleared wall space to display both sets of sticky notes.

Activity:
Concerns

- Ask people to empty their thoughts and share all the things they are concerned about in their lives at the moment. This may include anything from global warming and wars to things much closer to home such as what's happening in education and in your school. This is the reality we are facing, and it's challenging.
- Rather than have everyone sharing their concerns verbally with the whole group, ask individuals within the small groups to write their concerns on (for example, blue) sticky notes.
- Collect the sticky notes and position them close together on one part of the wall space. Read out the main concerns as you place them on the wall.

What you can influence

- Ask the whole group which of their concerns they can do something about. Remove these sticky notes from the wall and distribute them across the groups.
- In small groups, explore what action you all can take to influence change in these areas.
- Using different coloured (for example, yellow) sticky notes, ask the groups to write down the specific action(s) you can take to address the concerns.
- Position these (yellow) sticky notes in a different part of the wall.

The (blue) sticky notes remaining on the wall illustrate the things you can do little to change. Naturally, these can lower morale because they fall outside of your control. When people feel powerless to effect change, remind them they can still act. For example, they can vote, attend a peaceful protest, boycott goods and organisations, lobby their member of parliament, write to their local authority, and/or join special interest groups.

The (yellow) sticky notes in the different area of the wall have the potential to raise morale. You'll come back to these at stage 4.

Next, offer a different perspective on what is happening.

The change curve
Change is inevitable, and few changes are accepted by everyone. In my lifetime, I have seen and welcomed big picture changes, such as greater inclusion in our culture of people who are neurodiverse, people of colour, the sight-impaired, and those with different

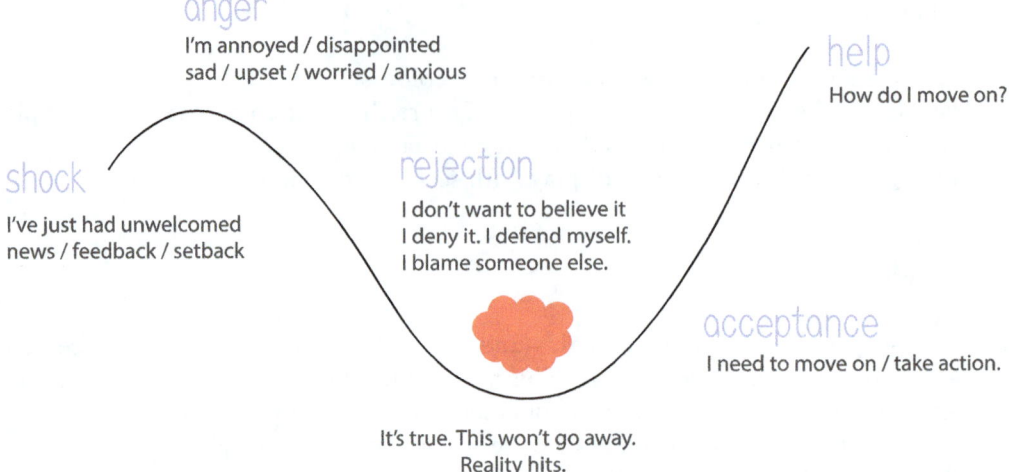

Figure 20.1 The change (SARAH) curve

gender orientations – to name a few. There is far to go, and the changes I have welcomed are still contested and are not fully embedded in our society.

You can use your own examples of how change has happened in society and also within your school. Remember together how people first reacted, how it took time to accept change, but once you do accept the new reality, it gets easier to receive help, offer help, and take action.

Talk people through the acronym and the stages of the change (SARAH) curve (Figure 20.1):

You announce, or people find out about the change, and they are shocked. **S**hock then peaks into **A**nger related feelings – frustration, annoyance, aggression – and then quickly dips into feelings of **R**ejection and denial. 'No, I won't do that.' 'Who do they think they are?' 'It will never work.' 'You won't get me doing that.' 'No way: I'm out.' And similar.

People get to the **R**ejection phase quite quickly, but it takes time for people to grasp the reality of what's happening or about to happen. When the realisation dawns that the change(s) will happen, that there are no choices, or only limited choices, you have the first step out of the dip towards **A**cceptance. When individuals are struggling at the lowest point of the change curve, a useful question for them to ask themselves is 'What is it that I am not accepting?'

When people move towards acceptance, they become more ready to ask for **H**elp, or more receptive to receiving help and progressing the change. Some will remain in the dip and take a while to emerge towards acceptance.

Knowing this process, as a leader, takes some of the heat out of the change and relieves some of the pressure. Change happens all the time. Some people can shift from **S**hock to **H**elp in a few minutes, while some may never accept the change.

Talk your people through the process of change so you all start to feel more confident you can get through this.

Shifting perspectives
Proud and grateful

- Get some discussion going. Ask the small groups to think of what they are proud of about this school.
- After a few minutes, ask them to say what is behind the pride they feel?
- What does that say about the people, the school?
- As they identify the qualities underpinning their feelings of pride, write them up on the flipchart/board.
- Now you have a list of core qualities in their words that describe what keeps you all going, what bonds you together. Add your own words to this list too. What makes this school your (plural) school?

Thank you

This is your chance to thank them, to give genuine heartfelt thanks. Share what you are proud of about them and how, with these qualities, you can work through difficult things and difficult times together. They will feel valued, meaningfully so, because this will touch them about why they do the job they do and why they work at this school. It's likely they don't hear this very often. It's a significant morale boost when they do.

From can do to will do

Now is the time to focus on what you can do.

- Distribute the yellow sticky notes from the wall across the small groups.
- Ask the small groups to discuss the specific actions and note down on flip chart sheets their suggestions for what they *will do*.

Depending on the content of each sticky note, group members will either be expressing their intent – the things they are prepared to do – or suggesting what other people in their respective roles can/should/will do.

- Ask each group member to create a simple action plan that acknowledges their responsibility for the changes they can make happen within school life.
  What actions will you take from the yellow sticky notes?
  What can you do to make a difference in these areas?
  What will you do to make a difference in these areas?

After the event, create a document from the flip chart notes and suggestions that you can share with every participant. Keep the document readily available to revisit at team meetings and in one-to-one discussions to keep the action going.

PEOPLE SOLUTIONS FOR SCHOOL LEADERS

Key points to consider

The following key points will help you to navigate your way through your ability to keep up with the pace of change and what to accept about other people's ability or resistance to change.

- People value honesty, transparency, and authenticity. Building trust will increase their loyalty and sense of belonging.
- Society is changing rapidly, and these changes often move faster than the infrastructure that is intended to support them. For example, you may have an ideological commitment to inclusion, but to achieve this, you need an environment where everyone, children and adults, can thrive: it takes time to create such an environment. Get really clear on what boundaries to have in place at this time and how to assert them.
- Stress and anxiety flourish when people feel helpless to change what's happening and unable to get on top of things. Clarify what to say yes to, what to say no to and, where appropriate, any points you can negotiate.
- The reality of today is that it's very difficult to arrive at any middle ground that's acceptable to everyone. This is where you have to stand strong in your resolve as a leader and do what your head and heart believe is right, in alignment with the school's vision and values, and in some cases, survival. This inner conflict takes its toll. The *Inner Truths* exercise in Chapter 21 can help you find your way through so you keep well.
- Flexibility is an essential trait to survive and progress. Hanging on to the past, no matter how fixed and passionate your views are, won't work. 'The way things used to be' is exactly that, it doesn't fit the future. The constants are your values and the importance of keeping well to be effective in your role.

Alternative option

If the culture of your school is low on trust, if people are not OK with openness and honesty, then omit the first two parts of the activity and start with the process of change at stage 3. There are many reasons why psychological safety is hard to achieve in a team or school. A few examples would be when staff haven't worked together for very long; if leaders are still relatively new to the school or their position; or if trust is low because of change, cuts, or conflictual relationships. If this seems familiar, it would be more beneficial to focus on establishing ground rules together (Chapter 18 *I, me, or we? Criteria for being a team player* and Chapter 12 *Clarifying expectations*).

Emotional equations as an additional tool

Emotional equations offer an easy way to understand the dynamics of emotions. They simplify the components of emotional experiences. If you discuss them and work them out, they offer solutions. (Conley, 2013)

$$Disappointment = Expectations - Reality$$

You can minimise disappointment when expectations are equal to the reality of the situation.

(NB. When people's expectations are low, they don't experience disappointment.)

Anxiety = Uncertainty x Powerlessness

To reduce anxiety, people need some certainty and to feel empowered.

Thriving = Frequency of Positive divided by Frequency of Negative

For people to thrive, they need a high ratio of positives to negatives.

Here are some questions to draw attention to positives over negatives, for a more optimistic culture:

- How do you want your school culture to be? And/or your leadership team culture?
- How do you not want your school culture to be?
- What are the aspects of the culture that you wish would change?
- Break those down into component parts or behaviours.
- Identify the behaviours you'd like to see instead. (Not this…but this…) Not moaning about everything that's wrong but focusing on small steps towards a solution. Not offloading only about what's been tough but adding a glimmer of what went well.
- How might you approach gradual cultural change towards gratitude, hope, and realistic optimism?
- How would that benefit your people – over time?
- Who can assist you with this?
- Note down your next steps.

Coaching approaches
Coaching yourself
- What differences are you aware of that are causing difficulties between people?
- How is this affecting morale?
- What's the real challenge here?
- And what else?
- And what else?
- So what's the real challenge?
- Who can you speak to about this?
- How can you address this?
- What's the most appropriate way and the most appropriate timing to do so?
- What approach will you take forward?

Coaching others
- Where are you currently focusing your energy and time? In your concerns or on what you can influence?
- What action can you take from what you can influence so that you feel differently about work and life?
- When will you start to take this action?

- Who will you talk to about this?
- How will you share what difference it makes?
- How will sharing that benefit others?

Coaching upwards
- How effectively do we ascertain and clarify the norm for this school?
- How do we find a way to enable people to resolve their inner conflicts and confusion about change and difference?
- How do we manage and develop people to work in the widening mainstream?
- How might you contribute to raising morale for the school?

Perspectives
When morale is low and people are feeling down:

Innovators – look for new beginnings elsewhere. What renewal can they find in-house?
Achievers – blame others. What action can they take to regain a sense of progress?
Perfectors – withdraw or close down. What action would bring them a degree of hope?
Harmonisers – want people to feel better. What actions would enable this?
Keep in mind – it's likely that the issues which affect your people weigh particularly heavily on those with disabilities or those who've been marginalised. For example, even though you may not be racist, parts of your school community may be. The cumulative impact of this, on top of other issues in a team member's life, can lower morale. Staying open to sometimes difficult conversations can help to support staff members to find more personal power.

Reference
Conley, C. (2013) *Emotional equations: Simple formulas to help your life work better.* London: Piatkus.

CHAPTER 21

Overstretched

Leadership and the widening parameters of inclusion

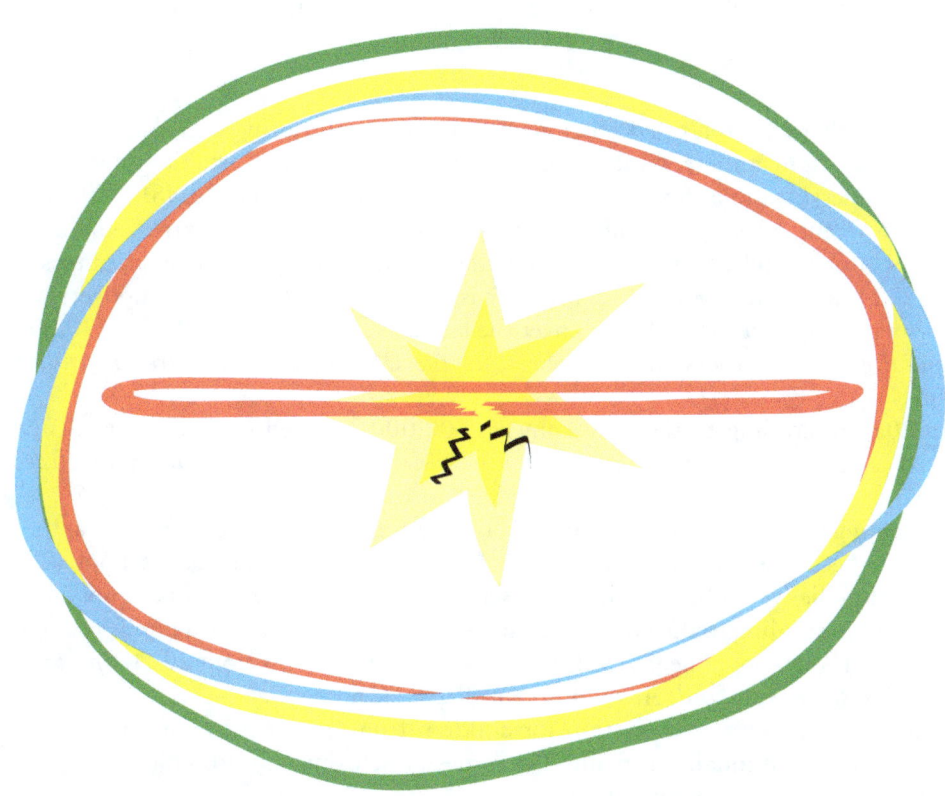

The missing peace

If I had to say what my coaching practice is about in one word, I would say 'peace'.

Peace of mind and a peaceful heart – cultivating those traits that enable you to keep well and be at ease with yourself. Feeling good about who you are and what you do.

When I first started coaching headteachers, a question I often asked was, 'What's keeping you awake at night?' because that showed where a sense of inner peace was missing. These days I feel confident that the major issue that's keeping Heads awake at night is inclusion. Leading a school that is actively committed to inclusion, year in and year out, is daunting, demanding, sometimes dispiriting, and, all too often, corrosive to peace of mind.

It's especially difficult to lead when your values are compromised, when you feel conflicted, and suppress your feelings of anger at the system and the injustice within it. You must put up with a lot that simply isn't right. This is what's making leaders ill, lose their joy, and leave the profession.

This isn't an easy chapter. It highlights what you're up against, offers some ways forward, and asks you to keep in mind how well you are doing...

The backdrop in figures

It's a given that children don't enter school on an equal footing and that some are at a particular disadvantage. Children coping with poverty; an unstable home life; life-limiting illness; trauma; Special Educational Needs and Disabilities (SEND); coming from a different culture; or combinations of these inevitably place extra demands on a school. Unfortunately, there are all too many children facing these disadvantages.

In 2024, according to the Rowntree Trust, 30% of children were impoverished, a figure that's stayed stubbornly high over the last 20 years or so. (*UK Poverty 2024: The essential guide to understanding poverty in the UK | Joseph Rowntree Foundation*, 2024)

In 2024, according to the Government, 400,000 children (or 1 in every 30) were classed as 'in need of help and protection. (*Children in need, Reporting year 2024*, no date).

According to the NHS, 87,000 children had life-limiting illnesses in England at the end of 2018 – this affects the children and their families, including siblings at school. ('B1675-specialist-palliative-and-end-of-life-care-services-cyp-service-spec.pdf.pdf', no date).

In 2024, according to the Government, there were over 1.6 million pupils in England with special educational needs (SEN) – an increase of 101,000 from 2023 (*Special educational needs in England, Academic year 2023/24*, no date).

Providing an inclusive education for children from one or more of these groups is essential but exceptionally difficult. The issues are chronically difficult, multi-agency, multi-faceted, and highly intractable.

How have we got here?
Budgets

- By 2024, real term funding barely matched 2010 levels – having dipped in the intervening period. Inevitably funding has impacted on staff numbers and, particularly, staff with specialist qualifications.

- The SEND reform in 2015 required local authorities to provide for SEND needs for children from zero to 25 years with no increase in resources, funding, or school place provision.
- The development of more special schools and resource provisions has not kept up with demand.

Lack of resource
- Lack of finances to equip schools with the right premises and facilities to support pupils with complex needs.
- Shortage of specialist advisory teachers to offer support and guidance to teachers in mainstream classrooms.
- Lack of funding to recruit and train the right people to support, assist, and care for pupils with additional needs. For example, managing medical needs and personal care, including toileting.

Without the right level of resources, it's hard for staff, pupils, and families to feel good about what's happening in their school.

Legal requirements
- Local authorities must comply with a parent's preference even when professionals do not believe this is in the pupil's best interests.
- Office staff and teaching staff must complete lengthy administration processes and record keeping for safeguarding and for pupils with SEND. This takes further time for staff to manage within an already overstretched organisational structure.
- Schools are required to do more with less. Inevitably, some pupils with SEND are not having their needs appropriately met in mainstream schools. Parents are increasingly challenging the system, and sometimes the school, and are turning to the courts to secure what their children are legally entitled to.

Concerns that widening inclusion affects school success

It's worth noting that the word 'inclusion' has no official definition within the school system…

There are, as there have always been, insistent demands that schools demonstrate that they are providing education to meet the needs of all pupils and to a high standard. The school day is full, and measures of success are detailed.

Schools that do not demonstrate sufficient levels of success when inspected are subject to close management. The pressure is always on. Unsurprisingly, the drive for success can easily be at odds with the drive for inclusion. In an effort to meet the challenge of the former, some schools resort to suspensions and exclusions. These numbers are also being monitored, so this is another factor that can influence decisions about admitting children with complex needs.

The everyday impact

In my experience, headteachers work hard to offer an education that is fit for all the needs of their children. But they have stories to tell about how tough it is to balance the everyday work of the school against the necessary but resource heavy aspects of supporting children with complex needs.

These are just some of the issues they describe:

- Persistent and frightening behaviours, including verbal and physical attacks on teachers and support staff.
- Complex legal processes that can quickly escalate and swamp time and energy.
- Limited or no extra support from the Government, local authorities, or other agencies. In particular, lack of emotional support and professional supervision.
- Lack of time to adequately support staff, especially new teachers, who may never have had to work with highly challenging children while keeping a class going.
- Hostility both from the parents of children with complex needs and other parents who worry for their own children who are exposed to more extreme behaviour and even violence.
- Lack of resource to support such basics for children as breakfast or a change of clothing.
- Long-term staff sickness and resignations because of stress.
- Resentment from staff who feel that a particular pupil should be excluded or disciplined for behaviour rather than being 'rewarded' with more attention.
- General demoralisation and the sense that little is being done to alleviate let alone fix the situation.
- A strong sense of their own powerlessness and fatigue in trying to address the legitimate needs of a child whilst knowing that their provision is not truly fit for purpose.
- A sense that some schools avoid sharing the load.

Shared Experience

A headteacher shares the reality of a parent's experience.

Most schools are feeling the stretch of resources and are struggling to accommodate new pupils with complex needs whilst maintaining the support for their current pupils on roll. It is becoming increasingly common for schools to say to parents, 'We cannot meet your child's needs, try the school down the road, they are much better at working with SEND.' Or sometimes confusing parents with complicated admissions processes, or, even worse, not getting back to parents at all.

This has meant a tipping point is quickly reached for those inclusive schools who follow the rules set out by the admissions code and are welcoming pupils with SEND within their school. After being turned down from six other schools, one parent asked me to thank my office team for being so welcoming and returning their calls – shouldn't all schools be doing that?

As a school leader, these dilemmas sap your energy and the energies of everyone around you, and they generate tensions that are hard to relieve. So how can you cope, keep up morale, and prioritise well-being for teaching and learning amid all these challenges?

Actions you can take

Since challenging the system alone won't change the reality of leadership in an inclusive school, here are five courses of action that will make some difference over time.

1. Stay open to your emotions.
2. Support your staff.
3. Create and clarify a school level response to the situation.
4. Adapt how the school operates.
5. Implement slow drip challenges to the system.

It's important to acknowledge time here. Progress can be very slow. There will come a point though where you see those cumulative changes come to fruition. The Shared Experience at the end of this chapter gives a very real example of this, of how one school has developed an approach to sustaining leadership, well-being, and inclusion.

Staying open to your emotions

It is extremely demanding to be responsible for the education of a child who has complex needs, who relies on your school to provide what is needed, but whose needs are beyond what you can offer. You may rationalise your situation and tell yourself you are doing all you can. Or you may rage against the system. Or you may try to avoid the issue. None of these options is likely to sustain you for very long.

Instead, you can face your feelings and use them as signposts towards courageous action. An excellent starting point is fierce self-compassion (see Figure 21.1 and Chapter 5) to bring results that are aligned with being true to yourself.

If you are experiencing some, or all, of the following, take some time to prioritise your emotional and mental health:

Figure 21.1 Fierce and nurturing self-compassion Venn diagram

- Simmering anger at the systemic load you are carrying.
- Persistent demoralisation in the face of the systemic problems that are pushing you and your school to the outer limits of what is sustainable.
- A chronic sense of injustice – there is a lot that is wrong.
- Impotence – you're a good person trying to do the best you can and to do right by others but what you believe in is getting harder to live out.
- Wear and tear – you're on the edge of what's acceptable within all the constraints and lack.

These feelings don't just go away if you ignore them. They sit in your body. They add shades of grey in places where you need light. The good news? They can be sources of breakthrough and creativity if you can find the courage to face them and act upon them.

Here is a way forward to get you out of the greyness, but go carefully and build yourself up gradually.

Step by step

Chapters 8 and 9 have personal development practices to choose from that you can use to build up to doing the following reflective process. The *Process Your Emotions* exercise in Chapter 8 would be a very good starting point.

Remember you are in charge of each process and can pause or stop if it gets too much.

Inner truths

Being true to yourself usually means facing up to what you're doing that doesn't align with your values, addressing where you feel guilt, and, most difficult of all, where you feel shame. Being true to yourself can feel awful, uncomfortable, awkward, and risky, which, I appreciate, isn't an enticing invitation. This is where change can start and remain in your control:

- Find a setting where you feel calmer and where there are no interruptions. Ideally with a notepad so you can jot down your thoughts and insights.
- Take a few deep breaths and allow your body, thoughts, and feelings to quieten a little.
- Focus on whatever is happening in your school that doesn't sit comfortably with you.
- Sit with this as best you can – detached, not judging, accepting this is very uncomfortable and that you can stop the process if it becomes too much.
- Notice and label your feelings.
- Find the cause behind the feelings. What's causing you to feel this way? Keep asking yourself until you get clearer on the cause(s). It's natural to feel anger, for instance, when your values are violated in some way.
- Give yourself time to notice any feelings of guilt, shame, or inadequacy. This is likely to become visceral. It's normal to feel squirmy, repelled. Hang on in there

if you can and remember to be kind on yourself. You're not a bad person. You're facing tough circumstances with no perfect answers or solutions. Judging yourself harshly does nothing to alleviate this.

- What's causing you to feel this way? Is it other people's expectations and judgements? Is it fear? Is it a sense of inadequacy?
- Be honest with yourself. Shame will be pleased if you stop at this point because it thrives if you keep your thoughts secret, if you stay alone with those feelings and if you give yourself a hard time because of them. So instead of stopping and avoiding these feelings, introduce empathy and kindness. Do whatever feels OK for you to reassure yourself, to soothe those visceral sensations, to wrap yourself in warm acceptance, to feel more at ease in who you are rather than tightly conforming to the needs or demands of others.
- Hold yourself in this space for as long as it feels right. Then note down any insights you've had and any action you want to take.
- Who can truly listen and empathise with how you are feeling?
- Who can you talk to develop your thinking – a confidante, coach, trusted colleague, other headteachers or leaders working in similar settings to you?
- What matters most?
- What would it take to transform the difficult feelings you are facing into contentment or pride?
- Where do you feel vulnerable? How might you turn this vulnerability into courage?
- What does that courage look like in action? What to say yes to? What to say no to?
- Who to say no to?
- Clarify your intentions and note them down. Experience what it feels like when you say them out loud – purposefully.
- What would you like to be proud of this time next year?
- Decide how to turn your intentions into action – small steps, gradual change, or direct (considered, fair, and reasonable) challenge.
- Take as long as you need to move from the reflective process of your inner world and adjust to whatever is happening right now in your outer world.

Group truths

If you have a small group of close colleagues who you trust and respect, you could use a group process to banish powerlessness, boost empathy, and bring you closer as professionals.

Use the graphics from Chapter 5 to explain what most people do when facing difficulties or setbacks and how shame thrives with this approach. Contrast this with the self-compassionate response.

Go around the group in turn asking people to respond to one question at a time. It's helpful for psychological safety in this kind of exercise if you go first and others follow your lead:

- Within all the complexities of these times, what is your greatest concern?
- What are your feelings (not thoughts) about this?

- What aspects of your leadership are you unhappy with or ashamed of? (Finish the sentence – I am unhappy with… I feel ashamed that…)
- How can we show empathy for one another through these difficult feelings and connect through empathy?
- How can empathy (for self and others) enable sustainable action?

Discuss, agree, and decide on any group action for keeping well, remaining true to yourself, and addressing what is in your influence.

Supporting your staff

As a leader, you're faced with a time, resource, and well-being conundrum. You want to be there for people, but this takes additional time. You want to role-model looking after yourself and managing your workload, but if a staff member is heading towards breaking point, you prioritise them over your to-do list. And so on…

This is where small, frequent, supportive actions can have a cumulative impact on the school culture and whole-school well-being over time. This means letting go of perfection and adopting more of a 'just right' approach. The following suggestions offer some ways in for small step (culture changing) actions.

Meeting with staff groups

- Set the scene – acknowledge the resource, time and well-being conundrum alongside the pressures and strain you know staff are under.
- Request their suggestions for a 'just right' approach. How can we look out for one another and give support where needed, when we are all working flat out, have no budget for bringing in another person, and making time for self-care isn't happening?
- What needs to stop? What needs to start?

Encourage as much creative thinking as possible as you generate ideas for:

- Meaningful and effective ways to check in with one another – especially when things are tricky. For example, visuals, cards, and/or shorthand vocabulary.
- Ways to offer regular debriefs or request a debrief when needed.
- Ways to build in supervision if circumstances become particularly challenging.
- Time saving ways to share what works for self-care – resources, links, posters, sharing your stories.
- How to share responsibility for making these small step actions happen and keep going over time so you all benefit from the cumulative impact?
- Get agreement from everyone that these suggestions are workable and welcomed.

Team reset

This technique can energise team meetings at the end of a school day when people are tired. It requires the leader to be time-focused and dynamic. It works best with a group of five to six people.

- Have a sheet of paper ready for everyone on arrival.
- Ask them to take two minutes to offload the difficulties and wind-ups from the day, in writing on the paper. No talking, just written off-loading.
- Put a bin in the middle of the group so that each person can screw up their paper and throw it in the bin after two minutes. No one reads what's there.
- Quickly, go around the group asking each person to take 30 seconds to share a meaningful moment from the day/week. You start – give a succinct example of something meaningful from your day or week.

The quiet process of offloading combined with the verbal expression of meaningful moments enables people to destress a little *and* be inspired. Both processes raise energy levels and, importantly, team members reconnect with their purpose, why they are doing this job.

Even though the situation you are facing may be overwhelming, the changes and developments you can make internally are within your control as a school leader. The following suggestions are clarifying, empowering, and enable you and your people to take more ownership.

Create and clarify a school level response to your situation

It's important to involve everyone in your school structure in open discussions about the reality of the level of additional needs amongst pupils. If you relate these discussions to the school values, this can usefully illustrate and support a response to gaps in meeting the needs of pupils.

Points for discussion:

- Inclusion means a commitment to supporting each pupil's individual needs. What are the parameters of what we *can* offer?
- How does what we *can* offer impact on pupils' learning across the school?
- How do we communicate this effectively to our stakeholders? How do you discuss this with governors? How do you clarify this with parents?
- Numbers of pupils with additional needs are increasing. How do we adapt? How do we future proof our school?

These discussions will not fix problems with budgets and workload, but they will reduce some tensions and uncertainties. Together you can establish a shared understanding of both where the school is currently and the required response for these times.

Staff training and development

Staff discussions about the school values and what the school can offer will raise awareness and enable people to understand where the school has positioned itself and why. As a starting point, this will highlight areas of expertise within the school, as well as gaps, where all staff may need some additional support or training.

For example:

Respect – What does this mean in our school for people with additional needs?
Achieve – What does this look like in our school for pupils with additional needs?
Responsibility – How do we enable responsibility in our school for everyone?

These discussions and subsequent training will gradually change attitudes. It's fair to acknowledge that some staff may react to challenging behaviours, automatically perceiving them as 'naughty' or 'bad'. Training and awareness raising will mean staff adjust their understanding of the needs behind the child's behaviour and can more readily cope and manage their own responses. Part of this is helping staff to reframe their understanding of pupil's behaviours from 'they won't do' to 'they find it difficult to do'. This shift in awareness moves people from seeing defiance to seeing lack of skill. They realise only education can fill this gap.

These discussions won't change the level of need, they will however ensure that everyone is aware of the situation, that it is not just a school issue, but a national one. This can go some way to mitigate a sense of failure, injustice, or powerlessness.

Challenging the system

Once your people are clear on both the level of need and the school's response within a values framework, they will be able to have informed conversations with parents and the local authority about additional needs in the school and where you have agreed to focus resources. This will enable everyone to be more at ease in themselves and more confident in the face of challenge, criticism, and directives.

Co-create Alternative Measures (see example in Figure 21.2) for your school to highlight successes that more meaningfully reflect your school's ethos and practice. Display these alongside the school values and the national data for your school to give a true picture of how amazing your school is.

Form a collective where headteachers locally or across a district share their approaches – what has worked, what hasn't, what they have learned. Cross-pollinate ideas and provide moral support through the pressures.

Shared experience

This SENDCo outlines the reality and the challenges of meeting complex needs as an inclusive Federation of schools.

We are an inclusive Federation of schools with high numbers of children with identified SEND (30–50% SEND in most year groups and 8% of the children in the junior school have EHCPs (Education, Health and Care Plan)). We have

Figure 21.2 Alternative measures

high rates of success when applying for EHCPs and have transitioned numerous children into specialist provision settings (sometimes via appeal/early tribunal proceedings).

Our reputation is growing. We have children transitioning to us because we are nurturing and go 'over and above.' We are extremely proud of these aspects as we aspire to progress our pupils towards national expectations. The reality though is that each new challenge threatens the already precarious balance we have meticulously orchestrated in attempts to meet the needs of our children.

Our best laid, strategic plans are often thwarted by the unexpected, e.g., an incident, a transition, a decision. Usually, this results in the requirement to go back to the drawing board (often literally scrawling names and multiple scenarios across sugar paper, strewn across the table, in attempts to puzzle a way forwards).

We continuously worry about staff well-being. We are alert to the consequences of staff experiencing/battling compassion fatigue or overwhelm. We work through the impact of children/parents sabotaging relationships. We fear budget implications. We face feeling disheartened by predicted progress data along with countless other barriers to success. However, we confront these challenges together as a team. Along the way, we reflect, adapt and enhance our SEND provision.

The fundamentals we believe have made a difference:

SEND is not solely the responsibility of the SENDCo, but every member of staff.

- Leaders in all areas monitor teaching and learning for children with SEND.
- Teachers are the advocates for the children in their year group with SEND.
- Teachers plan differentiation, teach utilising personalised provision; assess using a range of frameworks, and report on progress (academic as well as those specific to EHCP outcomes, targets set by health professionals, etc.).
- Senior leaders design continuous professional development to enable this and protect time for these actions, e.g., through a core, termly cycle of professional development meetings.

We have a 'grow our own' approach to staffing wherever possible.

After encountering an attitude of 'I shouldn't have to teach children like this,' on more than one occasion in the past, we are very cautious and:

- We sculpt recruitment to encourage transparency and commitment.
- We seek individuals who know the challenges our federation faces, understand the needs of our children, and share our values.
- We now have a dedicated team of people who are relentlessly patient and endlessly kind.
- We continually invest in training/outreach relating to SEND to further develop the expertise, confidence, and understanding of the team.

- We are committed to valuing and implementing external agency feedback and expertise.
- We involve the educational psychology service, behaviour service, and local specialist provision settings when personalising provision for individuals, groups, and cohorts.
- We review and shape whole school systemic change based on collaborative reflection with professional services.
- We have become more experienced at expecting the unexpected.
- Our staff have a level of flexibility that enables reactive changes in response to need.

We understand that behaviour is a communication of need.

- We have a behaviour policy which has been developed to meet the needs of our school by outlining our approach to behaviour expectations, rewards, and sanctions. This policy has a universal approach and a bespoke element to support individuals for whom the universal is inappropriate.
- Iceberg-informed Individual Behaviour Management Plans (IBMPs) are created for individual children and shared with all staff who encounter the child.
- Regular reviews of behaviour trackers, attendance for Reduced Hours Provision sessions, engagement with Alternative Provision Settings, Risk Assessments, IBMPs, and communication with parents, all inform the mass organisation of personalised packages of support.
- The evidence trail supports self-evaluation and conversations with the local authority regarding data, suspensions, etc.

For us to ensure sustainability, we understand the importance of staff well-being.

To foster a genuine culture of care, we are embedding:

- Supervision
- Debriefing opportunities
- Check-ins
- Problem-solving for managing workloads
- Signposting well-being resources
- Assigning regular time in CPD meetings to facilitate self-reflection and plan opportunities for self-compassion
- Promoting a healthy work-life balance

We have been on an arduous and emotive journey to arrive at this point. However, this is not a finite series of actions, leading to an end result but rather a perpetual, fluid process of reflecting and adapting.

Coaching approaches
Coaching yourself
These questions offer a checklist approach for small-step actions that make a significant difference over time and that will contribute to your peace of mind:

- What is your stance on inclusion in your school? In one sentence.
- What will progress look like in your school?
- How do you find confidence with your decision(s) – head and heart?

Decisions around suspending a pupil and protecting staff well-being and retention take their toll emotionally. Similarly, decisions for supporting a family when relationships feel broken.

- Who can you discuss the dilemmas with? For example, where can you access professional supervision?
- What does positive change mean for your school?
- How will you continue to challenge and support the system towards positive change?

Coaching others
- How do the school values relate to inclusion? Any examples?
- What can people see in your practice that supports the values and acknowledges the challenges?
- How do you know these are effective? How can you find out?
- How might you develop these traits in others?
- What would you like to hear your team saying about inclusion?
- What action will you take to make this happen?
- How will you have wider conversations with others about inclusion?

Coaching upwards
- How can we develop a position statement on inclusion that reflects the school's values and addresses the challenges of resourcing?
- How do we manage the parameters of education and inclusion here?
- How do we continue to support a pupil on our school roll who is attending alternative provision and waiting for specialist provision?
- How can we create meaningful data that truly represents our successes?
- What opportunities will you create for having further supportive discussions on inclusion with staff at all levels?

Perspectives
Different styles struggle with different aspects of adapting to changes in pupil needs. They may also struggle with their own anxiety about their skills in a new situation. Remind yourself and them:

Innovators – You can look at new ways of working and apply research evidence to practice.
Achievers – If you can tackle more of the low-level SEND issues, outcomes across the school can improve.

Perfectors – This is a significant opportunity to develop skills and enhance practice.

Harmonisers – By discussing this issue as a team, you can all be clear on what you need to be doing.

Keep in mind – Complex needs in others can trigger our own insecurities. If you have members of staff whose own needs were not met as children, they may need extra support in working through what the school can, and cannot do, for children who may be struggling just as they did.

References

Children in need, reporting year 2024 (no date) Available at: https://explore-education-statistics.service.gov.uk/find-statistics/children-in-need (Accessed: 23 January 2025).

Special educational needs in England, academic year 2023/24 (no date) Available at: https://explore-education-statistics.service.gov.uk/find-statistics/special-educational-needs-in-england (Accessed: 24 January 2025).

UK Poverty 2024: The essential guide to understanding poverty in the UK | Joseph Rowntree Foundation (2024) Available at: https://www.jrf.org.uk/uk-poverty-2024-the-essential-guide-to-understanding-poverty-in-the-uk (Accessed: 23 January 2025).

SECTION 7

Self-reliance

The demands on school leaders are relentless, making it easy to lose the joy and fulfilment you had when you started your teaching career.

Finding balance is sometimes not enough. It's important to re-establish that link with your drive and your deeper purpose so you find the courage within yourself for what the future needs.

Section 7 asks you to rise above the noise of everyday work and question what's really going on so that, if you choose, you can start to change things meaningfully.

CHAPTER 22

What really stops you prioritising your well-being?

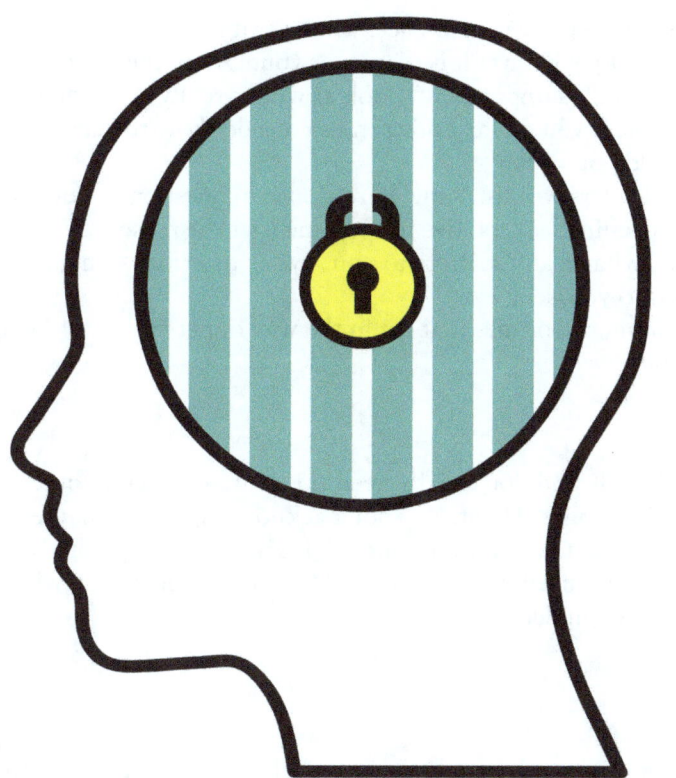

What really stops you prioritising your well-being?

Most people want to be fit and healthy with a manageable workload, to have time with friends and loved ones, and to have space to relax. What stops that? What gets in the way?

Usually it's attitude, particularly an individual's attitude, to change and risk.

Your attitude is a combination of feelings, thoughts, and beliefs that shape your approach to how you live your life.

What's your attitude towards putting your well-being first:

1. On a scale of 1–5 (where 1 is poor and 5 is excellent), how would you rate your self-care - the extent to which you prioritise your well-being?
2. What could you do to increase that self-care rating?
3. What would you be prepared to do to take better care of yourself and your needs?
4. What stops you from doing that?

Coaches frequently explore interference: whatever it is that gets in the way of you doing what you want to do, whatever it is that stops you. Often, the reason people give is only part of the problem. It's important to look at what's really going on behind your resistance and the choices you make, and then to consider how to start to shift some of the patterns that hold you back.

Most school leaders will list 'time' in response to question 4. But it's not time. In my experience of coaching leaders, I've found time isn't the reason. What you prioritise is. In other words, what really matters to you – your priorities – might be different from what you admit to yourself.

The most common attitudes that get in the way of personal well-being apply both at work and at home.

Slightly arrogant

You think you're OK and don't really need this stuff as much as others do.

You seem to be coping alright. You don't acknowledge this, but there's an underlying belief that it's weak to take time for yourself. It's not necessary. That's fine for others, of course, but you don't need it like they do. There's nothing wrong with you. You think you have everything under control.

Humble

You believe it's selfish.

You're caught in a virtue trap, believing others' needs are more important than your own, and all those things that need to be done should be given more priority than your needs. You encourage others to get enough sleep and have lunch breaks. You support them with your time, a listening ear, and by fixing their problems. Your work starts properly before people arrive and continues when everyone else has left for the day.

Self-judging

Strangely, self-care and self-compassion challenge your perception of being good enough in your different roles.

If you take time to exercise, choose to eat differently, or create some space for yourself, it's likely to go against what others have grown used to and may coincide with times other people need you. Then you feel like you're not being a good enough friend, a good enough partner, a good enough parent, or headteacher. If you are depleted and take time to restore your energy while there are still jobs to be done, you feel you're not good enough in your role. You seem unable to accept that you'll do things better with restored energy.

Uncomfortably familiar?

If you don't recognise, value, and take action to prioritise your needs, then your fears, beliefs, and thoughts override the common-sense practices for keeping well. You work later than you wanted, you skip lunch, or you remain sedentary all day. If all this sounds uncomfortably familiar, here are four approaches to consider that will change things for you, and inevitably, for those around you – at work and at home.

1. Demonstrating self-worth

You are not valuing yourself if you persistently ignore what keeps you well. In effect, you're allowing a form of self-neglect to override self-care. Consider how you show that you value yourself and your well-being:

- What are you doing that isn't doing you good?
- What small steps could you take towards changing this and keeping well?
- How will you tackle this?
- Plan what to say to communicate your well-being decisions to others.
- Find a good time to bring up the subject of self-care with those who need to be involved.
- Start communicating: not much will change until you do.

2. Sharing responsibilities

Ask for help. People may not realise you need help, especially if they have become dependent on you being super-capable:

- Finish the sentence 'I'd appreciate your help with...'
- Practise saying this out loud to yourself so that you feel more confident when you eventually articulate your request.
- Think through how you can share responsibilities, lighten your load, or create some time and space for yourself to do those common-sense activities that restore you.
- Imagine the result you want from this and picture the benefits in your mind's eye so it starts to feel possible and attractive.
- How can you negotiate these so it's fair for you?

3. Clarifying boundaries

It's easy to believe you have communicated what you want to say, but often, when we communicate change, we say things in a general way because the specifics feel awkward. We meander our way through the awkwardness, not realising the ambiguities or the points we've missed, how others are misinterpreting what we've said, or are only hearing what they want to hear.

Frequently, people really need things spelt out. They need clarity because they don't realise at first the knock-on effect of changing familiar patterns and routines. How will you spell things out for them? How will you know they've really grasped what this means?

Consider in advance:

- What time are you going to take for your well-being – from when to when?
- What will happen instead?
- How might you (plural) make it work?
- How can you grow together through this?
- Aim for clarity. Remove any ambiguity from the implications.
- Summarise the main points to check you've been understood. 'What this means is…'

4. Asserting

Assertiveness is based on respect – respect for yourself and for others. In simple terms, if you continually prioritise other people's well-being over your own, you are not treating yourself as an equal. Remember, you count too, and it matters (for everyone in the long term) that you respect your needs and that you respect (not disrespect) yourself. This may be a pattern you have fallen into, but it isn't sustainable for very long without adverse consequences for your mental, emotional, and physical well-being. You being well affects a lot of people.

Here are some popular assertiveness techniques and approaches you can adapt for different people in different professional and personal situations, especially when they impact you prioritising your well-being.

Saying no and turning down requests

What do you need to say 'no' to so that you can say 'yes' to valuing yourself and your well-being?

Rehearse your situation out loud and make sure you include the word 'no.'

'As we discussed in my performance management, I'm committing to leaving work by 6.00 at least three days each week. This means I'm saying "no" to attending Thursday's meeting.'

Making requests

What, and who specifically do you need to ask? What to say?

'As you know, I'm committed to leaving work by 6.00 at least three days each week. Thursday's meeting needs someone from the senior leadership team to be there. Please, would you attend?'

Negotiate a fair solution.

Disagreeing and stating your views

How will you respond when challenged or when facing a lack of cooperation? Here are some sentence starters:

'As I see it…'
'I believe…'
'I find that…'
'My experience is…'

Dealing with people who won't take 'no' for an answer

Vary what you say in response to each of the persistent comments:

- 'I understand you would prefer the headteacher to be present, but on this occasion, and for reasons I've explained, I have agreed the Head of Year will join the meeting.'
- 'I believe the Head of Year is perfectly capable of representing the leadership team on Thursday. I've seen their input in other meetings. I'm confident they will bring an important perspective to the group.'
- 'I'm not prepared to break my commitment to well-being. So, no, I will not be working four evenings that week.'
- 'I appreciate it's disappointing for you if the headteacher isn't present. We have other options and many factors to take into account.'
- 'I believe role-modelling decisions around well-being is an important option for Thursday.'

Negotiating

It's unlikely you'll get through all your to-do list, especially when people in authority keep involving you and asking more of you:

- Be clear in your own mind about your non-negotiables.
- Remember to pause and consider your response rather than automatically agreeing to something and then being annoyed with yourself afterwards.
- Have some go-to sentences that will help you negotiate:
    - 'I appreciate you need this done soon.'
    - 'I'm working on x, y, and z at the moment.' 'If I do this, I won't manage to do x and y until next week. What's the main priority?'
    - 'I'm at capacity. Can we explore some other options (people, time/deadlines)?'

Eyes wide open

Venturing into any of these four approaches brings risk, so you'll need your eyes wide open. You'll need to consider whether the risk is worth it. The risk here is being on the receiving end of the judgement, disapproval, or disappointment of people who matter. The risk of spending time away from them, of not doing as much as they expect of you, or have got used to.

Understandably, these risks form the main interference to what you know you 'should' do but don't. These risks block conversations that could be much easier. They get in the way of common-sense behaviour that would allow you to prioritise your well-being. You know how to take care of yourself, but you let things get in the way – not enough time, deadlines, people needing you, others not able to do things the way you do, and so on. It seems easier not to start to change those patterns.

There comes a point, though, where life twists and turns around you. Then the risks are no longer a choice; they become a necessity. You realise your attitude must shift; you have to wake up and face the reality of the strain, the pressure, and your situation.

Communicating, sharing responsibilities, establishing boundaries, and asserting will help you at that time. They'll help you even more if you start now, though.

Coaching approaches

Coaching yourself

What's your interference? Slightly arrogant, humble, or self-judging?

What risks are more challenging for you to address:

- self-worth?
- sharing responsibilities?
- clarifying boundaries?
- communicating assertively?

A great starting point would be to take some time to reflect and make notes on the above and decide on some steps, however small, to move in the direction of your well-being.

Coaching others

- How do you prioritise your well-being along with all your other competing priorities?
- What gets in the way?
- When have you taken good care of yourself in the past? What factors made that work?
- How can you do more of what works and less of whatever gets in the way?
- What easy steps can you put in place right away?
- When will you start?
- Who will you tell?

Coaching upwards
- Well-being is a school priority. In what ways are you role-modelling well-being to others?
- What stops you?
- What gets in the way?
- What could you do to change this?

Perspectives
What really stops the different Coaching Styles from prioritising their well-being?

Innovators – tend to avoid those areas that bring complications. They breeze over awkward topics and hope things will work out. It's hard for them to face or acknowledge the extent and impact of not taking enough care of themselves.

Achievers – fall victim to the belief that they are invincible. They delude themselves into thinking there will be a point when they will take things easy or slow down a little, usually after the next project, then the next one, and so on… It often takes something serious to make them slow down, when they no longer have a choice.

Perfectors – struggle to remove their blocks around the value of being good enough and doing work that is good enough. In their constant drive to do a faultless job and avoid criticism, they tend to work longer and longer with diminishing returns.

Harmonisers – face inner turmoil about putting their own needs first. The combination of other people's awkwardness at their request, followed by tension and resistance, is often just not worth the risk. They would rather not go there and simply accept their lot.

Keep in mind – some leaders find it especially difficult to assert themselves. Early trauma may have led to deeply ingrained people-pleasing tendencies, which sabotages efforts to break free. High levels of anxiety or the reduced energy of depression can also make assertion seem too risky. In these cases, people are likely to need extra support.

CHAPTER 23

Finding fulfilment

Finding fulfilment

When you are still and calm, even for a moment, there's a space where words, images, or ideas surface, a book title jumps out at you from the shelf, an email with a curious topic appears, and you notice. It turns out that's exactly what you're looking for or what you need.

The space must be there, though, momentarily, for noticing. You can create moments and spaces like that routinely, to switch off from the noise in your head, to rise above the clutter, to jump off the hamster wheel.

Inspiring yourself

To be a source of inspiration for others, you need to know how to inspire yourself. If you create a few moments of space and have the following within reach, you'll be able to find inspiration and boost your spirits whenever you need uplifting.

- Words that stir you.

    Quotes, lyrics, mantras – whatever works for you.
    Keep renewing them so they continue to surprise and delight you.

- Books, literature, or poetry.

    What books can you dip into that transport you to a higher place in yourself?
    Keep them nearby.

- Music and audio.

    Tracks or playlists to rouse you, calm you down, or rev you up.
    Make them easily accessible via your preferred device.

- Photos.

    Personal memories that represent what really matters to you.
    You may have these on display or about your person and they serve you as gentle reminders. Sometimes though, a few mindful moments of being very present with the images of those you love can activate a reset in your approach.

- Images.

    Art that resonates and that captures something meaningful for you.
    Make sure you can see art that sends messages to different parts of your brain, that gives you what you need to receive.

- Speakers – TED talks.

    How incredible to access inspirational individuals and absorb their learning over lunch.

- Nature.

    Always within reach – birdsong, flowers, geometry – whatever you're looking for.

- Purpose.

    Being in the moment with pupils – their imagination, learning, and experience. Again, always accessible to you.

- Kindness

    Seeing the good in people.
    Just look around. It's never far away in a school.

- Questions that bring stillness.

    What do you hear when you really listen? When you close your eyes and have space to hear a deeper wisdom?

Inspiring others

Ask questions that enable individuals to discover something inspirational within their reach. These conversations are highly likely to engage you and foster connection.

Share what inspires you and see how it inspires them, or invites them, to share something equivalent.

- Explore what music, book, film, creative expression, philosophy, or fun activity recharges you.
- Let them know what inspires you about them.
- Share three things you're glad about/appreciate these days.
- Ask people to recall a time when they felt inspired. Can they pinpoint what it was that made them feel that way?
- Share who you would choose as an inspirational role model (dead, alive, or fictional) and why.
- Share the thrill of emotional goosebumps. What moments made your spine tingle or the hair on the back of your neck stand up?
- Find some peak moments or high points from your life – no justification necessary, just tell the stories.
- When are you most at peace with yourself?
- What message would you give yourself to remember on waking each day?

Inspiring team meetings

Taking just a few minutes to share back on one of the following points is engaging and uplifting for everyone. You could make a routine of it. A voluntary go-around.

- Task team members to take a photo that simply represents what they most enjoy about working here. Share the story of why.
- Bring a quote that inspires you or words that are close to your heart.
- Select a quote (from a selection of pre-written slips) and say why it inspires you.
- Suggest random acts of kindness. Talk about them in the meetings that follow.
- Share something meaningful from today…
- Share something I'm proud of this week…
- A story that I can't tell without laughing is…
- I would use the word 'beautiful' to describe…
- A special moment in my professional life…
- What I most value about today…
- Suggest writing one short line a day. In a few words, capture something beautiful, something meaningful, or what you value each day. Then, at the end of the week, you might have a poem to share.

Just a few minutes at the start of every team meeting, especially if it's at the end of the day, renews energy levels and focus. There's a very significant by-product too – this process reconnects people with their purpose.

Inspiring Heads

From 2012 to 2020, I ran termly sessions for headteachers at a point in the term when energy was ebbing and people needed a boost to get through to the next break. These Thursday, early evening, sessions lasted two hours and offered headteachers time and space to connect and unwind. I facilitated the sessions so the Heads were able to engage in meaningful dialogue on a particular theme, talking in pairs, and sharing personal stories of creativity and inspiration. They had time to offload over tea and cake, followed by a 90-minute session when inspiration became the priority. How could 'Inspiring Heads' work in your area?

Tips for sessions
- Use a different venue each time so the patterns and dynamics are refreshed.
- Newness and doing things differently stimulate new perspectives and different ideas.
- Creative expression, however simple, facilitates different conversations. In my experience, Heads love colouring in.
- Take-aways – the sessions add value when Heads have resources to take away with them. Ideas they can use with their people. An 'Inspiration Thesaurus,' for example. Get everyone to discuss what inspires them, where they find inspiration, and what inspiration feels like. Then, divide out all the letters of the alphabet among the pairs or small groups and task them with finding a word or phrase beginning with that letter to capture inspiration. B is for Bravery. D is for Dawn and Daylight. M is for Moral compass. You have all the makings for a poster or infographic that's full of inspiration.

Coaching approaches
Coaching yourself
- When do you feel most alive?
- What are you most grateful for?
- What are you most proud of in life?

Coaching others
- In ten years' time, what will matter to you most about now?
- When do you lose track of time?
- What can you learn from that?
- What makes you smile?

Questions upwards
- What have you done that's worth remembering?
- How have you expressed yourself creatively – in your life, in this school?
- How have you made a difference to others?

Perspectives
In order to inspire others, remember:

Innovators – love the new. Fresh ideas, projects, initiatives, and/or unusual perspectives.
Achievers – love a sense of progress, particularly when their contribution is vital to the whole.
Perfectors – love quality and a calm focus on detail without the pressure to deliver 'good enough'.
Harmonisers – love to support others and help them through difficulties.
Keep in mind – we are all different. What inspires one person may leave another untouched. Giving people space in which to thrive, listening to them, providing the right kind of encouragement, and setting a good example by following your own inspiration, all help to inspire others and keep them inspired.

You are surrounded by children who are just trying to express themselves in their world and be accepted. You are surrounded by adults who are trying to express themselves in their world and be accepted. All those unique identities searching for expression, inclusion, and connection.

You are uniquely placed to enable this – especially with inspiration.

Shared experience

From interviews with people who attended Inspiring Heads.

What was school life like in the Ofsted window?

Four years after our last Ofsted inspection, we had been on 'high alert' from the start of the academic year, knowing that realistically, we could get 'the (dreaded) call' at any time. Waiting for Ofsted is a stressful and, quite frankly a depressing time for teachers and headteachers. There are such high stakes involved and the recent horrific news of headteacher Ruth Perry* was very much in staff's minds, knowing that an unreasonable judgement had taken such a tragic toll on a person's life.

We have always striven to ensure that school life for our children is an enjoyable and memorable experience. We have fought hard to ensure that the children in our school receive a balanced and exciting curriculum that also secured strong results, and where children enjoyed 'discovering the wonders of learning' (our motto).

Due to external pressure from Ofsted and the local authority, we could have focused our efforts purely on improving data, which would have been at the expense of an exciting and enriching curriculum. This was not the narrow tunnel we wanted to be forced down, as it would go against our core principles and values. So we held tight to what we knew in our hearts was the right thing to do and stuck to our values.

However, despite giving the children an education filled with lots of exciting opportunities and experiences within our financial constraints, combined with the reassuring knowledge that we were ticking many bullet points in the Ofsted handbook, there still remained the fear, the dread, and many, many sleepless nights for us all waiting for that call.

There were discussions in the staffroom on several occasions about how Ofsted, this huge, ominous, looming dark cloud, was responsible for ruining our enjoyment of teaching and our professional lives. And yet, despite having led my school through three successful Ofsted inspections, I was still reduced to feelings of immense stress, fear, and oppression.

When I thought about Ofsted, the word 'oppressive' came to mind. The dictionary defines this word as cruel, harsh, or tyrannical, to make anxious or depressed. This sums up our feelings about the process that is Ofsted.

How did things change after the inspection?

Despite achieving the outcome that we had hoped for following our inspection, when it finally came after 5 years and one term, we were initially all rather deflated. The realisation that the waiting was finally over and that we no longer needed to feel suppressed and obsessed by meeting Ofsted's many criteria gradually dawned on us.

Fast forward to a term later, and we are all starting to remember and experience the joy of teaching again without the constant worry or the sinking feeling that we had to carry for so long. All of my staff (myself included) are now starting to fully appreciate this time when we can more freely enjoy the creative and cultural aspects of our curriculum and be much more receptive to change and new ideas.

How did you find inspiration for yourself?

The deflated feeling I described above led me on a personal quest to find inspiration in my leadership. I gave a lot of thought to what or who had inspired me in the past and remembered the book by Sir John Jones 'The Magic Weaving Business'. I was lucky enough to listen to him at a conference a few years ago. I bought his latest book, 'Dusting off Thunderbolts', and am currently enjoying being reminded about the heart of leadership.

As part of our whole-school focus on improving mental health, I accepted an offer from a company offering a free mental health afterschool club for some of our older children. Their work on breathwork sounded really interesting and beneficial for both children and staff, so I asked them to deliver an Inset day for us. This Inset day experience then led the staff to want to learn more about breathwork, so we organised three practical twilight sessions so we would be in a strong position to share this practice with our children.

Our commitment to art, music, drama, dance, and creative workshops, along with the many trips to support learning in the humanities, ensures that the children at our school have a love of learning and experience a curriculum that is rich in cultural learning. This ensures that there is a balance between academic standards and the data-driven (English and Maths) push from the Department for Education and Ofsted. Our creative and cultural learning provides children who may not excel in academic subjects with an invaluable opportunity to flourish and enjoy another, equally important aspect of school life.

From a mental health and well-being perspective, it is my experience that cultural learning plays a significant part in supporting good mental health and well-being for children and young people. During a time when young people's mental health and well-being have never been so low, cultural learning increases children's happiness, resilience, and a sense of achievement. Therefore, I consider it imperative to make this an integral part of our curriculum.

How did you inspire others?

Staff could see the potential benefits of our breathwork sessions, not only for the children in their class but also for themselves on a personal level. I have regular, 'check-ins' during staff meetings to ask what teachers have tried with their classes and to get the staff to share amongst themselves what has worked well. This process has given staff a sense of accountability.

The cultural learning experiences in which our children participate give them a greater sense of achievement and enjoyment than academic success alone achieves. Children flourish with new challenges, which gives them far more than just academic achievement by which to measure themselves.

What does 'full of goodness' mean for you now?

For me, it's when you know, deep down inside, that what you're doing is a very good and positive thing to do for all involved. It's like a positive energy; it's something intangible, but you can feel the goodness in what's going on! And, it's exciting and feels completely right!

How does this contribute to society?

The most significant impact has been the improvement of our children's happiness and well-being (including resilience, confidence, and self-belief). This is due to the fact that children love coming to school. Learning is made irresistible because our curriculum has enriching cultural learning experiences interwoven throughout.

How are you changing the future lives of your pupils/families?

Through giving children cultural experiences that they may not have at home, we are hoping to broaden their minds, help them see the world differently, find enjoyment and appreciation, and learn new skills in areas that could otherwise have lain dormant.

The new knowledge and understanding about strategies to support and increase well-being, including breath work, are shared with our parents through parent workshops and with our children during the school day.

It's very early days, but we hope that this whole school focus on teaching children strategies to improve their well-being will help them to be better equipped to self-regulate, have a positive mindset, and be receptive to new learning.

Some children have commented that their sleep has improved and that they are beginning to use strategies to feel better much more quickly than before.

*Ruth Perry was a headteacher in Berkshire who died by suicide in January 2023 after learning her school was set to be judged Inadequate by Ofsted.

Ruth's family campaigns for the reform of Ofsted's inspection system to prioritise the welfare of school leaders and teachers, as well as of children.

CHAPTER 24

Creative self-compassion

- self care
- self management
- self awareness
- self worth
- self acceptance
- self compassion

Self-compassion is pivotal to well-being

When I first started reading about self-compassion, it was at a time when I had real concerns about where society was heading. More specifically, I felt exasperated by what education was focusing on, contrasted with what was happening in young people's lives.

> Extract from my journal 24th May 2018
>
> Increasingly we hear about how pressure is impacting on pupils, students and staff in schools – from social media and tests to judgements and comparisons in performance – all contributing to people not feeling good enough. Increasingly we read how this is manifesting in self-harm, all manner of mental and emotional health issues, medication, anxiety, addiction, and suicide. When you listen to the reasons behind these behaviours, data and grades become far less significant.

Around this time, I came across some of the reasons young people gave for why they self-harmed. These included 'overwhelming emotions' and 'not liking themselves'. What I found most heartbreaking, though, were their responses to what they wished they'd known earlier:

'I deserve better.' 'It was OK to talk.' 'How detrimental shame is to you getting better.'

In my role as a coach, I hear these same factors behind the fears and insecurities of adults. Judgements and comparisons in performance, not feeling good enough, the overwhelming emotion of shame you feel from critical comments about you or your school on social media, intense fear, and vulnerability from a complaint or judgement. Comparisons. Need for approval. Validation. Feeling alone.

The more I learnt about self-compassion and the more I practised it, the more I came to believe that it's not just necessary for well-being; it's pivotal. I realised that self-harm is the opposite of self-care and that one way to reduce the risk of neglecting yourself is by having the wherewithal, the inner resource, simply to feel a bit better. In this sense, and as I stated in Chapter 5, I believe self-compassion is the ultimate self-empowerment.

I felt very driven to do something about this. I created a website all about self-compassion for anyone to use, whenthetensiongoes.com, and then a residential programme for headteachers on self-compassion. I immersed myself in Kristen Neff's work and aimed to translate it into practices for the participants themselves, sharing ideas for how they might take it back to their own settings.

Up and down the cone

I created the cone graphic (Figure 24.1) to illustrate how I believe self-compassion to be pivotal to self-care. (It could just as easily be represented by a circle with self-compassion at the centre.) The point I want to illustrate is that if you nurture the self-compassion layer or core, it grows upwards through the layers and strengthens them all in turn.

If you start with some simple practices to show compassion to yourself, things soon start to change and usually feel better. This means you're much more likely to sustain these practices as your experience and perspectives change.

Figure 24.1 Self-compassion cone

Routinely practising those simple steps means you naturally start to accept yourself a little more. Accompanying that feeling of kindness to yourself is a sense that you matter (of course you matter). This is you validating yourself from the inside out, which means you need less validation or recognition from others because you are becoming more self-reliant.

It's more in the doing than the understanding

We know how important self-care is for a sustainable career in education, so that's where most approaches to well-being start, providing information on, and practices for, keeping well. These make good sense, and they are usually straightforward to understand, yet often they don't stick. (*You know it's good to keep hydrated but you don't continue drinking enough water throughout the day.*)

Moving down the layers in the cone illustration (Figure 24.1), we can see what's required to keep self-care going. Managing yourself (*Remembering to fill the water bottle and carry it with you.*). Remaining aware of what you need to make things work for you and where you get stuck. (*I carry my water bottle around but forget to use it.*)

Recall those times when you are only focusing on self-care, and it slips. You judge yourself because you didn't stick to your plan, and then if you keep forgetting, you lose your motivation and resolve. (*I'm useless at keeping the water bottle going, everyone else is better than me, I'm giving up on this one.*)

Contrast this with when you combine self-care and self-compassion. You notice, normalise, and reassure yourself (*It's midday and I haven't drunk any water yet. Deep breath. It's OK. I'm not the only one to forget their well-being habit. I'm glad I've noticed it now so I can keep it going through the afternoon.*) Then, with time, you accept yourself more and incrementally value yourself a little more.

When self-compassion enables you to accept yourself more and value who you are, your self-awareness really grows, and this is where so many personal insights start to happen about your well-being, your relationships, your roles, and how you live your life. This is where you 'get it'. You already understand all the analogies about how your well-being affects your performance (the wilting flower, the empty battery, the low fuel tank), but understanding these doesn't necessarily mean you keep taking good care of yourself. The awareness you get from putting self-compassion habits into practice means you will naturally change to keep yourself well. (Get the plant-watering right and watch it blossom, and so on.)

Tipping point

I've noticed when we neglect our self-worth and self-acceptance (and many of us do), there comes a tipping point of sorts. If our self-care, management and awareness are affected by not valuing who we are, and not accepting how we are, then we're much less likely to keep our intentions going. Our behaviour and lack of action topple the cone over. We let ourselves down and it doesn't feel good.

In other words, when you remember to value yourself, when you allow your self-worth to influence your self-awareness, you are letting self-compassion fulfil its purpose. All the layers are strengthened and so the cone keeps steadily spinning. Your relationship with yourself as a human being becomes less conditional, more accepting, and more liberating.

It's not selfish

It's fair to say as an educator, you are naturally compassionate towards others, much less so towards yourself. All that's needed then is to turn that compassion inwards! It sounds so simple but within minutes of any discussion on self-compassion, the word 'selfish' crops up. In this context, words like self-preservation are more truthful.

Valuing and respecting yourself really matters for leaders since you are role models and your example influences the culture. Your people want to be part of a culture that values them, and led by people who prioritise self-care, not stressed individuals who demonstrate a lack of respect for themselves; for example, by working too long or by always putting other people's needs above their own.

This many years on, having worked with headteachers on self-compassion, I've seen individuals becoming at ease in themselves, confident in their truth and their worth, arousing curiosity in others through continuing their self-compassion practices and sharing them with others in a timely way. They have learnt to shift shame and accept vulnerability, to motivate themselves with kindness not cruelty, to draw on their reserves of inner security at those times of external scrutiny, and to prioritise their well-being.

Lived self-compassion is when it's embedded in your approach to life. It means you know what to do, how to cope well with the hardship, tragedy, or setback that come your way. Lived self-compassion gives you a safety net that's there whenever you need it. Once embedded, being compassionate towards yourself is what will keep you well and stay making a difference in your remarkable profession. It will keep you enjoying who you are and what you do.

Lived self-compassion can only happen with regular practice. Chapter 5 provides a range of options for you to choose from and implement over time for yourself and your people. Here's an additional approach because a creative habit is excellent for anchoring you in your day and embedding compassion for yourself too.

Creative self-expression and self-compassion

A really simple way to start your self-compassion journey is with your creative self-expression. If I asked you right now to sketch something that's in your line of view, something on your desk, what you can see outside your window or in the room, how would you feel? If you're not used to drawing, you might feel apprehensive or uncomfortable at the prospect. All of us feel a bit awkward about some kind of creative activity that doesn't play to our strengths or talents, so please choose one that you feel uncomfortable about, and I'll explain how it could be a gift for starting to develop your self-compassion.

Pause for a moment and consider why you'd feel awkward doing that creative activity (singing, dancing, playing an instrument, collaging, knitting, etc.). Your reasons are likely to illustrate exactly what self-compassion is not – judging yourself as not being good enough and comparing yourself unkindly with others. You might even hide away your attempts; scrunch up your sketch and throw it, dissatisfied, in the bin.

Creative self-compassion involves recognising this simple task is just for you, no display or comparison is needed, and certainly no judgement. It can be an enjoyable experience of being present, mindfully absorbed for a little while in a different headspace, accepting yourself with kindness for whatever you create. Yes, just as you would with children.

The more you allow yourself some simple creative activities, the more you can learn to be kind to yourself and more self-accepting. If you allow yourself a few moments of creative self-compassion throughout the day, you're very likely to find yourself more content, patient, energised, and with more focus, and this will positively impact your well-being.

You can also use creative self-compassion as a way to offload and express your feelings privately. Identify what you're feeling and express it visually on paper through ink or pencil, through lines and shapes and colours. Try it and see how you feel better for doing so.

Expressing yourself creatively is such an important part of being human, whatever your stage in life. If you 'don't have time' for your creative expression, or, if like me, you discovered your creativity languishing at the bottom of your to do list, let it into your life again. Combine creative self-expression with self-compassion and watch the magic start to happen. Watch how ideas start to surface, over time, from a space inside. Experiment in those moments, play with ideas, and express them.

You're an educator. You don't need me to tell you how much children learn from creative self-expression and play. But as an adult, can I ask you, 'How much creative self-expression and play do you allow for yourself in your life?'

You're surrounded by children, those excellent role models. Let them inspire you to express yourself creatively or playfully. That's how you'll get life in perspective, that's how you'll take time to keep well, and that's where you'll rediscover the joy.

Conclusion

I have written a lot about self-compassion in this book. I want to finish by making a case for self-compassion as fundamental to your longevity, well-being, and leadership in your role.

A lot rests on you. You set the direction for your school. You energise your school's culture. You show by your actions what is acceptable and what is not. You create and maintain a community in which, you intend, all who live are welcome and supported. You look to the future as best you can, even as you wrestle with the present.

I've worked with many leaders who have brought energy and creativity to their work but have gradually succumbed to the pressures, dissonance, grind, and occasional sheer unpleasantness of the work they've had to do. We are all changed by experience, but we don't have to be diminished by it.

The one thing we can be certain of is that there will be times when things go wrong. Whether because we've failed to do the right things, or made a major mistake, or overlooked another's actions, been impulsive, or behaved badly, or given way when we should've stood strong. It's at these times when we have a simple choice: we either give ourselves a hard time and succumb to shame or despondency or guilt – or we extend kindness to ourselves (exactly as we would to a hurt child).

This choice, and we can always make it, has important consequences. If we give ourselves a hard time, we reinforce that we're only here for ourselves in the good times. We mustn't make mistakes. We make ourselves hostages to fortune. This is the road that leads, inexorably, to the loss of joy. If we extend kindness to ourselves in our darkest moments, we tap into an inexhaustible source of love and have the means to grow beyond our mistakes.

Only self-compassion will get you through the toughest times.

I'm very aware that I've portrayed this as a straightforward choice. But I know from my own experience that choosing self-compassion, and then practising it, is anything but easy. It takes commitment and persistence to practice self-compassion routinely. Of all the habits it's possible to gain though, this is the one that I believe can make the most difference for you and your people.

SECTION 8

Navigating towards a hopeful future

People Solutions for School Leaders covers the principles of emotional intelligence in practice. These principles never go away, but the applied practice changes year on year, just as your working relationships and circumstances change.

This consolidation chapter enables you to create and evolve a toolkit to use throughout your career.

Against a backdrop of societal change, this process offers you a personal development tool that covers values-led leadership, coaching, effective communication, attitudinal development, agility, school culture, morale, mental and emotional well-being, workload management, relational competence, difficult dynamics, team effectiveness, confidence, fulfilment, and self-reliance.

You can use it with your people too, throughout their careers, for their personal development reflection, performance management, and continuous professional development.

CHAPTER 25

Consolidating your personal development

Consolidating

As a school leader, you know how each term brings different challenges. Your personal development is informed by those challenges. Your growth and your well-being are directly related to those challenges.

Each chapter, with its explorations, coaching questions, and perspectives can contribute to your personal development term after term, year after year, by offering people solutions and exploring how to develop yourself as a leader through your relationships at work. And because each year is different, with different staff members and families, the areas you identify for your development will be different too.

The following examples show how to use the chapters to focus more specifically on what you want to develop. Choose the option(s) that work best for you.

You can download the outlines and templates from www.routledge.com/9781032945392.

Three options to explore
Option one

Reflect on your personal challenges over a specific time frame (determined by you):

- Note down the challenges.
- Identify the potential growth from them.
- Choose the personal development that is most important for where you are now and the phase you are entering (see the example in Table 25.1).

Revisit the contents and chapters and highlight those areas that are currently most relevant for you, and that will best serve you in your personal growth (see Table 25.2):

Use the coaching sections in those chapters to get more specific about your development areas.

Transfer your development needs to the template (see Table 25.3). You can adapt the template so that the wording and layout work for you:

Table 25.1 Personal challenges

Challenges – Autumn term	Potential growth	Most important for Spring term
Supporting staff through behaviour management issues. My personal resilience and crisis of confidence through this. Tiredness – keeping going. Keeping work in perspective. Switching off. Having more time for myself.	More ability to cope well and be less affected by other people's challenges, while remaining strong for them. Keeping well, being present at work, maybe even thriving. Fulfilment from enabling others. More detachment, objectivity. Some freedom and space in my head. A calmer me.	My personal resilience and crisis of confidence through this. Tiredness – keeping going. Switching off.

Table 25.2 Example of relevant chapters

Chapter 5 – Self-compassion
Chapter 7 – Personal organisation

Table 25.3 Example of personal development areas

	Personal development area	*Your action*
Chapter 5 Self-compassion	To better understand and practise mindfulness. To slow down my frenetic pace.	
Chapter 7 Personal organisation	To remember 'enough' is good for my well-being and confidence.	

Table 25.4 Example of personal development areas with actions

	Personal development area	*Your action*
Chapter 5 Self-compassion	To better understand and practise mindfulness. To slow down my frenetic pace.	To read *Fierce Self-Compassion* To do the self-compassion break every day at work before I go home.
Chapter 7 Personal organisation	To remember 'enough' is good for my well-being and confidence.	To remember 'interoception'. To stop when my body is signalling I've done enough.

Use the template to specify what action to take (see Table 25.4).
Decide on a tracker or how you will keep track of your progress (see Table 25.5).

Option 2
Use the contents list as a sifting tool to prioritise the area(s) you most want/need to develop. Table 25.6 lists all the chapter headings for easy reference:
Revisit the chapters and reflect on which specific areas of personal development to focus on.
Use the template (as shown in Table 25.7) to specify your development needs and how you will approach these:
Use the tracker to see and maintain your progress (see Table 25.5 and Table 25.8 as examples of completed trackers).

Table 25.5 Example of completed tracker

Date	Self-compassion break	Self-check interoception	Read Fierce Self-Compassion
Mon	☺	☺☺☺	
Tues		☺☺	
Weds	☺	☺☺☺	
Thurs	☺	☺☺	
Frid		☺☺☺	
Sat		☺	☺
Sun		☺☺	☺
Mon	☺	☺	
Tues	☺	☺	
Weds	☺	☺☺☺	
Thurs		☺☺	
Frid		☺☺	
Sat			
Sun		☺☺	☺
Mon	☺	☺	

Table 25.6 Example of chosen chapters for development

	Chapter	Your development choices
1	Respect – valuing yourself and valuing others equally	
2	Coaching Styles – Adapting the way you communicate and motivate	
3	Empowering others through (coaching) questions	
4	Embedding habits – keeping the momentum going for lasting change	
5	Self-compassion	
6	Choices for everyday well-beingEmpowering habits for creating your own feel-good brain chemicals.	
7	Personal organisation	
8	Mental and emotional fitness	
9	Responding to anxiety	
10	Workloads for everyone's well-being	
11	Living the school values	

(Continued)

CONSOLIDATING YOUR PERSONAL DEVELOPMENT

Table 25.6 (Continued)

	Chapter	Your development choices
12	Clarifying expectations	
13	Sharing responsibility	
14	Resilient relationships	
15	When parents get angry	✓
16	Necessary conversations	✓
17	Adding the human element to Inset days	
18	I, me, or we? How to be a team player	
19	Buzzing – EI in teams	
20	Getting real about low morale	
21	Overstretched. Leadership and the widening parameters of inclusion	
22	What really stops you prioritising your well-being?	
23	Finding fulfilment	
24	Creative self-compassion	
25	Consolidating your personal development	
	References – What to read, watch, study, listen to?	

Table 25.7 Example of development area and action

	Personal development area	Your action
Chapter 15 When parents get angry	To be more confident when meetings become emotional.	To print off the Vent Diagram and keep it within sight for each meeting. To consider Coaching Styles in my preparation so I understand more how they need me to communicate. To write down some affirming thoughts to reassure myself ahead of the meeting.
Chapter 16 Necessary conversations	To be better prepared for meetings I find difficult.	To reflect more in writing and aim to see things from other people's perspectives. To work through the coaching questions. To use the checklist in preparation for this term's meetings with AB and CD.

Table 25.8 Example of specific actions taken

Date	Action
5th	Prepped with reflective journal and coaching questions
6th	Kept VENT diagram and affirming message visible during phone call.
7th	Read more on Coaching Styles and applied to this situation with AB.
8th	Reflective journalling – why I find this situation/person so difficult.
9th	Went through checklist – breakthrough moment re how the situation could be sabotaged.
10th	
11th	

Option 3
As you consolidate your growth and development within the timeframe you have chosen, note down your strengths, opportunities, aspirations, and results so you recognise and value the progress you have made (see Table 25.9 SOAR analysis).

Personal Development
Note down what you want to develop to fulfil your aspirations and get the results you want.

Chapters
List the chapters that support your development.

Action
Summarise the specific action you need to take.

Table 25.9 SOAR analysis

strengths	opportunities
aspirations	results

Recommended reading

Bungay Stanier, Michael (2016) *The coaching habit: Say less, ask more and change the way you lead forever.* Box of Crayons Press.
English, Claire (2024) *It's never just about the behaviour: A holistic approach to classroom behaviour management.* Corwin.
Neff, Kristin (2011) *Self compassion: Stop beating yourself up and leave insecurity behind.* Hodder and Stoughton.
Neff, Kristin (2021) *Fierce self-compassion: How women can harness kindness to speak up, claim their power and thrive.* Penguin Life.
Paterson, Randy J. (2022) *The assertiveness workbook.* 2nd ed. New Harbinger Publications.
Rendle, Alison and Messenger, Kit (2023) *Curious not furious: Empowering children to take charge of their brains and behaviour. A practical toolkit.* Ember.

List of download files

The following resources referenced in the book as 'available for download' can be accessed via this link:
www.routledge.com/9781032945392

Chapter 1
Equal-II-se 1 Children's version
Equal-II-se 2 Adults' version
Equal-II-se 3 Advanced version

Chapter 2
How to adapt your Coacting Style
What are you like at work?

Chapter 4
Resilience habits and trackers:
Habits for taking care of yourself and managing your stress
Habits for keeping confident
Habits for keeping yourself organised
Habits for resilient relationships at work

Chapter 5
Family self-compassion habits
Self-compassion tracker 30 habits
Self-compassion tracker (blank)
Poster 'When the tension goes'
'Reassuring myself' 30 page booklet

LIST OF DOWNLOAD FILES

Chapter 6
Infographic poster – 20 feel good habits (DOSE) with trackers

Chapter 7
Keeping on track – Creating work/life harmony (termly, weekly, daily planner)

Chapter 8
Not taking things personally

Chapter 14
10 things you need to know about me
How to adapt your Coacting Style

Chapter 19
BUZZ Team questionnaire

Chapter 21
Alternative measures

Chapter 25
List of chapters
Templates

Index

Note: Entries in *italics* reflect terms that are currently used but that may be disputed and/or in flux as society develops its collective understanding

achiever *see* coaching styles
adaptability, own: changing own approach to others 30, 38; coaching styles 19–26, 176, 206; personal development 2–6; remind others to adapt 67; supporting others to adapt 96, 97, 127, 134, 138, 146, 151, 154; when being assertive 214
adaptability, team: in adversity 95; Inset activities 164, 186; working with difference 122, 201, 204, 205; working with people in authority 125, 126; *see also* personal development
anger, managing 74, 77, 140, 188, 194, 198; managing parents' 135, 141; *see also* assertiveness
anxiety, managing own and others' 51, 72, 81–89, 135, 141, 150, 190, 191, 206, 228
asking for help 213
assertiveness 51, 116, 118, 151, 214
attention-deficit/hyperactivity disorder (ADHD) 3, 68
attitude: respect 5, 12–18, 202; towards own and others' well-being 36, 62, 212, 216
authenticity 26, 53, 83, 139, 140, 159, 168, 183, 190
autism see neurodiversity

behaviour, influences on: attitude 13–18; careful self-management 33, 36, 39, 171; coaching styles 41, 119; different pressures 102, 134, 141–143, 148, 153, 196, 202; self-compassion 51, 70, 230; values 104–108, 175
belonging, sense of 2, 5, 47, 56–58, 172, 180–190
boundaries, coaching self 118; establishing own 51, 57, 63–67, 117, 190, 214, 216; 'us against the problem' shared experience 143, 144
brain chemicals *see* neurochemicals
Brown, B. 140
burnout *see* self-care
buzz in teams 172, 180–182

challenging: and coaching styles 22; challenging the system 2, 87, 128, 130, 131, 195, 197, 202–206; others 20, 153, 154, 173–175, 180, 226; responding when challenged 13, 47, 52, 67, 98, 108, 140, 191, 199, 212, 215, 236; self-care 7
challenging the system *see* challenging
change curve 148, 187, 188, 190, 214

245

INDEX

coaching: and emotional intelligence 1; extract from coaching conversation 102–103; leadership 186; the power of coaching questions 5, 30–33

coaching approaches to coaching others, self, and upwards 32, 40, 59, 67, 78, 88, 97, 107, 111, 118, 127, 140, 167, 176, 181, 191, 205, 216, 223

coacting compass *see* coacting styles

coacting style, achiever: at work 125, 158; characteristics 21–24

coacting style, harmoniser: at work 125, 158; characteristics 21–25

coacting style, innovator: at work 125, 158; characteristics 21–26

coacting style, perfector: at work 125, 158; characteristics 21–26

coacting styles, adapting 19, 25, 27, 239; coacting compass 21; communication needs of different styles 5, 20, 26, 127, 134, 153; flip-side of different styles 22, 98; raising awareness of needs of different styles 27, 125; teams 21–27

commitment, and respect 12; coaching others 41; coaching self 78; coaching styles 68, 79; encouraging in others 20, 105, 149, 180, 181; fuelling own 36, 38, 59, 64, 72, 214, 215, 224, 232; inclusion 190, 194, 201, 204

communication needs, others 5, 24, 127, 134; own 20, 153

competencies: individual 20, 32, 124, 146; team 172, 174, 175

conflict 2, 7; ground rules to reduce 110, 172; parents 134; working through 20, 23, 108, 119, 122, 177, 190

confrontation 14, 18, 141

Conley, C. 190

conversations: difficult 23, 106, 131, 144, 182, 192; necessary 21, 122, 145–154, 202, 206, 216; warm up 160, 161

courage 4, 13–18, 108; courageous action 84, 103, 106, 131, 197–199, 209; fierce self-compassion 51

creativity: creative self-compassion 227–232; others' creativity 102, 200, 225; own creativity 72, 221–223

demoralisation *see* morale
dependency, learnt 30
difficult conversations *see* necessary conversations
dopamine, oxytocin, serotonin, endorphins (DOSE) *see* neurochemicals
downloads, weblink to 15, 49, 51

Edlund, M. J. 75
EHCP *see* inclusion

emotional equations 190
emotional intelligence in teams, buzz 179–182
emotions managing others: anxiety 83; coaching 78; coacting styles 21, 60; necessary conversations 146, 147, 151, 153; neurodiversity 27, 123, 141; parents 134, 139

emotions, managing own: anxiety 82, 86, 87; as act of self-compassion 51, 52; coacting style 23; personal development 2, 5, 70, 74–75, 78, 94, 196–199, 206, 214

empowerment: coacting styles 25, 106; Equal–II-se 18; Ofsted 127, 129, 131, 144; of others 5, 18, 48, 57, 83, 86, 180, 186, 191, 201; of self 47, 53, 56, 82, 84, 124, 228; through questions 9, 30–34

Equal–II-se, model for behaving with respect 11–18, 105–106, 119

exclusion, impact of 195

executive function as essential part of personal organisation 62, 68

expectations: clarifying 109–112, 143, 149, 190, 191; communicating own 20, 154; managing others' 130, 142, 158, 205; managing own 38, 199

feeling valued 96, 137, 158, 186, 189

generational awareness 116
good enough: not striving for perfection 85, 99, 177, 223; sense of insecurity 14, 47, 48, 83, 213, 217, 228, 237
governors, communicating with 12, 20, 112, 122, 201
ground rules essential in teams 110, 112, 163, 172–174, 177
group truths 199
guilt, addressing 39, 48, 52, 64, 138, 198, 199, 232

habits: common but ineffective 30–33; feel-good chemicals 56–58; for self-compassion 49, 230, 232; for wellbeing 35–41
harmoniser *see* coacting styles
headteachers' shared experiences 7, 52, 72, 86, 94, 96, 102, 105, 128, 137, 141, 152, 196, 204, 224

help and support outside your organisation 85
honesty 38, 56, 87, 110, 140, 141, 173–175, 190, 199
human element *see* Inset days

icebreakers 25, 160, 161, 168
inclusion: additional needs 119; EHCP 144, 204; SEND 193–207; widening inclusion 152, 169, 190, 195, 197, 201, 206, 223

INDEX

individual effectiveness and personal organisation 63
innovator *see* coaching styles
Inset days 36: activities 117, 186, 225; adding the human element 157–169; inspiration 6, 103, 104; inspiring headteachers–regular get–togethers for local heads 222, 224–225; inspiring others 20, 127, 158, 168, 201, 221; inspiring, self 39, 53, 58, 84, 159, 220, 222, 223, 231
interoception, felt body sense 70, 126, 237, 238
interpersonal effectiveness 5, 124, 172
intrinsic motivation *see* performance management

jig–saw metaphor for bringing people together 161, 162
Jones, Sir J. 225
joy: discovering 53, 56, 58, 62, 71, 72, 136, 180, 222, 224, 225, 230, 231; loss of 6, 194, 209, 224, 232

laughter 56, 58, 71, 161, 162, 166, 167, 222
leadership 1, 6, 26, 32, 96, 146, 153, 186; coaching styles 22, 24, 83; developing 7, 18, 30, 32, 53, 56, 62, 110, 172, 175, 225; inclusion 193–206

making mistakes: different coating styles and 21–23, 34, 98, 169, 177; self–compassion 46, 232
managing anxiety 82–89; expectations 109–112; others including parents 134; self especially in difficult times 37, 146–154, 200, 229
managing staff; balancing performance and relationships 5, 113; coaching styles 22; confidence and necessary conversations 146; groundrules for managing expectations 110
mental and emotional fitness 69–70
mindfulness 38, 77–79
morale: demoralisation 196, 198; leadership 86, 87, 94, 112, 163, 197; raising and maintaining 186–192

necessary conversations 146–154
Neff, K. 46, 47, 51, 52, 71, 228
negotiating: how we do things here 18, 23, 136, 190; time and task management 63, 66, 84, 213, 215
neurochemicals 59: dopamine, oxytocin, serotonin, endorphins (DOSE) 56, 57
neurodiversity 2–4, 12, 27, 147, 152, 154, 187; *see also* perspectives

Ofsted 53, 128, 129, 131, 224–226
openness 190

overload and overwhelm *see* personal organisation and leadership
ownership as taking responsibility 25, 30, 32, 37, 40, 131, 172, 181, 201

parenting, *Pop Culture Parenting* 140
parents: challenging conversations with 82, 86, 134–144, 146, 195, 196, 204, 205; working with 2, 6, 12, 118, 119, 158, 201, 202, 226
peace of mind 4, 36, 63, 64, 86, 194, 205
perfector *see* coaching styles
performance management: clarifying expectations 110–112; coaching mindset 32; intrinsic motivation 47; others' accountability 20, 40, 105, 146, 149, 153, 172, 226; own accountability 2, 7, 20, 33, 39, 40, 59, 118, 214
Perry, R. 224, 226
personal development 7, 74, 198, 236: and adaptability 2
personal organisation: core approach 61–68; delegating 31, 32, 66, 83, 94; effective habits 31, 49, 51, 56–58, 230, 232; embedding habits 36–41; ineffective habits 30, 32, 33; overload and overwhelm 60, 62, 66, 68, 94–96; *see also* planners in resources
personal power 192
perspectives: how the different coaching styles may react to given situations 27, 33, 41, 59, 67, 79, 88, 98, 108, 112, 119, 123, 128, 141, 151, 169, 176, 182, 192, 207, 217, 223; keeping others' differences in mind 6, 12, 27
powerlessness 83, 191, 196, 199, 202
pressure *see* relationships (whole school)
psychological safety 127, 146, 150, 164, 167, 176, 190, 199

realistic optimism 175, 191
rehearsal circles for self–reliance 125–127
relationships: differences between coaching styles 22, 23, 27, 60, 68; difficult relationships with parents and children 137, 141–144, 204, 206; Equal–II-se 18, 108; leadership 1, 4, 5, 36, 37, 39, 111, 146; self–compassion 230; whole school relationships 117, 118, 122–124, 134, 168
resilience: and self–compassion 46, 51, 53; coating styles 22; as essential to relationships 122; habits 37, 38, 75; own 236
resistance, working with: others' 172, 186, 190, 217; own 97
resources for download, weblink to 15, 27, 49, 51
respect: across the whole school 103–108, 118, 119, 173, 174, 202; coaching styles

123, 151; differences between people 2; as the foundation of working relationships 5, 10, 12–18; leadership 30, 73, 117, 214, 230; parents 137; relating to people in authority 124; serotonin 56, 58

responsibility: for self 86, 87, 136, 213, 216; rights and responsibility 116, 119; support others to take responsibility 5, 20, 30, 32, 95, 96, 102, 106, 107, 143, 144, 172–174, 189, 201, 202

rights 116–119

role play and dialogue for psychological safety 126

safety: self–compassion 51, 230; serotonin 56, 58; supporting others to feel safe 86, 87, 94, 117, 119, 126, 127, 136–139, 150, 164, 167, 172, 176, 200; supporting self 72, 74, 85

SARAH curve, states of mind after a shock 188

self–care: burnout 67; feel good hormones 56; harmonisers 89; own 38, 70, 72, 181, 212, 213, 230; whole school 200

self–compassion lived 46–53, 71, 76, 138, 197, 199, 205, 212, 228–232

self–development activities: alleviate stress 74, 76, 82, 94–95; creative self–expression 231; raise own dopamine levels 56; raise own energy 56

self–doubt 14, 15, 124

self–regulation *see* habits

self–worth, prioritising 212–217

SEND *see* inclusion

shame: necessary conversations 146; self–compassion 46, 48, 51, 138, 198–200, 228, 230, 232; underlying difficult behaviour 3, 116

SOAR diagram: strengths, opportunities, aspirations, results 239

staff retention 87, 180

staff wellbeing 202–206; supervision 200, 205

suspension 195

taking things personally 73

team development activities: coacting styles 24, 88; ground rules 110, 173; Inset 159–167; low morale 186, 187; manage anxiety 84; presenting to people in authority 125, 126, 128; school values 103–106; team responsibility 117; working together 122

teams: allowing for differences 62; anxiety and pressures 84–86, 94, 96, 152, 153, 190; coaching styles 24–26, 123, 125, 192; good habits and team cohesion 40, 168, 172–177, 180–182, 186, 191, 201, 205, 221, 222; managing expectations 110, 111, 215; preparing for inspection 124, 126, 127, 131, 142; rights and responsibilities 117, 118; school values 73, 102, 103

templates 236–240

trauma: as source of difficult behaviour 2, 3, 83, 89; impact on self and others 138, 141, 146, 194, 217

values, living: own 75, 77, 230; team 110, 175, 182, 201; when compromised 134, 190, 194, 198; whole school 2, 12, 14, 73, 102–108, 143, 152, 159, 164, 181, 202, 204, 206, 224

vent diagram managing anger 135

Vine, T. 166

vision and values: actualising 36, 62, 105, 110; communicating 20; courage 4, 190; priorities 26

vulnerability: and neurodivergent people 153; anxiety and 87; necessary conversations 146, 147; self–compassion 199, 228

warm–up conversations *see* conversations

well–being: and anxiety 83; children's 144, 225, 226; enhancing own 46, 51, 56–58, 70, 75, 228–231, 236; protecting others' 67, 117, 122, 138, 175, 204–206; protecting own 31, 36, 62, 63, 149, 212–217

workload: and anxiety 83; managing others' 5, 26, 60, 67, 117, 205; managing own 3, 43, 62, 63, 152, 200, 212; reducing 93–99

For Product Safety Concerns and Information please contact our EU representative GPSR@taylorandfrancis.com
Taylor & Francis Verlag GmbH, Kaufingerstraße 24, 80331 München, Germany